Morphosyntax of Manipuri Verb

B. Premabati Devi

RAJESH PUBLICATIONS
NEW DELHI - 110 002

Morphosyntax of Manipuri Verb

ISBN : 978-93-83684-29-8 (H.B.)
ISBN : 978-93-83684-28-1 (P.B.)

Published by :
Sanjay Gupta
RAJESH PUBLICATIONS
1, Ansari Road, Darya Ganj,
New Delhi - 110002
Ph.: 011-23274550

Printed in India at :
Vijeta Offset Printers, Delhi

FOREWORD

Since the establishment of Department of Linguistics in Manipur University in 1985 many research works on Manipuri language as well as works on tribal language have started. This book, called Morphosyntax of Manipuri Verb, is an excellent work of Dr. B. Premabati Devi in the study of Manipuri language. In a language verb plays an important role in making a structure and in making his attitude to the addresses.

This book would be very significant because it analyses the vast area occupied by verbs, one of the most important word classes of Manipuri language. Manipuri verbs are naturally bound so they take another verbal affix to derive a free form. This book will reveal morphological complexity of Manipuri verb along with richness of semantics in the combination of verbs and verbal suffixes. This book will also show that there are many polysyllabic roots rather than monosyllabic ones. Another is the compound verbs which are not well discussed in other works of her predecessor linguistics.

In short, it can be said that this book has discussed Manipuri verbs and verbal affixes as a whole. It has focused mainly on the structural and semantic classification of Manipuri verbs. This book has revealed that the semantic combination of verbal affixes and sometimes verbs of the same group happens to imply different readings although they occur with the same suffix.

The present book is a concrete piece in the world of linguistics as well as to the scholars of the Sino-Tibetan languages in particular as it fills up the gap of linguistic analysis misinterpreted by many linguistics and it also brings out in light many structural and semantic analysis of Manipuri verbs along with the verbal affixes.

Prof. Ch. Yashawanta Singh
Department of Linguistcs
Manipur University

PREFACE

The book is a humble attempt to trace the nature of Manipuri verbs and the role of verbal suffixes which play an important role in the analysis of Manipuri language. Manipuri, being an agglutinating type of language, the occurence of verbal suffixes takes the major part in the study of Manipuri verbs. The semantic class of the verb decides the presence of the verbal suffixes.

The book has five chapters of which the first three deal with verbs while the last two focus on the verbal suffixes. The first chapter is about the identification of Manipuri verbs which mainly deals with verbs identified by negation, difference between verbs and nouns, adjectives and verbs, adverbs and verbs and finally, the non-inflectional feature of Manipuri verbs by tense, number, person and gender. The second chapter discusses the structural classification of Manipuri verbs into five classes. The third chapter deals with the semantic classification of Manipuri verbs into three groups. The fourth chapter discusses the verbal derivative suffixes while the last chapter is about the verbal inflectional suffixes.

Imphal **B. Premabati Devi**

ABBREVIATIONS

ablative .... ABL
accusative .... ACC
adverbial .... ADV
associative .... ASS
attributive .... ATT
benefactive .... BEN
causative .... CAU
command .... COM
comparative .... CMP
completive .... COMP
conjunction .... CONJ
conjunction particle .... CPART
contrastive .... CONT
copula .... COP
dative .... DAT
decorative .... DEC
definitive .... DEF
deictic .... DEIC
destructive .... DEST
determiner .... DET
directional .... DIR
downward .... DOWN
duration .... DUR
excessive .... EXC
feminine .... FEM
first person 1PP
generalized prefix .... GENP
genitive .... GEN
habitual .... HAB
honorific .... HON

inceptive	INCP
instrumental	INST
intentive	INT
interrogative	INTR
inward	IN
locative	LOC
modifier	MOD
negative	NEG
nominalizer	NMZ
nominative	NOM
non-potential	NPOT
non-realization	NREAL
outward	OUT
particularization	PART
perfective	PERF
permissive	PERM
plural	PL
potential	POT
progressive	PROG
prohibitive	PROH
prospective	PROS
purposive	PUR
question	Q
reciprocal	REC
reduplication	RED
reflexive	REF
second person	2PP
simple aspect marker	SAM
specific	SPF
specific duration	SPFD
suggestive	SUG
third person	3PP
upward	UP

CONTENTS

INTRODUCTION

1.1 Status of Manipuri Language

Manipuri is a Tibeto-Burman language mainly spoken in Manipur. The language is also known as Meeteilon/Meiteilon (**Meetei/Meitei**) 'the local people who inhabit in the valley' and **lon** 'language'). It is also spoken in some parts of Myanmar, Bangladesh, Tripura, Assam and Mizoram. It is the lingua-franca of 33 different mother tongues of Manipur. Thus, it occupies an important place in the day-to-day life of the people of Manipur.

According to Grierson (1904), in the classification of T.B. languages Manipuri language comes under the Kuki-Chin subgroup of the Burmese division. Shafer (1955, 1966, 1974) places Manipuri in the Meitei branch of Kukish section while Benedict (1972) puts Manipuri in Kuki-Naga of Kukish section.

Manipuri is the only T.B language included in the VIIIth Schedule of Indian Constitution since 20th August, 1992. Sahitya Academy, New Delhi also recognises Manipuri as a regional language long before its inclusion in the VIIIth Schedule. In 1974, ***Imphal Amasung Magi Ishing Nungshitki Phibham*** 'Imphal and its Climatic Condition' by Pacha Meitei, a renowned writer received the prestigious Sahitya Academy award and since then, many scholars are honoured with this award. Department of Manipuri Language and Literature, Manipur University has produced many Ph.D. Scholars in various fields of literature. This shows that Manipuri is a highly developed, culturally rich and advanced language. It has also been recognized by many academic bodies like Board of Secondary Education, Assam, Central Board of Secondary Education, New Delhi, Guwahati University, Delhi University, etc. All India Radio Imphal and Doordarshan Kendra, Imphal broadcast programmes through this language.

1.2 Script

Manipuri has its own script '**Meetei Mayek**'. During the reign of king Garibaniwaj (1709-1748) the religion of the state was converted into Hinduism and along with the change of religion, the script was also replaced by Bengali script. Since then, the script has been in use in schools, colleges, universities and all the text and literary works instead of the indigenous Meetei/Meitei Mayek (script). Accordingly, the VIIIth Schedule of Indian Constitution recognizes the language as 'Manipuri Language written in Bengali Script'. This is because of the controversy between the Meetei scholars. The first group supports 35 scripts (especially to read the ***Puyas***, the old text or archives) and another group supports 27 scripts. The state government has recognized the latter group officially. The state government has introduced **Meetei Mayek** in the institutions from the primary standard since 2006.

1.3 Review of the Literature

The adoption of Hinduism has influenced the language in a great deal. People used to learn Sanskrit, an Indo-European language and regarded it to be very prestigious and as a result of the close contact, many Sanskrit and Bengali words entered into the lexicon of Manipuri language. Many Sanskrit scholars began to write Manipuri grammar in the context of Sanskrit language. Some of them are: ***Manipuri Byakaran Kaumudi*** by Kalachand Shashtri (1964), ***Meiteilon*** by Nanadalal Sharma (1976), ***Manipuri Byakaran*** by Dwijamani Dev Sharma (1969), ***Meeteilon Byakaran*** by Narayan Sharma (1984). All these grammars are termed as traditional grammars by modern linguists. Traditional grammarians analysed Manipuri language on the basis of Sanskrit framework since they were not aware of the fact that the two languages exhibit different structures as they belong to different language families. As a tradition, they had a belief that grammatical categories are universal. The study of a Tibeto-Burman language like Manipuri on the framework of an Indo-European language like Sanskrit is considered to be theoretically inadequate and unauthentic by modern linguists for these traditional grammars are of prescriptive model and hence, fails to serve the purpose. After the introduction of English language in the state during the British Rule, Pettigrew (1912) and Primrose (1987) study Manipuri language on the framework of English which are also on the same track of the Sanskrit scholars. It is worth to be mentioned that Manipuri is an agglutinating type of language while Sanskrit is highly inflectional and English, on the other hand, is an isolating language.

In the later stage, modern linguists emerge in the scene and they start writing Manipuri grammar based on pure linguistic knowledge. Those pioneers' contributions are: ***Remedial Manipuri*** by Thoudam (1991), ***Manipuri Grammar*** by Bhat and Ningomba (1997), ***Manipuri Grammar*** by Yashawanta (2000), etc. These linguists analyse the language on the descriptive model. Some other works that are also found in the study of Manipuri on the linguistic approach, some of them are: ***A Study of Meitei Phonology*** by Tomchou (1976), ***A Study on Meiteilon Phonology with a Supplement of Morphology*** by Sonamani (1980), ***Meitei Lonmit*** by Ningomba (1992), ***Manipuri Phonology*** by Madhubala (2002), ***The Case for Case*** by Saratchandra Singh (2000), ***Meithei Grammar*** by Shobhana (1997), etc.

There are also a few studies on Manipuri as a part of Ph. D. programme that are directly or indirectly related to the verbs. ***A Meitei Grammar of Roots and Affixes*** by

Nonigopal (1986) is the first of its kind and comes out to be a significant piece. Some other works are ***Manipuri Verb*** by Bidyarani (2002) and ***Semantic Structure of Manipuri Verbs*** by Dolen (2002). Nonigopal studies both nominal and verbal roots and classifies them as action, stative and process. He also studies both nominal and verbal affixes, but does not classify the verbal affixes as derivational and inflectional; thus, he fails to give the semantic components of the verbal roots and affixes. He mainly focuses on monosyllabic verbal roots while there are many disyllabic, polysyllabic and even compound verbs and reduplicated verbs in Manipuri which altogether excelled monosyllabic verbal roots in number.

Bidyarani (2002), on the other hand, gives a few account of verb formation. Like Nonigopal she also classifies Manipuri verbs as action, stative and process on the semantic level but fails to give reason why a certain verb is assigned as action verb and on what basis and how it differs from other verb classes. She studied the use of Manipuri verbs in the syntactic level only as negative, imperative and interrogative constructions. She does not study the various types of verbal forms that result with affixation as she has almost skipped the analysis of verbal affixes.

Meanwhile, Dolen's (2002) ***Semantic Structure of Manipuri Verbs*** is purely based on semantic analysis. He studies the meaning of Manipuri verbs as denotative and connotative, synonymy, autonomy, polysemy, hyponymy, etc. His work is not related to the structural and semantic classification of verbs which is discussed in the present study. Thus, it has no co-relation with the semantic structure of Manipuri verbs.

1.4 Reason for taking up the study

Study of Manipuri verbs is incomplete without the study of affixation. Bound verbal roots are non-restricted in the sense that they cannot stand on their own without undergoing a morphological process of affixation. As a result, affixation also becomes an important part of study. A detailed classification of Manipuri verbs both structural and semantic and study of derivational and inflectional affixes involved in verb formation is needed for the purpose. This area has not yet been done by any linguist so far. All the earlier works focus mainly on root level analysis of monosyllabic verbs. They do not go further into the structural analysis of verbs. The present study tries to fill up this gap. The reason why the problem is taken up is for exploring the nature of the verbal roots and find out their functions and classify them as well as to discuss the semantic components of the verbal affixes which help to build up the different verb forms corresponding to time, aspect, etc.

1.5 Some Characteristic of Manipuri language

Manipuri has only two distinct word classes as nouns and verbs. Free forms like

jum 'house' **lairik** 'book', **cak** 'rice', **isiŋ** 'water', etc. and bound forms like **-hi** 'liquid' **-pəŋ** 'solid', **-cet** 'piece or fraction', etc. constitute the class of nouns. A generalized prefix **mə-** is attached to the above bound forms to derive free nouns like **khum-** 'cover' > **mə-khum** 'lid', **tət-** 'break' > **mə-tət** 'piece (of thread, rope, etc.), **kək-** 'cut' > **mə-kək** 'piece of something', **pun-** 'bind' > **mə-pun-** 'bundle', etc. Moreover, verbal roots may undergo another process of nominalization by suffixing **-pə ~ bə** to derive nominals like **ca-** 'eat' > **ca-bə** **'**to eat, eating', **cət-** 'go' > **cət-pə** 'to go, going', **i-** **'**write' > **i-bə** 'to write, writing', etc. However, the language has no verbalization rule which derives a verb from a noun. Kinship terms are always bound in Manipuri which may take the pronominal prefixes like **i-** (1PP), **nə-** (2PP) and **mə-** (3PP) and the generalized prefix **mə-** to form free nouns, *e.g.* **i-ma** 'my mother', **nə-ma** 'your mother', **mə-ma** 'his mother, mother'. Free nouns may also take these pronominal prefixes like **i-khoŋ** 'my leg', **nə-thəu** 'your duty or business', **mə-jum** 'his house', etc.

Verbs, on the other hand, are bound forms in nature and they become free only when verbal inflectional suffixes are attached to them, *e.g.* **ca-** 'eat' > **ca-i** 'eats' **ca-ri** 'is eating', **ca-re** 'has eaten', etc. The additions of verbal derivative suffixes do not make a verbal bound root a verb except for the nominalizer **-pə** and the adverbial **-nə** which are class-changing derivational suffixes as they make nouns and adverbs from verbal roots.

Manipuri is a SOV language. The verb comes at the end of a sentence. Verbal modifiers always precede the verb in a sentence. In case of two nouns occurring in a sentence, a copula verb **-ni** and its variants like **oi-ri** 'is', **oi-re** 'has become', etc. follow the last noun, *e.g* **əi memə-ni** 'I am Mema', **əi oɟa oi-re** 'I have become a teacher' etc.

Negation in Manipuri is denoted by the addition of negative suffixes like **-te**, **-loi**, etc. It may be mentioned that words that can take negative suffixes are verbs in Manipuri. The language exhibits a unique feature by allowing double negatives in a sentence which does not make the sentence an affirmative statement as found in English. Manipuri negative words like **pəŋnə** 'seldom', **pak** 'seldom', **khək** 'never' **kəja** 'hardly', etc. may occur in a sentence where the verb form has already taken a negative marker, *e.g.* **əi ca kəja thək-te** 'I hardly drink tea'. These negative particles are known as negative polarity as they strengthen the negative meaning.

Adjectives in Manipuri are derived from verbal nouns, *i.e.* word resulting from the suffixation of nominalizer **-pə ~ bə** like **ca-bə** 'eating'. An attributive prefix **ə-** is attached to the verbal nouns and thus, **ə-pai-bə** 'something that flies' is constructed from the verbal noun **pai-bə** 'to fly or flying'. The prefixation of **ə-** is restricted to monosyllabic verbal roots only. Otherwise, it is dropped when the verbal root is polysyllabic like **ca-gən-bə** 'someone who is a habitual eater' and when the adjective takes a modifier like

jam-nə 'very' in **jam-nə phəbə əŋaŋ** 'child who is very good'.

In Manipuri, adjectives derived from monosyllabic verbal roots may precede or follow the noun while the more common form is that of an adjective following a noun. On the other hand, adjectives derived from polysyllabic verbal roots or verbal nouns that have derivational suffixes like **ca-ri-bə** 'someone who is eating' always precede the noun. Some numeral adjectives which are not derived from verbal nouns like **khərə** 'some', **khəɟik** 'a little', **kəja** 'how many or how much' always follow the noun like **nupi khərə** 'some women', **cak khəɟiktəŋ** 'a small amount of cooked rice', etc.

The type of adjectives found in Manipuri occurs only in attributive position. They cannot occur in predicative position for verbs are the only words that come in the predicative position. Verbal roots semantically stative also take the verbal affixes as they perform the normal functions as verbs do in a sentence, *e.g.* **ləi əsi phəɟə-i** 'The flower is beautiful', **jum əsi cau-i** 'The house is big', etc. These adjectival verbal roots are translatable as adjectives in English while they are treated as verbs in Manipuri and can take the verbal suffixes.

As mentioned above, Manipuri is an agglutinative language which allows a verbal bound root to take a string of suffixes, *e.g.* **ca-khət-hən-ɟə-rəm-mə-gəni** 'might have caused to start eating (in the absence of the speaker)'. **ca-** 'eat' is the verbal root followed by five derivational suffixes and an inflectional suffix. The structure of the language allows as many as ten or more derivational suffixes to occur at a time.

Noun determiners follow the noun and the language (Manipuri) has no preposition like English does. In a noun phrase like **əŋaŋ-ədu/əŋaŋ-du** 'the child' the determiner **ədu/du** comes after the noun. **tebəl məthək-tə** 'on the table' is a prepositional phrase where **-tə** is the post positional marker functioning as locative which follows the noun.

One peculiar feature of Manipuri being a Tibeto-Burman language is that the velar nasal sound /ŋ/ can occur in all positions like **ŋəsi** 'today', **səŋai** 'brow-antlered deer' and **məŋ** 'dream'. The language is also a tonal language which distinguishes level from fall tone, *e.g.*, **pa-** 'read' is in level tone while **pa-** 'be thin' is in falling tone.

Manipuri is a tense less language. Traditional grammarians claim that Manipuri has tense as past, present and future as they analyse the language on the framework of Sanskrit and English languages. This claim is challenged by modern linguists like Bhat and Ningomba (1997) and Madhubala (1979). They observe that Manipuri shows two tense distinctions as future and non-future (both past and present). This claim is further challenged by linguists like Thoudam (1991) and Mahabir (1988). They argue that

Manipuri verbs are not morphologically marked by tense. Thoudam (1988) observes that the tense system found in Greek, Sanskrit, Latin, etc. is not found in Manipuri language. Tense, in this language, is shown by adverbial time element, not by morphological markers on the verb.

There is no agreement of number, person, and gender with verbs. In other words, Manipuri verbs are not reflected for these grammatical categories.

1.6 Significance of the study

There is no adequate work on the present area by any linguist so far except in some Ph.D. works as ***Manipuri Verbs*** (Bidyarani, 2002) and ***The semantic Structure of Manipuri Verbs***, (Dolen, 2002) and ***A Meitei Grammar of Roots and Affixes*** (Nonigopal, 1986). The present study would be very significant because it studies the vast area occupied by verbs, one of the most important word classes of Manipuri language. It would also be a significant piece in the world of linguistics as well as the students of linguistics especially those who study Tibeto-Burman languages as it fills up the gap of linguistic analysis misinterpreted by many linguists, and it also brings out in light many structural and semantic analysis of Manipuri verbs along with the verbal affixes.

1.7 Scope of the analysis

The present study is a descriptive analysis of Manipuri verbs and verbal affixes. It aims at the structural and semantic classification of Manipuri verbs as well the semantic analysis of verbal affixes. The thesis is divided into seven chapters including this introductory portion and conclusion. The body constitutes five chapters out of which chapter two, three, and four focus on verbs and chapter five and six deal with verbal affixes.

1.7.1 Chapterization

The first chapter is categorised into three parts dealing with the identification of Manipuri verbs. First, it studies the negative particles. Second, it tries to show verb as a distinct class which is different from other word classes as nouns, adjectives, adverbs, etc. The concluding part deals with the nature of Manipuri verbs in sentence level. It tries to show that they are not inflected for number, person, gender and tense. It also discusses the different readings implied by the combination of verbal roots and verbal suffixes occurred in negative environments. This chapter also examines Manipuri verbs closely whether they are inflected for tense or other time indicating parameters as this area has been controversial with modern linguists having different opinions.

The second chapter attempts to give the structural classification of Manipuri verbs. It discusses the syllabic patterns found in the verbal roots which are monosyllabic, disyllabic and polysyllabic. It also studies the compound verbs and reduplicated verbs which constitute the larger construction of Manipuri verbs. It tries to group the verbs into four classes as simple, complex, compound and reduplicated verbs. It also discusses the traditional concept of compound verbs as found in the earlier works of some linguists like Bhat and Ningomba (1986) and Loken (1997) in the combination of verbal roots with **niŋ-** 'wish', **thok-**, 'go out', etc.

The third chapter tries to examine the semantic classification of verbs as action, stative and process. It discusses the inadequacies caused by root level analysis of Manipuri verbs carried out by earlier scholars. It tries to study the verbs from other angles also. First, it elucidates the semantic properties of the verbal roots by means of three contrastive features. Second, it studies the three classes of verbs on functional level. Third, it analyses the overlapping of verb classes which causes a problem in assigning the semantic class of verbs. It also studies the notion of agentivity which occupies an important place in the semantic classification of verbs. Finally, the shifting of verb classes from one class to another often caused by suffixation is discussed.

The fourth chapter deals with the verbal derivative affixes. The chapter itself is divided into two sections as prefixes and suffixes and studies the verbal derivative affixes as grammaticalized and non-grammaticalized. First, it discusses the verbal derivative prefixes involved in reduplication. Second, it analyses the verbal derivative suffixes and further divides it into restricted and non-restricted grammaticalized suffixes. Third, it examines the other verbal suffixes like deictic suffixes, multi-functional suffixes, modifiers, etc. The final portion of the chapter focuses on contraction and deletion rules usually found in day-to-day use and even in texts. It observes the partial or complete deletion of verbal roots and suffixes when strings of suffixes are attached to a verbal root.

The fifth chapter analyses the verbal inflectional suffixes. It studies the aspect markers as realised and non-realised. In realised group, the aspectual suffixes like **-i**, progressive **-li** both in the present and past readings is discussed. It also examines the aspectual suffixes that indicate actions or events occurring in the past as well as perfective aspect. The various forms of copula **-ni**, a 'be' verb are also examined. This chapter highlights the non-realized aspect **-kəni** and its various interpretations when interrupted by other suffixes. Further attempts are made to analyse the other aspectual suffixes that indicate intention, suggestion, 'let' imperative, etc. This chapter makes a hypothesis that simple aspect marker **-i** is present in other aspectual suffixes like progressive **-li,** perfective **-le**, negative **-te**, etc.

CHAPTER 1

IDENTIFICATION OF MANIPURI VERBS

The important question that can be asked before the study of Manipuri verbs may be as follows: Does Manipuri language have a distinct class of verbs? If so, what are the criteria for distinguishing a verb from other word classes? The answers to the above questions are, of course, Manipuri has a distinct class of verbs that differentiates them from nouns. It would be more appropriate to give the criteria for verbhood before coming to the discussion of word-classes.

1.1 Manipuri Verbs identified by negation

All (and only) the words which may directly follow the negative adverb **ma** 'not' belong to Lahu verbs (similar criteria work for all Tibeto-Burman languages in Southeast Asia as Thai and Cambodian) (Matisoff, 1973: 193). The same case happens in Manipuri also where the negative particles **-tə** ~ **də** and **-loi** ~ **roi** follow only verbs and verbal suffixes. Negation, in Manipuri, can also be formed by an extra addition of negative adverbs like **pənə** 'seldom', **paknə** 'seldom' and negative modifier like **–phat** 'shortage of some quality' and negative polarity **suk**- 'never', etc.

The negative morpheme **-tə** ~ **də** is used as derivational suffix to form words like **ca-də-bə** (eat-NEG-NMZ) 'one who does not eat' **ca-gən-də-bə** (eat-HAB-NEG-NMZ) 'one who is not a habitual eater', etc. Such derived words occur only in phrases while **-te** ~ **de** **(-tə~də +i)** being an inflectional marker, can occur in the syntactic level.

-te~de: It is used to negate an affirmative sentence. It expresses a habitual action or event. **-te** occurs after voiceless sounds with some exceptions like **hau**- 'be tasty', **ləi**- 'be, have' and **həi**- 'be experienced or skilled (the phonological conditioning factors will be discussed with examples) and **-de** occurs after voiced sounds. The occurrence of the suffix **-te** ~ **de** with verbal roots may be studied under two sub-heads: (i) direct attachment of the suffix and (ii) attachment of the suffix at the end of a derived form.

The suffix **-te** ~ **de** can come closest to a verbal root. Possible occurrences of -te which come directly after the verbal roots are given below:

1. **thək**- 'drink'

məhak kophi thək-te
he coffee drink-NEG-SAM
'He does not drink coffee'

2. **hau-** 'be tasty'
ensaŋ əsi hau-te
curry this tasty-NEG-SAM
The curry is not tasty'

3. **həi-** 'be educated, be able to do something, know how to do something'

a. məhak lairik həi-te
he book educated-NEG-SAM
'He is uneducated'

b. əi ŋa thoŋ-bə həi-te
I fish cook-NMZ know-NEG-SAM
'I do not know how to prepare fish curry'

c. əi əŋkə-si hot-pə həi-te
I sum-DEM solve-NMZ know-NEG-SAM
'I do not know how to solve the sum'

4. **ləi-** 'be, have'

a. əi-khoi-gi ləu ləi-te
I-PL-GEN paddy field have-NEG-SAM
'We do not own/have paddy field'

b. nupa-du jum-də ləi-te
man-DEM house-LOC be-NEG-SAM
'The man is not at home'

In the above sentences, the verbal roots **thək-** , **hau-** , **həi-** and **ləi-** are used in the negative form by adding the negative suffix **-te**. The verbal roots **hau-**, **həi-** and **ləi-** are exceptionals where the marker **-te** cannot be voiced *i.e.* it cannot become **-de** even if it follows the vowel sounds /**au**/ in **hau-**, /**əi**/ in **həi-** and **ləi-**. It does not follow the general rule of voicing. **hau-** in the level tone having no contrast is one of the exceptions which cannot be easily explained. All other forms having /**au**/ at the end can take **-de** as **cau-de** 'is not big', **tau-de** 'does not float', **sau-de** 'is not angry', **kau-de** 'does not forget', **lau-de** 'does not shout', **phau-de** 'does not feel (pain, sorrow)', etc., **ŋau-de** 'is not mad', **wau-de** '(of colours) is not light-coloured, is not dirty (of person)', etc. In all the possible occurrences of /**au**/, **hau-** is the exception. Hence, a rule can be formed as follows: **-te** remains unchanged if the morpheme has /**h**/ in the beginning and ends in /**au**/. This is because, in all the possible occurrence of the vowels with /**h**/ in the beginning, the rule does not operate, *i.e.*, it changes to **-de**. For example, **ho-de** 'is not hollow',

hu-de 'does not steal', **ha-de** 'does not eat (an honorific word of **ca-** 'eat')', **həu-de** 'does not grow', **hi-de** 'does not lop', etc. Another exception with /**h**/ and /**l**/ in the beginning is **həi-te** 'is not educated', 'cannot do something' and **ləi-te** 'does not have, 'does not exist'. The tone in the above given verbs are level tones and in such cases they take **-te** instead of **-de**. The verbs have tonal contrast *i.e.*, falling tone as **hə̀i-** 'pour' and **lə̀i-** 'buy' take **-de** as seen in regular constructions: **hə̀i-de** 'does not pour' and **lə̀i-de** 'does not buy'. This holds true for all the possible occurrences of morphemes beginning with other consonants and ending in /əi/. Some of them are **pə̀i-de** 'does not pile up' **təi-de** 'does not apply (ointments, applying of hair oil)' **nəi-de** 'does not stir, does not oppress', **cəi-de** 'does not scold', **phəi-de** 'is not slant', **khəp-te** 'does not winnow', etc. From the above analysis a rule can be framed as follows: morpheme that begins with /**h**/ and ends in /**au**/ and morphemes that begin with /**h**/ and /**l**/ and end in level tone /əi/ do not follow the general rule that **-te** changes to **-de** when it follows a voiced sound.

As seen in the above analysis, morphemes ending in voiced sounds take **-de** (except some verbs).

5. **cau-** 'be big'
jum əsi cau-de
house this big-NEG-SAM
'The house is not big'

6. **pəi-** 'be slant'
jumbi əsi- pəi-de
pillar this slant-NEG-SAM
'The pillar is not slant'

Manipuri, being an agglutinative language, a verbal root can take a string of suffixes. Generally, derivative suffixes can occur one after another and inflectional suffixes always come at the end and they occur in the predicative position only. Hence, it is natural for the negative suffixes **-te** ~ **de** to come at the end of the derived form.

As mentioned above **-te** generally follows a voiceless sound and the suffixes that can precede **-te** are few in number. They are: **-lək** 'deictic' which means to perform an action somewhere and come towards the speaker, **-thok** 'outward directional' and **-khət** 'upward directional'. These three suffixes are multifunctional and they will be discussed under the following sub-sections in Chapter-IV (see **4.2**).

7. **ka-** 'attend'
roma ŋəsi skul ka-rək-te
Roma today school attend-DEIC-NEG-SAM
'Roma did not come to school (and attend the classes) today'

8. **pai-** 'fly'
ucek məca-siŋ-du məkon-dəgi pai-thok-te

bird small-PL-DEM nest-ABL fly-OUT-NEG-SAM
'The small birds did not fly out of their nest'

9. **ləŋ-** 'throw'
əi-nə bol-du jum-thək-tə ləŋ-khət-te
I-NOM ball-DEM house-UP-LOC throw-UP-NEG-SAM
'I did not throw up the ball on the roof of the house'

The allomorph **-de** follows the following suffixes: **-niŋ** 'wish', **-hən** 'causative', **-kən ~ gən** 'habitual', **-mən** 'excessive', **-pi ~ bi** 'benefactive', **-cə ~ ɟə** 'reflexive', **-nə** 'reciprocal, adverbial, purposive', **-həu** 'inceptive', **-minnə** 'together', **-sin** 'inward directional', **-thə** 'downward directional', **-lə**, **-lu**, **-lək** 'deictic', **-khi** 'definiteness', etc.

10. **jeŋ-** 'watch/see'
əi sinema jeŋ-niŋ-de
I movie watch-wish-NEG-SAM
'I do not want to watch the movie'

11. **pheŋ-** 'scour'
əi-nə ma-bu kon pheŋ-hən-de
I-NOM she-ACC utensil scour-CAUS-NEG-SAM
'I do not make her scour the utensils'

12. **thək-** 'drink'
ma-di ca thək-kən-de
he-PART tea drink-HAB-NEG-SAM
'He does not drink tea habitually'

13. **tum-** 'sleep'
əŋaŋ-du tum-khi-de
child-DEM sleep-DEF-SAM
'The child did not sleep'

14. **phəm-** 'sit'
əi-khoi əni klas-tə phəm-minnə-de
I-PL two class-LOC sit-together-NEG-SAM
'We do not sit together in the class'

15. **kən-** 'be strong'
ca-ri-bə-si-gə jeŋnə-bə-də məhak kən-
eat-PROG-NMZ-DEM-CONJ compare-NMZ-LOC he
mən-de
strong-EXC-NEG-SAM
'He is not strong enough as compared to his diet'

16. **ləi**- 'buy'
ma-nə əi-gi kərimətə ləi-bi-de
he-NOM I-GEN nothing buy-BEN-NEG-SAM
'He did not buy anything for me'

17. **cət**- 'go , visit'
əi-di memi-hoi-də əmuk-tə phaubə cət-lu-de
I-PART Memi-PL-LOC once-only even visit-DEIC-NEG-SAM
'I did not visit Memi even once'

18. **pi**- 'give'
ma-nə əi-ŋon-də lairik pi-rə-de
he-NOM I-DIR-LOC book give-DEIC-NEG-SAM
'He did not come here and give me the book'

19. **ŋəm**- 'able'
tombi-di isiŋ baltin əthənbə əmə phaubə thaŋ-bə
Tombi-PART water bucket full one even carry-NMZ
ŋəm-ɟə-de
able-REF-NEG-SAM
'Tombi cannot carry even a bucket full of water'

20. **lan**- 'give, offer'
imuŋ əni-du ensaŋ lan-nə-de
family two-DEM curry offer-REC-NEG-SAM
'The two families do not offer/exchange dishes'

21. **kəp**- 'cry'
əŋaŋ-du kəp-həu-de
child-DEM cry-INCP-NEG-SAM
'The child was not crying (when I left home)'

22. **hap**- 'put'
phurit-tu əi-nə upu-də hap-cin-de
shirt-DEM I-NOM almirah-LOC put-IN-NEG-SAM
'I did not put the shirt in the almirah'

23. **cen**- 'run'
əŋaŋ-du siri-də cen-thə-de
child-DEM stair-LOC run-DOWN-NEG-SAM
'The child did not run down the stairs'

24. **thoŋ**- 'cook'
əi əjuk-ki cak thoŋ-ŋəm-de (-ləm-de)

I morning-GEN cooked rice cook-COMP-NEG-SAM
'I did not cook/prepare lunch (before coming here)'

The suffix -**niŋ** in sentence (10), causative suffix -**hən** in (11), habitual suffix -**kən** in (12), definitive suffix -**khi** in (13), suffix -**minnə** 'together' in (14), -**mən** 'excessive' in (15), benefactive suffix -**pi** in (16), the deictic suffix -**lu** in (17) and -**lə** in (18), reflexive suffix -**cə** (-**ɟə**) in (19), reciprocal suffix -**nə** in (20), -**həu** 'inceptive' in (21), -**sin** (-**cin**) 'inward directional' in (22) and -**thə** 'downward directional' in (23) and -**ləm** 'completive' in (24)will be discussed in **4.2.**

-loi: It is the derivative suffix which indicates negative mood of a speaker when it occurs with action verbs (as action verbs are agent-oriented). When it goes with stative and process verbs *i.e.* non-dynamic verbs, it gives a sense of futurity that the referent will not be so and so (it will be discussed with examples just below). In both cases of action and non-dynamic verbs the suffix takes another suffix -**i** (simple aspect marker) which is not seen at the surface level because of the identical vowel deletion rule *i.e.* -**loi-i** > -**loi** and the aspect marker is represented by a zero morpheme. The suffix has six allomorphic variations as -**loi** ~ **roi** ~ **poi** ~ **moi** ~ **ŋoi** ~ **oi**. -**loi** follows morphemes that end in /**t**/ and /**n**/ while -**roi** occurs with morphemes that end in vowels, -**poi** with /**p**/ ending morphemes, -**moi** with /**m**/ ending morphemes, -**ŋoi** with /**ŋ**/ ending morphemes and -**oi** with /**k**/ ending morphemes. The suffix can be attached either directly to the verbal root or after a derived form.

The suffix –**loi** can occur next to the verbal root.

25. **thət**- 'pluck'
əi ləi-si thət-loi
I flower-DEM pluck-NPOT-SAM
'I shall not pluck this flower'

26. **pən**- 'mention'
əi hirəm-si-də nəŋ-gi miŋ pəl-loi
I matter-DEM-LOC you-GEN name mention-NPOT-SAM
'I shall not mention your name in this matter'

The verbs in (25and 26) are agent-oriented verbs and they imply the speaker's intention of 'not to do something' and in one sense, this may be interpreted as an assurance from the speaker's side to the hearer. For example, in (26) the speaker shows his intention 'not to pluck the flower' and he is giving a sense of assurance that he will not do such a thing.The sense implied by the suffix -**loi** when it goes with action verbs is contrasted with stative and process verbs. Consider some examples with non-dynamic verbs.

27. **tət**- 'break'
thəuri-si pak tət-loi

rope-DEM seldom break-NPOT-SAM
'This rope will not break easily'

28. **cau-** 'be big'
u əsi cau-roi
tree this big-NPOT-SAM
'This tree will not be big'

29. **lum-** 'be warm'
phəiɟup əsi lum-moi
quilt this warm-NPOT-SAM
'This quilt will not be warm (enough)'

The verbs in the above given sentences are non-dynamic and they are not agent-oriented. The suffix **-loi** when occurred with such verbs gives a sense of futurity as well as a simple negative statement that the referent will not be such and such. For instance, in (27) the suffixation of **-loi** to the verb **tət-** 'break' implies that the referent *i.e.* 'the rope' will not break easily. It does not show any sense of intention as found in sentences which have action verbs *e.g.* sentences (25 and 26).

With action verbs the suffix **-loi** can follow almost all the suffixes.

30. **phəm-** 'sit'
əi nəŋ-bu cəuki-si-də phəm-həl-loi (-hən-loi)
I you-ACC chair-DEM-LOC sit-CAUS-NPOT-SAM
'I shall not let you sit in this chair'

31. **thaŋ-** 'carry'
əi tebəl-si məpan-də thaŋ-dok-oi (-thok-loi)
I table-DEM outside-LOC carry-OUT-NEG-SAM
'I shall not take the table outside the house'

-loi and its allomorphs can occur with almost the derivative suffixes as **cət-minnə-roi** 'shall not go together', **pu-rək-loi** 'shall not bring', **ca-rəm-moi** 'shall not eat (until you come back), **thaŋ-ɟil-loi (-sin-loi)**'shall not bring', **ləŋ-thə-roi** 'shall not throw down', **ka-khət-loi** 'shall not climb up', etc.

-loi may give a different meaning which is conditioned by its neighbouring suffixes. The combination of **-khi** with **-roi** gives a sense of temporal negation.

32. **thoŋ-** 'cook'
əi cak thoŋ-khi-roi
I cooked rice cook-DEF-NPOT-SAM
'I will not cook (for sometime or right now)'

In (32) the combination of the suffixes **-khi** and **-roi** gives the meaning that the action of 'cooking' will not be performed right at the time of the speech in the sense that it will be held in suspension for some time and the speaker intends to perform the action after sometime. The temporal meaning is inherently present in the verb form itself. That is why the sentence does not need any temporal adverb like **həuɟik** 'now', **ŋaihak** 'for time being', etc. in the surface form. .

Another construction is with **-lə** 'prospective' where the speaker's intention is not to do something. It optionally gives a sense of simple negative statement or stoppage of a habit and sometimes a promise.

33. **ca-** 'eat'
    əi cak ca-rə-roi (-lə-roi)
    I rice eat-PROS-NPOT-SAM
    'I will not take meal (today)'

34. **ca-** 'eat'
    əi ŋa ca-rə-roi (-lə-roi)
    I fish eat-PROS-NPOT-SAM
    'I will not eat fish'

35. **thək-** 'drink'
    əi ca thək-ə-roi (-lə-roi)
    I tea drink-PROS-NPOT-SAM
    'I will not drink tea'

Sentence (33) gives the meaning of stoppage of something for some time *e.g.* the verb implies that the speaker will not take meal for a particular day only. The verbs in (34) and (35) imply the speaker's intention to promise himself to stop a habit (for **-lə** 'prospective' see **4.2**).

The combination of the suffixes **-lə** and **-loi** again be preceded by definitive marker **-khə** which intensifies the statement by giving a sense of promise.

36. **thək-** 'drink'
    əi əmuk hən-nə ju thək-khə-rə-roi
    I once repeat-ADV liquor drink-DEF-PROS-NPOT-SAM
    'I will never drink liquor again'

37. **ɟwar sannə-** 'gamble'
    əi əmuk hən-nə ɟwar sannə-khə-rə-roi
    I once repeat-ADV gamble play-DEF-PROS-NPOT-SAM
    'I will never gamble again'

38. **ŋaŋ-** 'speak'
 əi mə-ŋon-də əmuk hən-nə ŋaŋ-khə-rə-roi
 I 3PP-DIR-LOC once repeat-ADV speak-DEF-PROS-NPOT-SAM
 'I will never talk to him'

The above sentences imply a sense of promise made by the speaker. In (36) the speaker is fed up of drinking wine and intends to make a promise that 'he' will drop the habit totally. Sentences (37) and (38) also imply the same intention from the speaker's side to drop the habit of 'gambling' in (37) and to develop a gap between the speaker and the referent in (38).

The suffix **-loi** cannot go with **-kən ~ gən** 'habitual', **-mən** 'excessive', deictic suffixes -lə 'towards the speaker' and **-lu** 'to go somewhere and perform the action there'. Excepting the above mentioned four suffixes it can go with almost every suffixes; it can go with the four directionals: **-sin**, **-thok**, **-khət**, **-thə**; **-lək** 'deictic', **-ləm** 'completive', **-nə** 'reciprocal', **-minnə** 'together', **-cə~ɟə** 'reflexive', **-həu** 'inceptive', **-pi ~ bi** 'benefactive', **-lə** 'prospective', etc. It should be mentioned that verbal roots can take a string of suffixes in Manipuri because of its being an agglutinating type of language (the other two are isolating and inflectional). The above given examples show only the possibilities of the occurrence of the derivative suffixes which can be attached directly before **-tə ~ də** and **-loi ~ roi**.

An interesting point to be noted here is that all the verb forms that end in **-loi** can also be followed by some other suffixes to make an interrogative sentence. In such constructions where **-loi** is followed by other suffixes, it should not be confused that it is derivative suffix -**loi**. On the other hand, **-loi** when it comes at the end of a sentence, it is followed by **-i** 'simple aspect marker'. Consider the following sentences where **-loi** is contrasted with **-kə** 'potential' as a derivative suffix.

39. **cət-** 'go'
 pabuŋ! cət-thok-pi-roi-də-bə-ra?
 Father go-OUT-HON-NPOT-SPF-NMZ-INTR
 'Father! Will you not go out?'

40. **cət-** 'go'
 nəŋ skul cət-khi-roi-də-bə-ra?
 you school go-DEF-NPOT-SPF-NMZ-INTR
 'Will you not go to school now?'

41. **ca-** 'eat'
 nəŋ cak ca-rə-roi-də-bə-ra?
 you rice eat-PROS-NPOT-SPF-NMZ-INTR
 'Will you not take meal?'

The suffix **-ra** is an interrogative marker which can be attached to noun, pronoun and adjective. It cannot be attached directly to verbal root. Hence, it is necessary to nominalize a verb form to take suffix **-ra**. /ə/ of **-bə** and this nominalizer **-bə** can optionally be deleted in spoken or sometimes in written forms (see also **4.3**).

cət -thok-pi-roi-də-bə-ra

cət-thok-pi-roi-də-bra by contraction rule /ə/ in -bə is deleted.

cət-thok-pi-roi-də-ra /-**bə**/ is deleted.

cət-thok-pi-roi-dra /-ə/ in **-də** is deleted.

There are other forms of negative markers showing different aspects and sentence forms. They are **-tə-ri (-tri) ~ də-ri (-dri)**, **-tə-re (-tre) ~ də-re (-dre)**, **-kənu ~ gənu**, **-nu** alone; **-kum ~ gum,** etc.

-tə-ri~də-ri (-tri~dri): It is the combination of a negative marker **-tə ~ də** + progressive marker **-ri** (**-li**) as a medial suffix in the sense that it can be followed by other derivational suffixes like **ca-də-ri-bə/ca-dri-bə** 'one who has not taken meal yet', **ca-riŋəi-də** 'while eating', etc. But when the suffix comes at the end of a sentence the suffix **-li** takes an aspect marker **-i** which can be shown as following:

42. **ca-** 'eat'

əi cak ca-də-ri (-dri)
I rice eat-NEG-PROG-SAM
'I have not taken my meal yet'

In the sentence given above, the suffix **-ri (-li)** is followed by an inflectional marker **-i,** *i.e.* a simple aspect marker (SAM). The aspect marker is represented by a zero morpheme in the surface structure as it has been deleted by identical vowel deletion rule. The two suffixes **-tə-ri ~ də-ri** can be contracted by deleting vowel /ə/ of the **-tə ~ də** as **-tə-ri ~ də-ri > -tri ~ dri**.

The suffixes **-tə-ri ~ də-ri** (**-tri ~ dri**) mean that the activity has not yet started. For instance, when someone says **əi cak ca-də-ri (-dri)** (42) may be analysed in a way. In the underlying structure, it may mean that a situation of 'not doing the action' still remains or continues. In this sense, the progressive suffix **-li** has contributed some meaning in the negative environment. Of course, one may argue about the meaning of progressiveness in the negative environment as there is no sense of realization or continuation in the negative environment. Negative environments always imply an action or event which is not realized and probably have no sense of progressiveness. This confusion may be cleared in the following way when the function of **-li** is always found both in positive and negative environments.

43. **ca-** 'eat'

a. i-ma cak ca-ri
1PP-mother rice eat-PROG-SAM

'My mother is eating'

b. i-ma cak ca-də-ri (-dri)
1PP-mother rice eat-NEG-PROG-SAM
'My mother has not taken meal yet'

The verb **ca-ri** in (43a) may be analysed in the underlying structure as **ca-dunə-ləi-ri** 'the action of eating has already started and it still continues'. Contrasting this environment in the negative construction in (43b), the verb **ca-də-ri** may also be analysed as **cak ca-də-nə ləi-ri** 'the action of eating has not yet started and the situation of not eating still continues. From the above analysis, it may be concluded that negative marker **-tə** when followed by progressive suffix **-li** does not necessarily mean to stop an action while it is going on. Thus, **pa-də-ri** does not mean 'stop while reading'. It gives a sense that the action of reading has not yet started and the situation of not reading still goes on.

Another implication present in the construction of **-tə-ri** ~ **də-ri** is that it has the prospect of doing the action after sometime. Thus, the verb **ca-də-ri** may mean that the action of eating has not yet started but may be doing it after some time. This implication is not present in **ca-de** 'do not eat' in the sentence that it has no prospect of doing the action after sometime. The two forms of negation are illustrated in the following environments which will make the point clear.

44. **ca-** 'eat'

a. nəŋ cak ca-ri-bə-ra?
You cooked rice eat-PROG-NMZ-INTR
'Are you taking your meal?'

b. əi cak ca-ri
I rice eat-PROG-SAM
'I am taking my meal'

c. əi cak ca-de
I rice eat-NEG-SAM
'I do not take my meal'

Sentence (44a) enquires something while (b) gives the answer in positive environment and (c) answers the question in negative environment. The last sentence may imply a habitual sense as "I do not eat rice", instead "I eat bread (roti in Hindi), fish or pulse".

An important point to be noted in the above sentences is that the question has progressive marker **-li** as in **ca-ri-bə-ra** 'are you eating' in (44a) while the answer given to this question in negative environment is that **ca-de** 'do not eat', (c) which does not have the suffix **-li**. The question supposed to be asked when someone says **ca-də-ri** 'has not eaten yet' does not have the suffix **-li** either. It has the perfective suffix **-lə** instead.

45. **ca-** 'eat'

a. nəŋ cak ca-rə-bə-ra?
you rice eat-PERF-NMZ-INTR
'Have you taken your meal?'

b. əi cak ca-re
I rice eat-PERF-SAM
'I have taken meal'

b. əi cak ca-də-ri (-dri)
I rice eat-NEG-PROG-SAM
'I have not taken my meal yet'

As mentioned above, sentence (45c) implies that the action of eating will be performed after sometime.

46. **cət-** 'go'
caubə skul cət-tə-ri (-tri)
Chaoba school go-NEG-PROG-SAM
'Chaoba has not yet gone to school (but he might go after sometime)'

Sentence (46) denotes actions which are not realized yet. In certain circumstances, it may mean to stop doing an action for sometime, *e.g.* due to an illness the action of going to school may be stopped for some days, weeks or months. In such circumstances, the sentence may be as follows:

47. **cət-** 'go'
məhak na-bə-dəgi skul cət-tə-ri (-tri)
he ill-NMZ-ABL school go-NEG-PROG-SAM
'He has been absent from school due to illness'

Now consider the following sentences:

48. **cau-** 'be big'
əŋaŋ-si cau-də-ri (-dri)
child-DEM big-NEG-PROG-SAM
'The child has not yet grown up'

49. **mun-** 'be ripe'
həinəu-si mun-də-ri (-dri)

mango-DEM ripe-NEG-PROG-SAM
'The mango has not yet become ripe'

50. **kəŋ**- 'be dry'
phi-siŋ-du kəŋ-də-ri (-dri)
cloth-PL-DEM dry-NEG-PROG-SAM
'The clothes have not yet dried up'

51. **kau**- 'forget'
əi nəŋ-bu kau-də-ri (-dri)
I you-ACC forget-NEG-PROG-SAM
'I have not yet forgotten you' or 'I still remember you'

The verb **cau-də-ri** 'has not yet grown up' in (48), **mun-də-ri** 'has not yet become ripe' in (49) and **kəŋ-də-ri** 'have not yet dried up' in (50) refer to conditions or states in which the desired degree has not been achieved yet. This is the first assumption of meaning just perceived at the first glance of the verbs. The verb **kau-də-ri** 'has not yet forgotten' in (51) is a process verb.

For stative verbs, the second assumption is conditional where the conditions imply that the referents expect an opposite situation. For example, in (48) the verb **cau-də-ri**, gives the idea that the child might have grown up as compared to his age. But the situation was not so as desired by the speaker. The same condition applies to **mun-də-ri** in (49) and **kəŋ-də-ri** in (50) respectively. In such conditions, the speaker expects a change. This is the reason why ***nəu-də-ri** 'has not yet become younger, ***ten-də-ri** 'has not yet become short', ***pik-tə-ri** 'has not yet become small' are not semantically acceptable. One cannot expect to become younger instead of becoming older; hair, rope, etc. cannot become shorter by itself and one cannot think of a child to become small instead of growing up. It is quite natural for animates (human beings, plants, etc.) to grow old, (of hairs) to become longer and of children to grow up. Hence, the verbs like **nəu-də-ri**, **ten-də-ri**, **pik-tə-ri**, etc. are not semantically acceptable. It is also quite natural for human beings to forget and that is why, **kau-də-ri** in (92) is semantically acceptable.

-tə-re ~ -də-re (-tre ~ dre): According to the different semantic scope of the verbal forms the suffixation of **-tə-re ~ də-re** to verbal roots may refer to different situations. It may give the meaning of stop, drop, or give up a habit.

52 a. nəŋ ju thək-li-bə-ra
you liquor drink-PROG-NMZ-INTR
'Do you keep on drinking liquor?'

b. əi ju thək-li
I liquor drink-PROG-SAM
'I keep on drinking liquor'

c. əi ju thək-tə-re
I liquor drink-NEG-PERF-SAM
'I have given up drinking liquor'

Sentence (52a) enquires somebody whether he is still keeping on his habit of drinking while sentence (b) gives the answer in a positive sense and sentence (c) gives the answer in negative sense that he has given up the habit of drinking liquor.

In case of stative verbs like **noi-** 'be fat', **ŋəu-** 'be fair, white', **cau-** 'be big', **sa-** 'be sunny, hot' the suffixation of **-tə-re ~ də-re** may give two alternative meanings. The first implication is 'stoppage of an action or event' (same as action verbs just given above) and another is a situation which does not show any kind of change; a situation which remains as it is.

53. **noi-** 'be fat'
lәta-si noi-d-re (-dre)
Lata-DEM fat-NEG-PERF-SAM
'Lata has not become fat (despite efforts)' OR 'Lata is not fat any longer'

54. **ŋəu-** 'be white'
phi-si ŋəu-də-re- (-dre)
cloth-DEM white-NEG-PERF-SAM
'The cloth has not become white'
(even if it is washed *i.e.* it remains as it is)

55. **cau-** 'be big'
əŋaŋ-du cau-də-re (-dre)
child-DEM big-NEG-PERF-SAM
'The child has not grown up (remains as short as before)'

56. **sa-** 'be sunny'
nuŋsa **sa-də-re** (-dre)
sunlight sunny-NEG-PERF-SAM
'It has not become sunny (It remains as cloudy as before)' OR
'It was sunny before but now it becomes cloudy'

In the above examples the verbs show two implications as an unchanged in the first sense and a changed in the second one except the verb **cau-də-re** in (55) where the verb implies only one sense that is a situation which remains as before. The sense of change is not found in this verb because of the semantic structure of the verb which does not allow a change from 'big' to 'small' or 'tall' to 'short'.

The implication of two-way meaning may be removed by adding adverbs like **–hannə gumnə** 'as before, as usual' and **həuɟikti** 'at present'. The two adverbs can occur singly or both and in both situations, the meaning remains the same. The additions of the adverbs show a sense of comparison between an earlier and the present situations (at the time of uttering the sentence).

57 **kən-** 'be strong'

a. əi həuɟik-ti hannə-gum-nə i-sa
I now-PART before-like-ADV 1PP-body
kən-də-re (-dre)
strong-NEG-PERF-SAM
'I am not as strong as before'

b. əi həuɟik-ti i-sa kən-də-re (-dre)
I now-PART 1PP-body strong-NEG-PERF-SAM
'I am not as strong as before'

c. əi hannə gum-nə i-sa kən-də-re (-dre)
I before like-ADV 1PP-body strong-NEG-PERF-SAM
'I am not as strong as before'

The three sentences (57a, b and c) denote the same idea. The addition of both the adverbs and removal of one of them does not bring any significant difference in the meaning of the sentences.

58. **pum-** 'get rotten'
həuɟik-ti niŋthəm tha oi-rə-bə-ni-nə ŋa
now-PART winter month be-PERF-NMZ-COP-CONJ fish
thoŋ-bə pum-də-re (-dre)
cook-NMZ rot-NEG-PERF-SAM

'Fish curries do not get rotten nowadays as it is winter'

In the above sentence there are two means of indicating adverbial form. The first is **həuɟik-ti** 'now' and the other is the phrase **niŋthəm tha oi-rə-bə-ni-nə** 'being winter'. Without the first adverb of time **həuɟik-ti** 'nowadays' the phrase can give the idea clearly.

59. niŋthəm tha oi-rə-bə-ni-nə ŋa thoŋ-bə
winter month be-PERF-NMZ-COP-CONJ fish cook-NMZ
pum-də-re (-dre)
rot- NEG-PERF-SAM
'Fish curries do not get rotten as it is winter now'

The adverb of time indicated by the phrase is because of the suffix **-ni** 'copula'. It gives the realized situation. In other words, it gives the meaning that winter has already started/ prevailed. If **-ni** 'copula' is replaced by - **bədi** 'if' the whole sentence structure will be changed.

60. niŋthəm tha oi-rə-bədi ŋa thoŋ-bə pum-moi
winter month be-PROS-if fish cook-NMZ rot-NPOT-SAM
'If it is winter, fish curry will not get rotten'

The verb takes a negative non-realized suffix because of the conditional suffix **-bədi** while **-ni** 'copula' refers to a realized action. It should be noted that **-rə** in (59) is perfective while **-rə** in (60) is prospective. The suffixation of **-tə-re ~ də-re** (**-tre ~ dre**) can also refer to an action or event where something expected does not happen.

61. **lak**- 'come'
məhak puŋ məŋa-də lak-kə-də-bə-ni ədubu
he hour five-LOC come-POT-SPF-NMZ-COP but
lak-tə-re (-tre)
come-NEG-PERF-SAM
'He was to come at 5 o'clock but he did not turn up'

62. **tek**- 'collapse'
ŋəra-gi noŋ- nuŋsit-tu-də jum-du
yesterday-GEN storm-DEM-LOC house-DEM
tek-tə-re (-tre)
collapse-NEG-PERF-SAM
'The house has not collapsed in yesterday's storm'

The suffixation of **-tə-re ~ də-re** may also denote a situation where something is not functioning or of failure of an engine, mechanism, etc. which are supposed to be functioning.

63. **ja**- 'be in working condition'
əi-gi gari-gi horn ja-də-re (-dre)
I-GEN vehicle-GEN horn function-NEG-PERF-SAM
'The horn of my vehicle is not working'

64. **cət**- 'be in working condition'
əi-gi ghəri cət-tə-re (-tre)
I-GEN watch work-NEG-PERF-SAM
'My watch is not functioning'

-nu/-kənu ~ gənu: The suffix **-nu/-kənu ~ gənu** denotes prohibition of an action when attached to verbal roots. **-nu** is mainly used in spoken form to prohibit someone when the action is about to perform or carry out. But in most written works, **-kənu ~ gənu** is used as prohibitive marker. Both **-nu** and **-kənu ~ gənu** cannot occur with uncontrollable verbs like **mu**- 'be black' as ***mu-gənu** 'do not be black', **waŋ**- 'be tall' in ***waŋ-gənu** 'do not be tall', **si**- 'die' in ***si-gənu** 'do not die', etc. This prohibitive marker **-nu/-kənu ~ gənu** indicates a negative command, *i.e.* to ask somebody not to do something, to stop something as the marker usually goes with controllable verbs only.

-nu is used to prohibit somebody when the action is about to perform. For example, when somebody is about to eat something the following sentence may be used to prohibit him from eating. It denotes a sudden expression.

65. **ca**- 'eat'
cak cəɟik-tu ca-nu
cooked rice stale-DEM eat-PROH
'Don't eat the stale rice'

66. **pai**- 'hold'
khau-du pai-nu
bag-DEM hold-PROH
'Don't hold the bag'

-kənu follows any morpheme that ends in voiceless sounds.

67. **nok**- 'laugh'
mi-jam tin-bə məphəm-də kən-nə nok-kənu
public gather-NMZ place-LOC loud-ADV laugh-PROH
'Do not laugh loudly in public places'

68. **nəp**- 'stick'
phəklaŋ-də ce nəp-kənu
wall-LOC paper stick-PROH
'Do not stick bill on the wall'

The suffix **-gənu** can occur after any morpheme that ends in voiced sounds.

69. **laŋ**- 'make noise'
mi-nə lairik təu-riŋəi-də laŋ-gənu
man-NOM book study-SPFD-time make noise-PROH
'Do not make noise while somebody is reading'

70. **tən**- 'be lazy'
nə-sa-gi nə-thəu təu-bə tən-gənu
2PP-body-GEN 2PP-duty do-NMZ lazy-PROH
'Do not be lazy in doing your own duty'

71. **pəŋ**- 'be foolish'
pəŋ-gə-nu mi-gi m-wa-də cət-kə-nu
foolish-PROH man-GEN 3PP-speech-LOC go-PROH
'Don't be foolish! Don't follow other's instruction'

The verbs **laŋ-gənu** in (69), **tən-gənu** in (70) and **pəŋ-gənu** in (71) give the meaning of prohibition as well as advice in some sense.

-kum ~ gum: The suffixation of **-kum ~ gum** refers to negative proposal of an action. It is always followed by suggestive marker **–si** (see **4.2**). It can occur only with controllable verbs as one cannot propose not to become small as in ***nem-gum-si** 'let us not be small or short'. The subject will always be in plural form of first person, *i.e.* **əi-khoi** 'we'.

The suffix -**kum** comes after morphemes that end in voiceless sounds.

72. **cət**- 'go'
əi-khoi həjeŋ mə-khoi-də cət-kum-si
I-PL tomorrow he-PL-LOC go-NEG-SUG
'Let us not visit him tomorrow'

73. **thək**- 'drink'
əi-khoi ŋəsi ca thək-kum-si
I-PL today tea drink-NEG-SUG
'Let us not drink tea today'

The suffix -**gum** always occurs after morphemes that end in voiced sounds.

74. **theŋ**- 'be late'
həjeŋ-di əi-khoi theŋ-gum-si
tomorrow-PART I-PL late-NEG-SUG
'Let us not be late tomorrow'

75. **həŋ**- 'ask'
əi-khoi mə-ŋon-də wa əmə-tə həŋ-gum-si
I-PL 3PP-DIR-DAT speech one-only ask-NEG-SUG
'Let us not ask him anything'

Negative Polarity Items *suk-, -phat, -pəŋ* : Words that are used only in negative environment are called negative polarity item (NPI). The main functions of these words are to strengthen the negation. In Manipuri, they are available in two forms: (i) affix and (ii) adverbs.

In Manipuri the prefix that functions as negative polarity item is **suk**- 'never' and a suffix -**phat** 'slightly'. There is also another prefix **pəŋ**- 'seldom' which can occur in both positive and negative environments with different meanings.

suk-: The addition of this prefix to a verbal root demands a reduplicative form of the verbal root.

76. **ləu**- 'take'
əi mə-ŋon-dəgi lairik suk-ləu ləu-de
I 3PP-DIR-ABL book never-take take-NEG-SAM
'I never took the book from him'

77. **noi**- 'be fat'
nəŋ nəsa suk-noi noi-de
you 2PP-body never-fat fat-NEG-SAM
'You are not fat at all'

78. **hau**- 'be tasty'
ensaŋ-si suk-hau hau-te
curry-DEM never-tasty tasty-NEG-SAM
'The curry is not tasty at all'

Unlike English, the verb takes negative marker as usual when one more negative item is occurred in the sentence. In English, negative meaning is carried by the negative adverb 'never, seldom', etc. whereas in Manipuri both the negative polarity marker and negative marker occur in a sentence.

-phat: It occurs in negative environment only. It cannot occur in a positive sentence. The addition of this suffix to a verbal root gives the meaning of 'slightly, less to the necessary degree'. In other sense, it denotes quality or degree of a state or quality. It cannot go with action verbs as the semantic boundary of the suffix demands a state or quality only.

79. **seŋ**- 'be distinct'
photo-si məmi seŋ-phat-te
photo-DEM picture distinct-MOD-NEG-SAM
'This picture in the photograph is not distinct enough'

80. **ŋəu**- 'be white'
nəŋ-n su-bə phi-si ŋəu-phat-tə-ri
you-NOM wash-NMZ cloth-DEM white-MOD-NEG-PROG-SAM
'The cloth you have washed has not yet become white enough'

81. **mun**- 'be properly cooked'
cak-si mun-phat-te
rice-DEM properly cook-MOD-NEG-SAM
'The rice is not properly cooked'

pəŋ-: The prefix **pəŋ**- can occur in both positive and negative environments. The prefixation of **pəŋ**- demands the verbal roots to be reduplicated.

82. **ŋaŋ-** 'speak'

a. məhak-ti wa pəŋ-ŋaŋ-də ŋaŋ-ŋi
he-PART speech RED-speak-LOC speak-SAM
'He speaks too much'

b. **ŋaŋ-** 'speak'
məhak-ti mərəm ləi-tə-nə wa pəŋ-ŋaŋ
he-PART reason have-NEG-ADV speech RED-speak
ŋaŋ-de
speak-NEG-SAM
'He does not speak too much without any cause/reason'

83. **noi-** 'be fat'

a. nupi-si mə-sa pəŋ-noi-də noi
woman-DEM 3PP-body RED-fat-LOC fat-SAM
'This woman becomes too fat'

b. nəŋ nə-sa pəŋ-noi noi-de
you 2PP-body RED-fat fat-NEG-SAM
'You are not too fat'

The prefix **pəŋ-** can occur in both environments *i.e.* positive and negative. But the suffix -**tə** ~ -**də** as found in all positive sentences cannot occur in negative environments with state verbs. It is ungrammatical to take -**tə** ~ -**də** with state verbs and that is why -**tə** ~ -**də** is dropped in (84b and 85b). The prefix **pəŋ-** refers to do something at random, do something without purpose or do something irregularly (see **4.1**).

Adverbs denoting negative polarity: -pak ~ paknə, pəŋnə, khək, kəja, kəidəuŋəidə ~ kəidəuŋəidəsu/kəidəunuŋdə ~ kəidəunuŋdəsu, kənamətə ~ kənasu, əmuktə phaubə are negative adverbs.

pak ~ paknə: Functionally the word **pak** 'seldom' functions as a negative adverb in a sentence. But semantically it functions as a negative polarity item as it strengthens the degree of negative sense in a sentence.

84. **lak-** 'come'
məhak əi-khoi-də pak lak-te
he I-PL-LOC seldom come-NEG-SAM
'He seldom comes to our place'

85. **waŋ-** 'be tall'
u-si pak waŋ-de

tree-DEM seldom tall-NEG-SAM
'This tree is not tall enough (while others have become tall)'

86. **kai-** 'break'
kəp-si pak kai-de
cup-DEM seldom break-NEG-SAM
'This cup hardly breaks'

The adverb **pak** when it goes with action verb **lak-te** in (84) mean seldom. But when it goes with stative verb **waŋ-de** (85) it refers to a lesser degree or quality. But when it comes before process verb **kai-de** in (86), it indicates that an event does not happen easily.

pak can be reduplicated without disturbing the semantic structure of the sentence.

87. **lak-** 'come'
məhak əi-khoi-də pak pak lak-te
he I-PL -LOC seldom come-NEG-SAM
'He seldom comes to our place'

But when it goes with stative verb as in (90) the reduplicated adverb **pak** refers to a meaning totally different from the non-reduplicated sentences.

88. **waŋ-** 'be tall'
u-si pak pak waŋ-de
tree-DEM seldom tall-NEG-SAM
'The tree takes a long time to grow tall'

When **pak** is non-reduplicated as found in (87), it refers to a degree which is less than the necessary degree or quality. But when it is reduplicated, it refers to time taken by the subject (tree) to become tall.

The negative adverb **pak** can be replaced by **pak-nə** 'seldom' without any semantic disturbance. The adverb **pak** takes an adverbial suffix **-nə** and this forms **pak-nə** and it cannot be reduplicated as **pak pak**. The form ***paknə paknə** is ungrammatical.

89. **lak-** 'come'
məhak əi-khoi-də paknə lak-te
he I-PL-LOC seldom come-NEG-SAM
'He seldom comes to our place'

90. **waŋ-** 'be tall'
u-si paknə waŋ-de
tree-DEM seldom tall-NEG-SAM
'The tree is not tall enough (while others have become tall)'

pəŋnə: This is another adverb used in negative environment only. It occurs with animate subjects only.

91. **lak**- 'come'
məhak əi-khoi-də pəŋnə lak-te
he I-PL-LOC seldom come-NEG-SAM
'He seldom comes to our place'

92. **waŋ**- 'be tall'
*u-si pəŋnə waŋ-de
tree-DEM seldom tall-NEG-SAM

93. **kai**- 'break'
*kəp-si pəŋnə kai-de
cup-DEM seldom break-NEG-SAM

The adverb **pəŋnə** is derived from **pəŋ** 'be fool' and that is why it cannot go with inanimate subjects (for details see **4.1**).

khək: This adverb also occurs in negative environments only. It strengthens the negative meaning of the sentence in which it occurs.

94. **təu**- 'do'
mi-gi thəmoi sok-pə thəbək khək təu-gənu
man-GEN heart hurt-NMZ work never do-PROH
'Never do anything that will hurt others' feelings'

95. **ja**- 'be possible'
wa-də-nə nuŋŋai-bə khək ja-roi
suffer-NEG-ADV happy-NMZ never possible-NPOT-SAM
'It will never be possible to get happiness without hard work'

In the above examples, **khək** strengthens the negative meaning of the sentences. In English, this word 'never' carries the negative meaning and the verb need not be in negative constructions. But in Manipuri, there are always two negative words in such constructions. To indicate a negative sense, negative markers are added to the verbal roots and to strengthen the negative meaning, negative adverbs and affixes are used. Such negative strengthening items are termed as negative polarity items. There are also other means of indicating negative modifiers. They are **kəja** which can be found in both environments (affirrmative and negative) but with different meanings and other adverbs like **kəidəuŋəidə** ~ **kəidəuŋəidə-su** 'never', **kəidəunuŋdə** ~ **kidəunuŋdə-su** 'never', **kənaməte** ~ **kənasu** 'no one or nobody', **kəriməte** 'nothing', **kərisu** 'nothing', **kədaidəsu** 'nowhere'.

kəja :This adverb can occur in both constructions of negative and positive environments.

96. lairik-si-gi   məməl   kəja-no
book-DEM-GEN   price   how much-Q
'What is the price of this book?'

97. əŋaŋ   kəja   əmə-su   sannə-ri
child   many   one-also   play-PROG-SAM
'Many children are also playing'

98. məhak   əphəbə   pautak   kəja   ləu-de
he   good   advice   hardly   take-NEG-SAM
'He hardly takes many a good advice'

99. əŋaŋ-si   mə-sa   kəja   phət-te
child-DEM   3PP-body   hardly   good-NEG-SAM
'This child is not so healthy'

It may be noted that the verbal root **ph**- 'be good' in (99) has undergone regressive assimilation where -**te** influences the preceding vowel and /t/ is doubled as: **phə-te** > **phət-te**. The general phonological rule may be **phə-de** while this form is restricted for indicating prohibition that one should not do such and such things like **ca-phə-de** 'ought not eat', **thək-phə-de** 'ought not drink', **təu-phə-de** 'ought not do', **jeŋ-phə-de** 'ought not look', etc. In order to give the different meanings, the negation of **phə**- 'be good' might have adopted the regressive assimilation resulting to **phət-te**.

kəidəuŋəidə ~ kəidəuŋəidəsu/kəidəunuŋdə ~ kəidəunuŋdəsu: These are the adverbs which can occur in negative environment only. All the four forms have same meaning and they can be replaced by one another.

100. kəidəuŋəidə/kəidəuŋəidə-su/kəidəunuŋdə/kəidəunuŋdəsu
never

ma-gə   khətnə-gənu
he-ASS   quarrel-PROH
'Never fight with him'

kənamətə ~ kənasu: Both the words function as nouns rather than adverbs in a sentence. They have the same semantic value and can be replaced by each other and they have personal reference.

101. **u**- 'see'
əi   jum-si-də   kənamətə/ kənasu   u-de
I   house-DEM-LOC   no one   see-NEG-SAM
'I don't see anyone in this house'

The above examples show that **knamətə** and **kənasu** function as nouns in the sentences. They can take the case markers as regular nouns do.

When they take case suffixes the forms will be as follows:

kənəmətə ~ kənamətə-nə	nominative
kənabusu	accusative
kənagisu ~ kənamətə-gi	genitive
kənagəsu	associative
kənadəsu	dative
kənadəgisu	ablative/source
kədaidəsu	locative

The addition of **-su** to the **kə-** pronouns (**wh-** pronouns) gives negative meaning in a sentence, otherwise they remain as question words. Example of **kədaidə-su** having non-personal reference is given below:

102. lairik-tu məphəm kədaidəsu phəŋ-də-re (-dre)
book-DEM place nowhere find-NEG-PERF-SAM
'The book could not be found anywhere'

Other expressions: There are also other expressions used only in negative environments. They are **əmuktə phaubə** 'not even once/never' and **ima-nə hek pok-pə-dəgi** 'since my birth (since my mother gave birth to me).

103. əsuk phəɟə-bə məphəm-di əmuktə phaubə
such beautiful-NMZ place-PART not even once
u-ɟə-də-ri (-dri)
see-REF-NEG-PROG-SAM
'I have never seen such a beautiful place (in my life)'

104. əsuk phəɟə-bə maithoŋ-di i-ma-nə hek
such beautiful-NMZ face-PART 1PP-mother-NOM just
pok-pə-dəgi u-rək-tə-ri (-tri)
born-NMZ-ABL see-DEIC-NEG-PROG-SAM
'I have not seen such a beautiful face since my birth'

The negative adverbs **əmuktə phaubə** in (103) and **imanə hek pokpə-dəgi** in (104) express something very exciting and very interesting. From the above examples, it can be concluded that two negative items can occur in a negative sentence in Manipuri. Prefixes, suffixes, nominals and adverbials which are found only in negative environments are termed as negative particles and they occur in negative sentences only. Thus, two negative items are found in Manipuri where the first one is negative polarity item like **suk, pəŋnə, pak, phat** etc. and the last one being the negative makers that are attached to the verbal roots. The construction found in Manipuri is ungrammatical in English. It is ungrammatical to say ***'I did not see none on the road'***. The correct form will be ***'I saw none on the road'*** or ***'I did not see anybody on the road'***. English language does not allow having two negative items like 'not' and 'none' and the last negative word is replaced by anybody or anyone which can occur in both positive and negative environment.

105 a. *This book will be useful to any student.*

b. *I have not seen anybody in the garden.*

*c. *I have not seen none/no one in the garden.*

However, negative prefixes are allowable even if there is a negative word in the sentence, but such sentences are not as clear as positive sentences (K.M. McCarthy, 1980: 101). He further mentions that at any rate, there is usually a different emphasis, depending on whether the sentence is more negative or more positive.

106 a. *The elephant was not really dissatisfied.*

b. *The elephant was satisfied.*

107 a. *Gimmy was not unhappy.*

b. *Gimmy was happy.*

108 a. *The door mat read 'Not Unwelcome'.*

b. *The door mat read 'Welcome'.*

Such situation is also found in Manipuri where double negative gives a positive sense.

109. məhak ju thək-tə-bə nətte
he liquor drink-NEG-NMZ not-SAM
'He drinks liquor' OR 'It is not that he does not drink liquor'

110. nupi-du mə-sək thi-bə nətte

woman-DEM 3PP-face ugly-NMZ not-SAM
'The woman is not ugly' OR 'The woman is beautiful'

111. əi thəbək-tu təu-bə ŋəm-moi hai-khi-de
I work-DEM do-NMZ can-NPOT say-DEF-NEG-SAM
'I did not say that I could not do the work' OR 'I can do the work'

112. məhak ŋəsi ŋa ca-roi hai-khi-de
he today fish eat-NPOT say-DEF-NEG-SAM
'He did not say that he would not eat fish today' OR
'He will eat fish today (as usual)'

In (109) the negative marker **-tə ~ də** is in the nominal form forming a nominal complement **thək-tə-bə** with another negative word **nətte**. In (110) the nominal complement is **thibə nətte** 'not ugly'. Both the nominal complements **thək-tə-bə nətte** 'not that (he) does not drink' means **thək-i** 'drinks' and **thibə nətte** 'not ugly' means **phəɟəi** 'is beautiful'. The degree of emphasis whether the sentence is more negative or more positive depends on the context. Sentences (111) and (112) have two clauses: one dependent clause and another independent or main clause, each having a negative marker. Such complex sentences which have two negatives in each clause convey a positive meaning in Manipuri.

1.2 Verbs and Nouns

Before identifying a word to be a verb or a noun we can consider some examples of words used in our day to day life. **əŋaŋ** 'child', **lairik** 'book', **isiŋ** 'water', **ca** 'tea', **cak** 'rice/ cooked rice', **kok** 'head', **ŋa** 'fish', **u** 'tree', **cəphu** 'pot', **nupa** 'man', **nupi** 'woman', **jum** 'house', etc. on the one hand and **ca-**'eat', **thək-** 'drink' , **tum-**'sleep', **i-** ' write', etc. on the other hand, constitute the lexicon of Manipuri language. Words of the first group can stand independently without the help of others whereas words of second group are constructed with roots and suffixes. The first morpheme in **ca-niŋ-ŋi** 'wishes to eat' is **ca-** 'eat', **thək-** 'drink' in **thək-kənu** 'do not drink', **tum-** 'sleep' in **tum-mi** 'is sleeping', and **i-** 'write' in **i-ri** 'is writing' are bound forms as they need help from another bound form to make up a word. The above examples clearly illustrate that there are two forms of roots: free and bound.

David Crystal (1985: 267) defines a root as the base form of a word which cannot be further analysed without total loss of identity. It is that part of the word left when all the affixes are removed. It may be of two types: free and bound. A tree diagram showing a detailed classification of roots is given below:

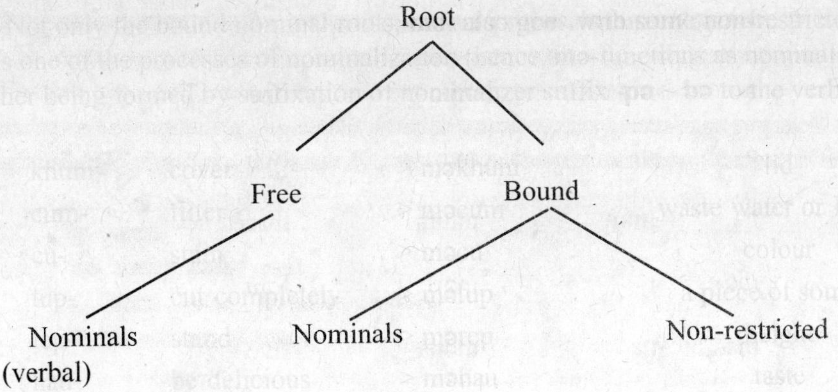

Non-restricted bound roots are the roots (other than nominals) which can generally take inflectional suffixes indicating aspect, moods, time etc. These bound roots are not restricted to one class of word only (as nominals do), instead, they can take derivative suffixes to form different word classes as adjectives, adverbs and nominals. This is the reason why the term non-restricted is used in the classification of roots. However, these non-restricted bound forms take inflectional suffixes to form verbs in Manipuri which is a major word class. There are only two major word classes which can distinctly contribute in the study of Manipuri language and they are nouns and verbs. Adjectives and adverbs come under the group of verb as they are derived from the non-restricted bound roots. To make the study more systematic and smooth, it will be convenient to term the non-restricted bound forms as verbal roots and throughout the study it will be used.

The reason, why bound roots are categorized as nouns and verbs, are given here. As mentioned earlier in **1.1** bound roots that can take the negative markers are verbal roots, they can take inflectional suffixes for predicative use and derivational suffixes to form different word classes for phrasal use. Apart from the verbal roots, there are some bound roots like kinship terms, basic numerals, body parts of animals and other non-human objects. They cannot take the inflectional suffixes like aspect, mood, etc. These bound forms take certain prefixes to form free words. It is clear that both bound forms need affixation to make free words either to function as verbs in sentences while those bound roots which take prefixes to make free words function as subjects and objects in a sentence. Hence, they come under noun category and the bound roots which become nouns are termed as nominal bound roots.

Kinship terms with pronominal prefixes *i-*, *nə-* and *mə-*

First person ***i-***	pa	father	i-pa my father	nə-pa your father	mə-pa his father
Second person ***nə-***	ma	mother	i-ma my mother	nə-ma your mother	mə-ma his mother
Third person ***mə-***	ce	sister	i-ce my sister	nə-ce your sister	mə-ce his sister

Basic numerals with prefixes

ə-	-mə	>	əmə	one
ə-	-ni	>	əni	two
ə-	-hum	>	əhum	three
mə-	-ri	>	məri	four
mə-	-ŋa	>	məŋa	five
tə-	-ruk	>	təruk	six
tə-	-ret	>	təret	seven

Body parts of animals with prefixes

mə-	-ci	>	məci	horn
mə-	-məi	>	məməi	tail
mə-	-soŋ	>	məsoŋ	body
mə-	-phəi	>	məphəi	thigh

Other non-human objects with prefixes

mə-	-pan	>	məpan	bank
mə-	-jai	>	məjai	centre
mə-	-thək	>	məthək	up
mə-	-kha	>	məkha	down
mə-	-na	>	məna	leaf
mə-	-nai	>	mənai	servant
mə-	-pum	>	məpum	whole
mə-	-cet	>	məcet	piece
mə-	-ton	>	məton	top
mə-	-nuŋ	>	mənuŋ	inner, etc.

Not only the bound nominal roots, **mə-** also goes with some non-restricted bound roots. This is one of the processes of nominalization (hence, **mə**-functions as nominalizer prefix) and the other being formed by suffixation of nominalizer suffix **-pə** ~ **bə** to the verbal bound roots.

khum-	cover	> məkhum	lid
cum-	filter	> məcum	waste water or liquid
cu-	stain	> məcu	colour
tup-	cut completely	> mətup	a piece of something
lep-	stand	> mərep	height
hau-	be delicious	> məhau	taste
nəm-	smell	> mənəm	smell
cən-	contain	> məcən	ingredients, etc.

The generalized **mə-** can also go with some free nouns like **khoŋ** 'leg' > **məkhoŋ** 'leg of an animal/somebody', **mai** 'face' > **məmai** 'face of somebody/an animal', **tu** 'body hair' > **mətu** 'fur of an animal', **mit** 'eye' > **məmit** 'eye of somebody/an animal', etc.

From the above given examples, it can be observed that nominal bound roots take prefixes to form a free noun. In English, nouns are free words whereas in Manipuri, it can be free and bound. Free nouns are large in number while bound forms are few. These derived nominals can function as a free noun in sentences.

Inflection is one of the processes of word formation which signal grammatical relationship such as case, aspect, mood, etc. (see Chapter-V). According to the kinds of bound roots as nominal and verbal (non-restricted), the inflectional suffixes they take also vary. Nominals (both free and derived) take case suffixes, number. Verbal bound roots, on the other hand, take both derivatives and inflectionals like aspect, mood, etc.

Case suffixes:

Nominative	-nə
Accusative	-pu ~ bu
Genetive	-ki ~ gi
Associative	-kə ~ gə
Ablative /source	-təgi ~ dəgi
Locative/dative	-tə ~ də
Instrumental	-nə

Number suffixes

-siŋ	>	əŋaŋ-siŋ	children
		lairik-siŋ	books
		jum-siŋ	houses
		khau-siŋ	bags
		mə-cet-siŋ	pieces
		mə-cən-siŋ	ingredients
		mə-khum-siŋ	covers,etc.
-khoi	>	əi-khoi	we
		nə-khoi	you (plural)
		mə-khoi	they

The plural suffix **-khoi** is derived from **khwai** 'many people'. It has another variation -**hoi** which occurs with any third person while **-khoi** is restricted to pronominals. Both number and case suffixes can occur with a nominal where number suffixes always come first and case suffixes follow them.

əŋaŋ-siŋ-gi lairik-siŋ
child-PL-GEN book-PL
'Children's books'

113. əŋaŋ-siŋ-gi lairik-siŋ-du mə-khoi-gi khau-siŋ-də
child-PL-GEN book-PL-DEM he-PL-GEN bag-PL-LOC
hap-cil-lu
put-IN-COM
'Put the children's books in their respective bags'

In the sentence number marker **-siŋ** precedes the case marker. Nouns in Manipuri can also take particles like **-ti ~ di** 'particularization', **-si** demonstrative meaning 'this', **-du** demonstrative' meaning 'that', **-mək** 'self', **-su** 'also', etc.

Verbal roots can be nominalized by suffixing **-pə ~ bə** as in **ca-bə** 'eating', **cət-pə** 'going', **tum-bə** 'sleeping', **i-bə** 'writing', **phəm-bə** 'sitting', **cak-pə** 'burning', etc. But there is no verbalization rule through which a noun becomes a verb as found in English: peace > pacify, class > classify, identity > identify, etc.

Manipuri, being a SOV language verbs always occur in predicative position.

114. əi-nə kəithel-dəgi lairik əmə ləi-rək-i
I-NOM market-ABL book one buy-DEIC-SAM
'I bought a book from the market'

There are also sentences in which noun comes in the predicative position. In such situations the subject noun and the predicative noun are linked by a copulative **-ni** or interrogative **-la ~ ra**.

115. tombə oɟa-ra?
Tomba teacher-INTR
'Is Tomba a teacher?'

116. tombə oɟa-ni
Tomba teacher-COP
'Tomba is a teacher'

These types of sentences are called equational sentences where nouns can occur in predicative position. R.L. Trask (1993) defined an equational sentence as a sentence in which one noun phrase is identified with another one (see **5.1** for more detail).

Another process of nominalization involves suffixation of **-pə ~ bə** to the verbal roots.

ca-	eat	+	-bə	>	ca-bə	to eat
cen-	run	+	-bə	>	cen-bə	to run
pi-	give	+	-bə	>	pi-bə	to give
wai-	borrow	+	-bə	>	wai-bə	to borrow
ŋai-	wait	+	-bə	>	ŋai-bə	to wait
tak-	teach	+	-pə	>	tak-pə	to teach
lak-	come	+	-pə	>	lak-pə	to come
nok-	laugh	+	-p	>	nok-pə	to laugh
jeŋ-	look	+	-bə	>	jeŋ-bə	to look
iŋ-	be cold	+	-bə	>	iŋ-bə	to be cold
ten-	be short	+	-bə	>	ten-bə	to be short
lu-	be deep	+	-bə	>	lu-bə	to be deep
waŋ-	be tall	+	-bə	>	waŋ-bə	to be tall
səŋ-	be green	+	-bə	>	səŋ-bə	to be green, etc.

The nominalizer suffix **-pə ~ bə** can be added after progressive suffix **-li ~ ri**, perfective **-lə ~ rə** and many derivational suffixes.

ca- 'eat'

ca + ri + bə > ca-ri-bə (one who) is eating

ca + rə + bə > ca-rə-bə (one who) has eaten

ca + rəm + bə > ca-rəm-bə (one who) was eating

ca + ru + bə > ca-ru-bə (one who) went somewhere and ate there

ca + niŋ + bə > ca-niŋ-bə (one who) wants to eat

ca + gən + bə > ca-gən-bə (one who) is a habitual eater

ca + mən + bə > ca-mən-bə (one who) eats too much

ca + sin + bə > ca-sin-bə (one who) eats more than enough

ca + rək + pə > ca-rək-pə (one who) ate somewhere and come here, etc.

The derived nominals like **ca-bə** 'eating/to eat', **pa-bə** 'reading/to read', **hek-pə** 'plucking/to pluck' and derived nominals with other derivatives like **ca-ri-bə, ca-rə-bə,** etc. can be found in the nominal positions and can take copulative **ni**

117. memə-di noi-bə-ni
Mema-PART fat-NMZ-COP
'Mema is fat' (when others are not)

The derived nominal **noibə** can also be replaced by a verbal form. Free nouns like in the sentence **tombə oja-ni** 'Tomba is a teacher' on the other hand, cannot have alternatives. They remain as it is and they cannot be expressed in another way.

118. memə-di noi
Mema-PART fat-SAM
'Mema is fat'

The derived nominals can also take verbal modifiers like **kən-nə cen-bə** 'fast running' in the following sentence:

119. əŋaŋ-du kən-nə cen-bə-ni
child-DEM fast-ADV run-NMZ-COP
'The child runs fast'

1.3. Adjectives and Verbs

Adjective is a term used in the grammatical classification of words to refer to the main set of items which specify the attributes of nouns. They generally modify a noun. The languages of Tibeto-Burman family are quite different from those of Dravidian as well as Indo-Aryan family. Unlike the Dravidian languages, these languages do not have the adjectival bases functioning as a sub-group of verbs rather than that of nouns (Bhat, 1991: 673). The reason why they come under the group of verbs is that they are able to take the verbal suffixes and function as a normal verb in Manipuri. Moreover, they are derived from verbal bases by affixation. The process of derivation of adjectives can be classified into two as: derived with prefix ə- and another is without ə-.

Adjectives Derived with ə-: Verbal roots are first derived to nominals by suffixing nominalizer suffix **-pə ~ bə**. These nominalized forms are termed as verbal nouns by some linguists. Adjectival prefix ə- is attached to verbal nouns to derive an adjective.

Nominals		Adjectives		
kəp-pə	crying	ə-kəp-pə	əŋaŋ	crying baby
cak-pə	burning	ə-cak-pə	məi	burning fire
iŋ-bə	cold	ə-iŋ-bə	isiŋ	cold water
hau-bə	tasty	ə-hau-bə	ensaŋ	tasty curry
cen-bə	running	ə-cen-bə	gari	running vehicle
tum-bə	sleeping	ə-tum-bə	əŋaŋ	sleeping child
waŋ-bə	tall	ə-waŋ-bə	u	tall tree
pik-pə	small	ə-pik-pə	pambi	small plant
nəu-bə	new	ə-nəu-bə	wari	new story
ŋəu-bə	white	əŋəu-b	ləi	white flower
pət-pə	rotten	ə-pət-pə	həi	rotten fruit
cau-bə	big	ə-cəu-bə	jum	big house, etc.

A sound change takes place where /**a**/ of **cau**- 'be big' changes to /ə/ when adjectival or attributive prefix ə- is attached to the verbal noun **cau-bə**. It should be noted here that ə- can be attached to monosyllabic verbal roots. It cannot be added to disyllabic or polysyllabic verbal roots. :

Nominals		Adjectives
ca-nə-bə	suitable	*ə-canə-bə
pannə-bə	supervised	*ə-pannə-bə
cennə-bə	involved	*ə-cennə-bə
phəɟə-bə	beautiful	*ə-phəɟə-bə
nuŋsi-bə	love	*ə-nuŋsi-bə
hərau-bə	happy	*ə-hərau-bə

However, there are some exceptions where the prefix ə- can be added to some verbal roots which do not have a verbal noun. They are:

ə-kəknə-bə	special, particular, exact
ə-thomnə-bə	specially added
ə-təmnə-bə	deliberate, intentional
ə-tak ə-phoŋnə-bə	open secret
ə-khənnə-bə	special

In the above examples, the verbal roots when derived with suffix **-nə** may give another meaning which is not related to the adjectives. For example, **kək-nə-bə** may mean 'to cut each other or one another' (of two lines) or 'to separate', **thom-nə-bə** may mean 'to hit with something like stones with each other or one another'. **təm-nə-bə** is a derived verbal root meaning haunting and **khənnə-bə** is also a derived verbal root meaning 'discuss' or 'consult' whereas the reduplicated form **tak phoŋ-nə-bə** is not a derived verbal root and does not function as a word even if the roots have meanings as **tak**- 'teach, inform' and **phoŋ**- 'be open (no more a secret)'. The reduplicated form cannot become a word until ə- is attached to it.

Adjectives derived without ə-: Complex verbs (see **2.2**) and compound verbs can function as adjectives when they are nominalized with **-pə ~ bə**. They do not take prefix **ə-** because of the syllabic nature of the verbal roots.

Adjectives formed by complex verbal roots

cennə-bə mi	person involved
khennə-bə mə-oŋ	different forms
cətnə-bə kaŋlon	agreed rule
khənnə-bə waphəm	discussed topic
mannə-bə səktəm	similar appearance
pəknə-bə phiɟol	suitable dress
canə-bə paukhum	appropriate answer
kannə-bə pautak	useful advice
təmthi-bə nupa	wicked man
kəremnə-bə wahəi	mocking word
cəmotnə-bə phi	dirty clothes

The adjectives (in **bold** letters) in the above examples are derived from complex verbal stems (see **2.2**). They are disyllabic and polysyllabic in nature.

Adjectives formed by Compound forms: Both types of compound nouns incorporation and verbal compounds (**2.3**) can be formed into adjectives by adding a nominalizer suffix **-pə ~ bə**.

khunda-bə mi	person who has settled down
ləllon-bə mi	business man
nəmthi-bə mənəm	bad smell
koirau-nə-bə mit	big and round eye
khoithumnə-bə wahəi	sweet or healing words
phopcaunə-bə əŋaŋ	big and stout boy
pomsatnə-bə ləi	flower (like rose, lotus, lily, etc.) which is not yet bloomed fully
khəjaknə-bə ensaŋ	a salty curry
səŋmun-nə-bə ləphoi	a fully matured banana but yet to ripe
koida-nə-bə maithoŋ	round face

In the above examples, both noun incorporation and verbal compounds modify the following noun.

Adjectives formed by adding other suffixes: Derivational suffixes can be followed by a nominalizer suffix **-pə ~ bə** and such derived forms can function as an adjective in Manipuri.

Adjectives formed with derivational suffixes: Derivational suffixes like progressive -**li ~ ri** and perfective -**lə ~ rə** can be followed by a nominalizer suffix **-pə ~ bə** and the derived form can become an adjective.

Progressive *-li ~ ri*

ca-ri-bə mi	person who is eating
ŋaŋ-li-bə mi	man who is speaking, etc.

Perfective *-lə ~ rə*

kai-rə-bə likli	bottle that has been broken
tət-lə-bə məri	relationship that has been broken, etc.

Causative *-hən*

ca-hən-bə əŋaŋ	child who has been made to eat
nok-hən-bə pau	news that has made somebody laugh, etc.

Habitual *-kən ~ gən*

kəp-kən-bə əŋaŋ	child who is a habitual crier
sau-gən-bə nupa	man who gets angry quickly, etc.

Definiteness ***-khi***

pu-khi-bə lairik	book that has been taken (from here)
ləi-khi-bə khau	bag that has been bought (yesterday), etc.

Deictic – not here, not now (indicating past time) ***-ləm ~ rəm***

lak-ləm-bə əŋaŋ	child who came (yesterday)
pa-rəm-bə para	lesson that was reading, etc.

Deictic – come here after performing an action somewhere - ***lək ~ rək***

khullək-pə pəisa	money that has been found/pick up from the road
wai-rək-pə satin	umbrella that has been borrowed, etc.

Deictic – go somewhere and perform an action there ***-lu ~ ru***

təu-ru-bə thəbək	work done somewhere
pa-ru-bə sireŋ	poem read somewhere, etc.

Deictic – come here and perform an action ***-lə ~ rə***

ca-rə-bə nupa	man who came here and ate
li-rə-bə wari	story which had been told here, etc.

Numerals: Ordinal numerals precede the noun that modifies and cardinal numerals follow the noun and some other numeral adjective also follow the noun.

Ordinal numerals:

əhan-bə əŋaŋ	the first child
əni-subə əŋaŋ	the second child
əhum-subə əŋaŋ	the third child, etc.

Cardinal numerals:

ləi **məŋa**	five flowers
ucek **məri**	four birds
mi **təret**	seven persons
jum **əhum**	three houses, etc.

Other numerals:

cini **khərə**	some sugar
nupi **khərə**	some women
ca **khəɟiktəŋ**	small quantity of tea
ceŋ **khərədəŋ**	small quantity of rice, etc.

All the above given examples are the possible form of adjectives. It may be noted that adjectives formed by prefixing ə- will not have ə- when it takes a modifier like **jamnə** 'very'.

ə-phə-bə nupa > jam-nə phə-bə nupa
good man very good man

ə-cəu-bə jum > jam-nə cau-bə jum
big house very big house

ə-saŋ-bə wari > jam-nə saŋ-bə wari
long story very long story, etc.

Adjectives, in English and many Indo-European languages like Hindi, serve as the head of an adjective phrase. Used alone or with one or more modifiers, they have two characteristic functions: pre-modifier of a noun and the subject predicative. Most adjectives can be used both attributively and predicatively. Attributive adjectives attribute a quality or characteristic to what is denoted by the noun they modify: beautiful flower, nice guy. Predicative adjective are part of the predicate, linked to the subject by a copular verb such as **be** or **seem**: ***The flower is beautiful***, ***The guy is nice.*** Examples of attributive adjective in English:

120. *He gave her a* ***beautiful*** *flower.*

121. *A* ***cool*** *breeze is blowing*

The words in bold letters are attributive adjectives. In Manipuri also attributive adjectives are found in sentences. Attributive adjectives can be used in sentences in the following way.

122. **canə-bə** paukhum 'appropriate answer'
wahəi əmətəŋ-nə canə-bə paukhum
word one-only-NOM appropriate-NMZ answer
pi-ju
give-COM
'Give the appropriate answer in one word only.'

123. **ə-khənnə-bə** phiɟol 'special dress'
ə-khənnə-bə phiɟol-du set-ləgə nupi-du
special-NMZ dress-DEM wear-CPART woman-DEM

tho-rək-ləm-mi
come-OUT-DEIC-SAM
'The woman came out by wearing her special dresses'

Examples of predicative adjectives in English.

124. *The flower is* ***beautiful***.

125. *The boy is **naughty**.*

The **bold** words are the adjectives used in predicative position in English. In Hindi also, both attributive and predicative adjectives are found. For predicative uses, the noun and adjective is linked by a 'be' verb 'hai' which has many forms of inflection with number, person and tense.

126. *main lamba: hoon* 'I am tall'

127. *tu sundar hai* 'You are beautiful'

In English, there are some adjectives which are used only in attributive position *i.e.*, before a noun. They cannot be used in the predicative position. They are **utter**, **sheer**, **sole**, **chief**, **very**, etc.

128. *That is **utter** nonsense.*

129. *I only agreed out of **sheer** desperation.*

130. *He is the **sole** surviver of the family.*

The position of adjectives in an attributive use in English is that it always precedes a noun. But in Manipuri, under certain circumstances, adjectives can follow a noun. All monomorphemic verbal roots (see **2.1**) when they are formed into adjectives can precede a noun as well as it can also follow it. Adjectives derived from complex verbal roots cannot follow a noun. A verbal root may be monosyllabic, disyllabic or polysyllabic but monomorphemic in function. Syntactic illustrations of monomorphemic verbal roots when they are derived to adjectives are given below:

131. əŋaŋ **ə-kəp-pə** 'crying baby'
əŋaŋ ə-kəp-pə-du **ləu-khət-lu**
child ATT-cry-NMZ-DEM take-up-COM
'Pick up the crying baby.'

132. isiŋ **ə-iŋ-bə** 'cold water'
isiŋ ə-iŋ-bə-nə iru-ɟə-thok-u
water ATT-cold-NMZ-NOM bath-OUT-COM
'Take a bath with cold water.'

Adjectives derived with ə- can either precede or follow a noun. However, that of following a noun is more common in Manipuri. The change of position does not cause any disturbance in the semantic structure of the sentence. It can be noticed that the suffixes that are generally attached to a noun are found to be attached to the adjectives when they follow nouns in the above sentences.

Adjective preceding the noun		**Adjective following the noun**	
ə-kəp-pə əŋaŋ-du	>	əŋaŋ **ə-kəp-pə**-du	'the crying child'
ə-iŋ-bə isiŋ-nə	>	isiŋ **ə-iŋ-bə**-nə	'by/with cold water'
ə-cen-bə gari-dəgi	>	gari **ə-cen-bə**-dəgi	'from the running vehicle'
ə-pik-pə pambi-siŋ-si	>	pambi **ə-pik-pə**-siŋ-si	'these small plants'

Adjectives formed by derived verbs cannot occur after a noun. They can only precede the noun. When the position is altered, it will give an otherwise meaning.

133. ma-nə pi-bə paukhum-du ca-nə-bə khərə
he-NOM give-NMZ answer-DEM proper-NMZ some
wat-li
shortage-SAM
'The answer that he has given is somewhat improper.'

The sentence has two clauses: a dependent clause and a main clause. It can be written as:

(a) ma-nə paukhum pi
he-NOM answer give-SAM
'He gives answer'

(b) paukhum-du ca-nə-bə khərə wat-li
answer-DEM proper-NMZ some shortage-SAM
'The answer is not somewhat proper'

The two clauses are connected by **pi-bə** and it is a 'relativizer'. In the above example, it has been seen that relativizer in Manipuri functions as an adjective. In sentence (133) the relativizer **pi-bə** 'given' functions as an adjective. Then, what is the function of a derived nominal **canə-bə** 'suitable' which was once an adjective in sentence (122)? But in sentence (133) the derived nominal **canə-b** comes in the main clause and it functions as a complement which is formed by nominalization (see Yashawanta, 2000:176). From this analysis, it can be concluded that adjectives derived from complex verbal roots when nominalized cannot follow a noun. It is ungrammatical for such types of adjectives to come after a noun.

Plato and Aristotle considered that the most typical function of both adjective and verb was that of predication whereas the most characteristic function of noun was that of naming the subject of predication (Lyons, 1968:324). In English when an adjective occurs in predicative position, it does not take verbal suffixes like tense, aspect, mood, etc. Instead, it takes a dummy verb 'be' to carry out the necessary inflectional functions. The difference can be seen from the following examples.

134. *Mary is beautiful.*
135. *Mary dances.*
136. *Mary would have been beautiful.*
137. *Mary would have danced.*

The predicative forms in the above sentences (134) and (136) are adjectives while in sentences (135) and (137) are verbs. The position of adjectives cannot be replaced by verbs nor can the verbs take the position of adjectives as the outcome will not be grammatical in English.

138. **Mary is dance.*
139. **Mary beautiful-s.*
140. **Mary would have been danced.*
141. **Mary would have beautiful-ed.*

It has been clear from the above examples that adjectives in English cannot go with the verbal suffixes and verbs, on the other hand, cannot be placed in the position of adjectives. Of course, verbs can be derived as adjectives by adding the suffix –ing as in ***singing** boy*, ***dancing** girl*, ***crying** baby,* etc. But these derived forms cannot occur in predicative position as they are in phrasal form functioning as attributive adjectives.

The situation is totally contrastive in Manipuri where the adjectives do not have a distinct word class. They come under the sub-group of verbs as all adjectives are derived from verbal bases. Of course, Manipuri has two distinct word classes as nouns and verbs but not adjectives and adverbs. The above examples show the position of adjectives in Manipuri.

142. nupi ədu phəɟə-i
woman that beautiful-SAM
'The woman is beautiful.'

143. əŋaŋ-siŋ-du mərəm ok-i
child-PL-DEM obedient-SAM
'The children are obedient.'

In the above sentences no adjectives are seen in the predicative position. This is the point of difference between Indo-European languages like English and Hindi and Tibeto-Burman languages like Manipuri, Lahu, etc. English and Hindi have adjectives in both attributive and predicative positions while Manipuri and Lahu have attributive adjectives only. Vadj's (Verb adjectives) are generally translatable by English adjectives or past participles, since they have meanings referring to states or qualities rather than actions: **daʔ** 'good, pretty', **mɔ** 'long (of time)', **i** 'little, **chu** 'fat', **lɛ** 'late', **qhâ** 'bitter', **lȷ̈** 'ruined, wretch', **kɨ** 'rotten', **bɛ** 'infected, purulent' etc. (Matisoff, 1973). Adjectival or stative forms (see Chapter-III) in Manipuri can go with the verbal inflectional suffixes like aspect, mood marker, etc. For English, to be stative is normal for the class of adjectives, but abnormal for verbs; to be non-stative is normal for verbs, but abnormal for adjectives (Lyons, 1968). Sentences (134-141) clarify this statement. But for Manipuri, it is normal to be stative for both adjectives and verbs because all adjectival bases like **phəɟə**- 'be beautiful', **mərəm ok**-'be obedient', **məm**-'be dim', **hau**-'be tasty', **saŋ**-'be long', **cin**-'be tight', **ŋaŋ**-be red', **cau**-'be big', **ten**-'be lazy', **noi**-'be fat', **məsa phə**-'be healthy', **khu**-'be narrow', **lau**-'be broad', etc. can function as a normal verb in Manipuri. One more point to be noted here is that in Manipuri it is normal for action verbs also to be adjective especially when the verb is intransitive. This holds true for Lahu and Tibeto-Burman languages. In this context, consider the statement of Shobhana (1997: 164) 'A nominalized verb in a relative clause can refer to a state (8a) or an action (8b). Adjectives on the other hand, can describe only states'. The examples given by her are as follows:

(8.a) *jam-nə* *sau-gən-bə* *mərup*
hot-ADV anger-REPEAT-NOM friend
'The friend who is very angry'

(8.b) *hÚy* *hat-pə* *nupa-di*
dog kill-NOM person-DLMY
'The man who kill dogs'

Adjectives can also be derived from action verbs by prefixing ə- to a verbal noun or without ə-. Some of them are: **əpai-bə** ucek 'flying bird', **əcenbə** gari 'running vehicle', **əkəppə** əŋaŋ 'crying baby', **ca-ri-bə** mi 'man who is eating', **pa-ri-bə** lairik 'book which is reading' etc. In Lahu also, it is normal for adjectival bases to precede or follow a noun when they function as noun modifiers. For example, the stative base **da** 'pretty' in a relative clause may be as follows:

da`ʔ ve ŋâ 'pretty birds'

This phrase can be written in the following way where the stative base can follow the noun **ŋa** `ʔ 'birds' as:

ŋa`ʔ da` ve 'pretty birds'

From the above examples it is clear that stative bases can precede and follow a noun as well. But for action verbs, it is normal to precede a noun. It can follow a noun only when a Pv (verb particle) **t** follows it. Thus, the position of action verbs used as modifiers in a relative clause may be as follows:

pò ve ŋâʔ 'flying birds'

pò 'fly' precedes the noun **ŋâʔ** and **ŋâʔ pò t ve** 'flying birds' where **pò** 'fly' follows the noun **ŋâʔ** 'birds' with an addition of verb particle **t**.

1.4 Verbal modifiers

Verbal modifiers are derived from verbal roots by suffixing **-nə**. They always precede the verb.

144. **kən-** 'fast'
nupa-du kən-nə cel-li
man-DEM fast-ADV run-SAM
'The man runs fast'

145. **sau-** 'angry'
nupi-du sau-nə ŋaŋ-ŋi
woman-DEM angry-ADV speak-SAM
'The woman speaks angrily'

The modifiers **kən-nə**, **sau-nə** in the above sentences can be reduplicated.

146. nupa-du kən-nə kən-nə cel-li
man-DEM fast-ADV fast-ADV run-SAM
'The man runs fast'

147. nupi-du sau-nə sau-nə ŋaŋ-ŋi
woman-DEM angry-ADV angry-ADV speak-SAM
'The woman speaks angrily'

The reduplicated forms of the adverbs do not cause any disturbance in the semantic structure of the sentences given above. But adverbs which are derived from action verbs cannot be used without reduplication.

148. əŋaŋ-du cen-nə cen-nə lak-i
child-DEM run-ADV run-ADV come-SAM
'The child came (by) running'

149. məhak kəp-nə kəp-nə cət-li
he cry-ADV cry-ADV go-SAM
'He goes (while) crying'

There are also other adverbs like adverbs of time (indicating time) durative adverb, adverb of quantity and adverb meaning 'slightly'.

Adverb of Quality: The verbal roots **hen-** 'be greater in number or quantity', **wat-** 'be less in number or quantity' and **jam-** 'be more in number or quantity' are derived to adverbs of quantity by suffixing adverbial suffix **-nə**.

150. məhak-nə məjam-dəgi hen-nə ca-i
he-NOM others-SUP more-ADV eat-SAM
'He eats more than others'

151. cak-tu wat-nə ca-u
cooked rice-DEM less-ADV eat-COM
'Take your meal in less quantity'

152. wa jam-nə ŋaŋ-gənu
speech much-ADV talk-PROH
'Don't talk too much'

Durative Adverbs: They are formed by adding **-tunə** or **-dunə** to the verbal roots. **-tunə** comes after voiceless sounds while **-dunə** follows voiced sounds.

153. sən-gi thəuri tət-tunə ləi-re
cow-GEN rope break-ADV be-PERF-SAM
'The rope of the cow has been snapped'

154. nupi-du bəs-tə ui-dunə toŋ-li
woman-DEM bus-LOC doze-ADV sit-PROG-SAM
'The woman is dozing while travelling by bus'

Adverb meaning 'slightly': They are formed by adding the following suffixes to the verbal roots. Some of them can also be used both singly and in reduplicative forms while others are used in only reduplicative forms. There is no difference in the meaning for both uses:

-ləp ~ rəp

mu-rəp	~	mu-rəp mu-rəp	slightly black
sil-ləp	~	sil-ləp sil-ləp	slightly sour
kha-rəp	~	kha-rəp kha-rəp	slightly bitter
cau-rəp	~	cau-rəp cau-rəp	slightly big
sa-rəp	~	sa-rəp sa-rəp	slightly hot

Verbal roots ending in **p, t, k, m, n,** and **ŋ** take **-ləp** while those ending in vowel sounds take **-rəp**.

-tək

sin-tək	~	sin-tək sin-tək	slightly sour
ŋaŋ-tək	~	ŋaŋ-tək ŋaŋ-tək	slightly red
noi-tək	~	noi-tək noi-tək	slightly fat
pa-tək	~	pa-tək pa-tək	slightly thin
kom-tək	~	kom-tək kom-tək	slightly loose
pet-tək	~	pet-tək pet-tək	slightly soft

kon-tək	~	kon-tək kon-tək	slightly bent
kəu-tək	~	kəu-tək kəu-tək	slightly short (of dress), etc.

-li* ~ *ri* ~ *mi: They are used only in reduplicative form.

-li	mul-li mul-li	slightly ripe
	tel-li tel-li	slightly short
	col-li col-li	slightly long (of dress)
-ri	wau-ri wau-ri	slightly light coloured
	mu-ri mu-ri	slightly black
	ŋəu-ri əu-ri	slightly white
-mi	nok-mi nok-mi	smiling
-pet	thum-pet thum-pet	slightly sweet
-phet	ci-phet ci-phet	at intervals
	nok-phet nok-phet	smiling
	cəm-phet cəm-phet	slightly tasteless
	ku-phet ku-phet	twinkling
-bu	lum-bu lum-bu	lukewarm/feverish

155. phurit-si əi-ŋon-də kom-tək təu-i
shirt-DEM I-DIR-DAT loose-ADV do-SAM
'The shirt is slightly loose to me'

156. əhən-du təp-li təp-li cət-li
old man-DEM slow-ADV slow-ADV go-SAM
'The old man goes slowly'

157. ensaŋ-du ci-ri ci-ri thoŋ-ŋu
curry-DEM in small quantity cook-COM
'Prepare the curry in small quantity'

1.5 Manipuri Verbs are not inflected for tense, number, person and gender

Tense: It is a category used in the grammatical description of verbs (along with aspect and mood) referring primarily to the way the grammar marks the time at which the action denoted by the verb took place (Crystal, 1985). Traditional grammarians recognized three distinctions of tense as past, present and future. Comrie (1985a) defined tense as 'grammaticalized expression of location in time'. The difference between ***Jack goes*** and ***Jack went*** in English is one of tense; whereas that between ***Jack goes*** and ***Jack is going*** is rather one of aspect.

Traditional grammarians considered tense to be a universal phenomenon. This concept is challenged by modern linguists and proved that tense is expressed by means of grammatical categories, for instance in Hindi, English, etc. Lyon (1968) claimed that tense is not found in all languages. It should be mentioned that time and aspect are language universal while tense is language specific.

Tense, in Tibeto-Burman languages (TB) is not distinct. This indistinctiveness of tense is one of the structural features of the TB languages. Bauman (1975) remarks that morphologically unmarked status of tense is a feature of TB languages. Again, Zograph (1980) opines that tense (a relative time) is usually expressed by the addition of supplementary focussing words. Traditional Manipuri grammarians namely Kalachand Shastri (1964), Nandalal Sharma (1976), Dwijamani Dev Sharma (1969) and others were of the opinion that Manipuri has tense. They studied Manipuri on the framework of Sanskrit, Hindi, Bengali, etc. But the influence of Indo-European languages like Sanskrit, Hindi, Bengali, etc. on a TB language like Manipuri is not acceptable. Yashawanta (2000: 111-114) observed that aspect is more prominent than tense in Manipuri. The view of traditional grammarians is challenged by modern linguists like P.C. Thoudam (1991) and others while Bhat and Ningomba (1997) are of the view that Manipuri has tense distinction of future and non-future. Thoudam (1991) argues that the tense system found in Greek, Latin and Sanskrit is not found in Manipuri language. Tense, in the language, is shown by an adverbial element, not by morphological markers. He further strongly claims that the markers – present **-i**, past **-rəm** ~ **ləm**, **-khi-**, future **-kəni** ~ **gəni** which are regarded by traditional grammarians as tense markers are not, in fact, tense markers. They are aspect markers. To support this point he gave the following examples where past markers go with future marker.

ca-khi-gəni eat-past-future	will continue eating
ca-rəm-gəni eat-past-future	may be eating
ca-khi-rəm-gəni eat-past-past-future	may be eating
ca-khi-rəm-khi-gəni eat-past-past-past-future	may be still eating

Another scholar, Mahabir (1988) in one of his seminar papers ***'Meiteilon (Manipuri): as a Tenseless Language'*** claims that a verb form can occur with different temporal adverbs that refer to different times without any change. It proves that time reference is not grammaticalized.

158. məhak ŋa ca-i
He fish eat-SAM
'He eats fish'

159. məhak ŋəraŋ ŋa ca-i
he yesterday fish eat-SAM
'Yesterday he ate fish'

160. nəŋ-nə ŋəsi ŋa ləi-də-rəbədi həjeŋ həwai
you-NOM today fish buy-NEG-if tomorrow pulse
ca-i
eat-SAM
'If you do not buy fish today, then tomorrow we will naturally eat pulse'

The verb **ca-i** remains in all the three sentences. Sentence (159) means that 'he' generally eats fish that he is a non-vegetarian. Sentence (160) means that 'he' ate fish particularly on the previous day. Sentence (161) indicates a future time with the same suffix **-i**. The same verb form **ca-i** gives three different meanings when it is used with or without temporal adverbs. The verb form can occur with **ŋəraŋ** 'yesterday' in (160) while in (161) it goes with **həjeŋ** 'tomorrow'.

The marker **-le ~ re** can also be used with temporal adverbs indicating future time like **həjeŋ** 'tomorrow' to give a future meaning *e.g.*

161. nəŋ jau-də-rəbədi əi-su həjeŋ tok-e
you join-NEG-if I-also tomorrow drop-PERF-SAM
'If you are not in the party, I will also drop it tomorrow'

162. nəŋ-nə həjeŋ ŋai-rəm-də-rəbədi əi ədum
you-NOM tomorrow wait-DEIC-NEG-if I naturally
lak-tə-re
come-NEG-PERF-SAM
'If you do not wait for me tomorrow, then I will not come'

163. məhak ka-si-də cəŋ-lək-ləbədi əi cət-khə-re
he room-DEM-LOC enter-DEIC-if I go-DEF-PERF
hai-nə khəl-lo
connector think-COM
'In case he enters this room, think that I will leave this place (at once)'

The three conditional sentences show that the temporal adverbs **həjeŋ** 'tomorrow' which denotes future time can occur with the suffixes **-le ~ re ~ khə-re** which generally indicate completion of an action. In normal conditions, the future time is indicated by the suffix **-kəni ~ gəni** with or without the temporal adverb **həjeŋ** 'tomorrow'.

164. əi kəithel cət-kəni
I market go-NREAL
'I will go to market'

165. əi həjeŋ sinema jeŋ-gəni
I tomorrow movie look-NREAL
'Tomorrow I will see a movie'

In the above sentences, the suffix **-kəni ~ gəni** gives the meaning of future time. It indicates an action which is not realized. This is the point where Bhat and Ningomba (1997) argue that Manipuri has tense distinctions of future and non-future. But this claim is not applicable in all conditions where the so-called future suffix can occur with other suffixes and does not give the meaning of futurity. The analysis of the above sentences shows that Manipuri has no tense.

Tense indicates location of an event on a linear time scale, Comrie (1976:6) defines aspect as the internal temporal structure of the event (as complete or on going, beginning or ending, occurring once or several times, etc.). Mood, on the other hand, denotes the actuality of the event (as real/not real, seen, heard or inferred; possible, probable or certain; necessary/unnecessary, etc.) Bhat (1999: 130) thus describes mood to be more speaker-oriented than situation-oriented. For the study of Manipuri language, it would be more convenient to study aspect markers that are attached to verbal roots. Aspect markers in Manipuri are: simple aspect marker -i, progressive marker **-li ~ ri**, perfective marker **-le ~ re** and non-realized or irrealis marker **-kəni ~ gəni**. The aspect markers are discussed in detail in Chapter-VI.

Simple Aspect Marker *-i*: It denotes a simple statement, habitual meaning and universal truth. The marker has seven allomorphic variations as **-i ~ li ~ pi ~ mi ~ ŋi ~ ri** ~ merged into diphthong. The distribution of allomorphs will be discussed in detail in Chaper-V.

166. əi puŋ məŋa-də həu-gət-li
I hour five-LOC get-up-SAM
'I get up at five o'clock'

Progressive Aspect *-li ~ ri*: The suffix is attached to verbal roots to denote progressiveness of an action. It denotes that an action is going on. The suffix has six allomorphic variations as **-i ~ li ~ ri ~ pi ~ mi ~ ŋi** (the conditioning factor of the allomorphs and their distribution will be discussed in detail in Chapter-V).

167. əi phi su-ri
I cloth wash-PROG-SAM
'I am washing clothes'

Perfective *-le*: The suffixation of this marker to verbal roots generally denotes a perfective action. It shows that an action is completed. The suffix has six allomorphic variations as **-e ~ le ~ re ~ pe ~ me ~ ŋe** (the conditioning factor of the allomorphs and their distribution will be studied in detail in Chapter-V).

168. əi cak ca-re
I meal eat-PERF-SAM
'I have taken meal'

Nonrealized or irrealis *-kəni ~ gəni*: he suffix is attached to verbal roots to denote nonrealization of an action (the distribution of this suffix will be discussed in detail in Chapter-V).

169. məhak həjeŋ imphal-də lak-kəni
he tomorrow Imphal-LOC come-NREAL
'He will come to Imphal tomorrow'

Hindi verbs, on the other hand, are influenced by tense, number, person and gender.

170. *tombə skul ɟa:ta: hai*
'Tomba goes to school'

171. *tombə skul gaya: tha:*
'Tomba went to school'

172. *tombə skul ɟa:ye-ga:*
'Tomba will go to school'

a:ta: hai 'goes' in (169) is in present tense. In (170) the verb ***gaya: tha:*** 'went' is the past form of the verb ***ɟa:*** 'go' while in (171) the verb ***ɟa:ye-ga:*** is the inflected form of future tense. This clearly shows that Hindi has tense like other Indo-European languages. It is a totally different language from Manipuri. English has also tense as ***John eats*** and ***John ate*** showing two distinct forms of tense as past and non-past. The verb form of present tense is different from past tense in English. It can be shown as:

I go – I went

He goes – He went

I am going – I was going

You are going – You were going

He/She is going – He/She was going.

is, am changes to ***was*** while ***are*** changes to ***were*** in English. ***go*** and ***goes*** change to ***went***. This clearly shows that English has tense.

Number: It is a grammatical category used for the analysis of word classes displaying such contrast as singular, plural, dual (two), etc. as in English ***boy*** versus ***boys***, ***he walks*** versus ***they walk*** (Crystal, D. 1985). The change caused by the singularity or plurality of the subject in a sentence on the verb form is termed as inflection of number on the verb. Manipuri has number on the noun *e.g.* **əŋaŋ əmə** 'one boy', **əŋaŋ əni/məjam/əŋaŋ-siŋ** 'two/boys, many boys' are the number of nouns. But this number on the nouns does not have any inflection on the verb. For instance, the subject of a singular noun or plural noun does not affect the verb. The verb remains unchanged whether the subject is singular or plural.

173. nupa-məca əmə cel-li
man-small one run-PROG-SAM
'A boy is running'

174. nupa-məca məjam cel-li
man-small many run-PROG-SAM
'Many boys are running'

175. nupa-məca məŋa cel-li
man-small five run-PROG-SAM
'Five boys are running'

In the above sentences, the verb **cel-li** is found unchanged. This means that verbs, in Manipuri, do not have concord with number. The same can happen to pronouns also which are:

	Singular		**Plural**	
First person	əi	I	əi-khoi	we
Second person	nəŋ	you	nə-khoi	you
Third person	məhak/ma	he/she	mə-khoi	they

176. əi koleɟ cət-li
I college go-SAM
'I go to college'

177. əi-khoi koleɟ cət-li
I-PL college go-SAM
' We go to college'

The verb **cət-li** is common for both (175) and (176). The pair of sentences shows that the verb is not inflected for the number of the subjects. But this case is not found in English and Hindi.

178. *I am going to college.*

179. *We are going to college.*

Hindi is also another Indo-European language which has number inflection on the verb. It can reflect on both main verb and auxiliary verb.

180. *larka: skul ɟa:ta: hai*
'The boy goes to school'

181. *larke skul ɟa:te hain*
'The boys go to school'

182. *main skul ɟa:ta: hun*
'I go to school'

183. *ham skul ɟa:te hain*
'We go to school'

184. *tu: skul ɟa:ta: hai*
'You go to school'

185. *tum skul ɟa:te ho*
'You go to school'

Person: It is a category used in the grammatical description to indicate the number and nature of the participants in a situation (Crystal D, 1985). Usually, a three-way contrast is found: first person, in which the speaker refers to himself, or to a group usually including themselves (*e.g.* I, We); second person in which the speaker typically refers to the person he is addressing (*e.g.* you); and third person in which other people, animals, things, etc. are referred to (*e.g.* he, she, it, they). Generally, the distinction of persons is marked on the verb and /or on the associated pronouns. But in Manipuri, the distinction is not marked on the verb but only on the associated pronouns *e.g.*

First person -	singular	əi	I	plural	əi-khoi	we
Second person -	singular	nəŋ	you	plural	nə-khoi	you
Third person -	singular	məhak/ma	'he/she'	plural	mə-khoi	they

These pronoun forms of the three classes of persons do not inflect on the Manipuri verb. The following examples will clarify the statement.

186. əi ca thək-i
I tea drink-SAM
'I drink tea'

187. nəŋ ca thək-i
You tea drink-SAM
'You drink tea'

188. məhak/ma ca thək-i
he tea drink-SAM
'He drinks tea'

The three classes of persons in the above sentences take the same verb form. The verb form taken by first person is same to both second and third persons. The examples clearly show that Manipuri verb is not inflected for person.

While in English and Hindi, the situation is different. The personal pronouns of both languages have different verb forms for different class of persons. Consider the following sentences in Hindi.

189. *main ga:na: ga:ta: hun*
'I sing a song'

190. *ham ga:na ga:te hain*
'We sing a song'

191. *tu: ga:na: ga:ta: hai*
'You sing a song'

192. *tum ga:na ga:te ho*
'You sing a song'

193. *caubə ga:na: ga:ta: hai*
'Chaoba sings a song'

194. *bachche ga:na: ga:te hain*
'Children sing a song'

Hindi has concord of person between the subject and verb in a sentence. With first person singular the verb is ***ga:ta: hun;*** in plural it is ***ga:te hain***. With second person singular and plural the verb forms are ***ga:ta: hai*** and ***ga:te ho***. With third person singular and plural the forms are ***ga:ta: hai*** and ***ga:te hain*** respectively'.

Gender: It is a grammatical category used for the analysis of word-classes displaying such contrasts as masculine/feminine/neuter, animate/inanimate, etc. Discussion of this concept in linguistics has generally focused upon the need to distinguish natural gender, where items refer to the sex of real-world entities, and grammatical gender, which has nothing to do with sex, but has an important role in signalling grammatical relationships between words in a sentence (Crystal, 1985). Hindi has grammatical gender while Manipuri has no such type of gender. The gender difference found in Manipuri is natural gender. It differentiates between male and female not to inanimate objects. Some examples of gender difference found in Manipuri are given below.

Male		Female	
nupa	man	nupi	woman
labə	male	əmom	female
məma	mother	məpa	father

195. nupa-du cak ca-ri
man-DEM meal eat-PROG-SAM
'The man is having his meal'

196. nupi-du cak ca-ri
woman-DEM meal eat-PROG-SAM
'The woman is having her meal'

In the above pair a male and female subject are doing the same thing. The verb **ca-ri** is same in both sentences. This shows that there is no gender agreement between the subject and the verb and finally, it can be concluded that Manipuri verb is not inflected for gender.

Hindi, on the other hand, is a language which has gender agreement between the subject and the verb. The subject can be differentiated by the verb. In other words, a given verb form can be masculine as well as feminine.

197. *main skul ɟa:ta: hun*
'I go to school'

198. *main skul ɟa:ti: hun*
'I go to school'

199. *tomba ba:ɟa:r gaya:*
'Tomba has gone to market'

200. *mema ba:ɟa:r gayi:*
'Mema has gone to market'

The verbs ***ɟa:ta: hun*** and ***gaya:*** denote that the subjects in the sentences are masculine (in sentences 198 and 200) while ***ɟa:ti: hun*** and ***gayi:*** denote feminine (in 199 and 201). This clearly proves that Hindi verb agrees with the subject when the verb is intransitive. Grammatical gender, on the other hand, plays an important role on the verb. When the verb is transitive, the gender agreement is between the gender of the object and the verb. In other words, the verb agrees with the gender of the object instead of the subject. If the object is a feminine gender like **roti:** the verb will take feminine marker.

201. *tomba ne roti: kha:yi:*
'Tomba ate bread'

In the above sentence, the subject is masculine while the verb takes feminine marker. There is no concord between the subject and the verb as the verb is transitive. The verb follows the gender of the object. It would be ungrammatical if the verb agrees with the subject **Tomba** in the following sentence.

202. **tomba ne roti: kha:ya:*

But in intransitive sentences, the concord between the subject and verb is grammatical as seen in (198-201). It is grammatical to have concord between the object and verb in (202) while it is ungrammatical to have concord between the subject and verb when there is an object in the sentence as in (203). When there is no object the verb agrees with the subject of the sentence.

Another point of agreement with verbs is in possessive adjective. The subject takes the gender of the following noun. A male subject will take a feminine marker if the following noun is feminine and a female subject will take a masculine marker if the following noun is masculine.

tomba ki: ma:ta:ɟi:

ra:ni: ka pita:ɟi:

**tomba ka: ma:ta:ɟi:*

**ra:ni: ki: pita:ɟi*

It is ungrammatical to say ***tomba ka: ma:ta:ɟi:*** because the noun ***ma:ta:ɟi:*** is female and it should be ***ki:*** even if the possessive adjective is masculine. Similarly, it is ungrammatical for ***ra:ni:*** to take ***ki:***

A male subject will say ***meri: ma:ta:ɟi:*** while a female subject will say ***mera pita:ɟi***. Such type of gender distinction is not found in English and Manipuri. For English, some parts can be analysed in the use of personal pronouns (he/she) and possessive adjectives like 'his' and 'her'. Compared to Hindi, Manipuri is a totally different language.

Finally, it may be concluded that Manipuri verbs are not inflected for tense, number, person and gender unlike Indo-European languages like English and Hindi. One cannot distinguish tense, number, person and gender by looking simply at a given verb form **cət-li** 'go/ went'. It cannot indicate tense, *i.e.*, it can indicate both past and present by an addition of a temporal adverb like **ŋəraŋ** 'yesterday' or **ŋəsi** 'today'. The subject of the verb can also be singular or plural as there is no difference in the verb form. Further, the subject can be first person, second person or third person since the three classes of persons do not bring any change in the verb form. Finally, the subject can also be both masculine and feminine. From the above analysis, it can be claimed that Manipuri verb is neutral in all conditions given above and does not have concord with tense, number, person and gender.

In this chapter, identification of Manipuri verbs by negative morphemes, difference between verbs and other word classes, non-inflectivity of verb with number, person, gender and tense have been discussed. Subsequent to this, the next chapter aims at the classification of Manipuri verbs on structural level mainly focussing on their larger constructions.

CHAPTER 2

STRUCTURAL CLASSIFICATION OF MANIPURI VERBS

There are two major lexical categories in Manipuri language namely noun and verb. Adjectives and adverbs do not show distinctive feature of their own as they are derived from verbal roots and they come under subgroups of verb (see Chapter-I). Nouns may be free and bound whereas verbs are always bound and they become a free form only when verbal suffixes are attached to them.

The structure of Manipuri verbs fall into five groups namely (i) Simple or Monomorphemic verbs, (ii) Complex verbs, (iii) Compound verbs, (iv) N + V and (v) Reduplicative verbs.

- Verbs
  - Simple or Monomorphemic Verbs
    - Monosyllabic
    - Polysyllabic
  - Complex Verbs
    - Disyllabic
    - Polysyllabic
  - Compound Verbs
    - N + V (Noun Incorporation)
    - V + V (Coordinate Compound)
  - N + V
    - N Dependent (clitic)
    - N Independent (non-clitic)
  - Reduplicated Verbs
    - Reduplicated Verbs 1
    - Reduplicated Verbs 2

2.1 Simple Monomorphemic Verbs

Verbal roots that have a single morpheme are termed as simple verbs. They are always monomorphemic in nature and they cannot be divided further as meaningful units. They may be sub-grouped into two on the basis of the syllables they constitute as: monosyllabic and polysyllabic.

Simple Monosyllabic Verbs: Verbal roots that have only one syllable are called simple monosyllabic verbal roots. These are the roots that are most widely used by many linguists in the analysis of Manipuri verbs.

saŋ-	be long
pa-	read
waŋ-	be tall
cen-	run
jəi-	hit
ləŋ-	throw
cai-	scatter
ta-	fall
jeŋ-	look
sau-	be angry
ok-	be enough, satisfied, welcome
kau-	kick
kai-	break
təp-	be slow, etc.

1. **i-** 'write'
   i-ce cithi i-ri
   1PP-sister letter write-PROG-SAM
   'My sister is writing a letter'

2. **sat-** 'bloom'
   həinəu mə-pan sat-le
   mango GENP-flower bloom-PERF-SAM
   'The flower of the mango tree has bloomed'

3. **nan-** 'be clean/smooth/slippery'

   a. ka əsi nal-li (nan-li)
      room this clean-SAM
      'This room is clean'

   b. ləmbi əsi nal-li, ceksin-nə cət-lu
      path this slippery-SAM careful-ADV go-COM

'This path is slippery, go carefully'

c.	u-pak	əsi	nal-həl-lu (nan-hən-lu)
	plank	this	smooth-CAUS-COM

'Make this plank smooth'

Note:-/**n**/ of **nan**- changes to /**l**/ when followed by /**l**/ and /**h**/ as seen in sentences (3a, b and c).

Most of the Manipuri verbal roots are monosyllabic and it can be assumed that every syllable has a meaning.

Simple Polysyllabic Verbs: It refers to the verbal roots that display more than one syllable but has only one morpheme. It should be mentioned that sometimes more than one syllable *i.e.* two or three syllables may constitute a single morpheme and they cannot be cut further. Such types of verbal roots are few in number.

olaŋ-	be hot and sultry
thəmai-	hypnotize, mesmerize
lairə-	be poor
hərau-	be happy
thaɟə-	believe, trust
ikai-	feel shy
pammu-	dear
nuŋsi-	love
həŋgoi-	detest, hate, abhor
tonan-	be pampered, indulgent
kəram-	be greedy
hakətcə-	be itchy, tingle
tukətcə-	hate, detest
lakcə-	get insulted
niŋsiŋ-	remember, remind, etc.

4. **əurai**- 'read, rehearse'
   əi lairik əurai-ri
   I book read-PROG-SAM
   'I am reading'

5. **oinəm**- 'has a good taste or flavour'
   ensaŋ əsi oinəm-mi
   curry this have a good flavour-SAM
   'The curry has a good flavour'

6. **kəllək-** 'envy, jealous'
   əphəbə mi-siŋ-di pumnəmək-nə kəllək-i
   good man-PL-DEM all-NOM envy-SAM
   'Everybody envies good people'

The verbal roots given above have two or three syllables. Semantically they do not allow morpheme cutting within the syllables, as the syllables in compact, represent one morpheme each. The verbal root **hakkətcə**-'be itchy or tingle' has three syllables. But the morpheme cutting cannot be done here like **hak-kət-cə**-. They are structurally polysyllabic but semantically monomorphemic.

2.2 Complex Verbs

Verbs that result after affixation are termed as complex verbs. Affixation is a process of word-formation and the role of derivational and inflectional affixes will be studied in Chapter-**IV** and **V** respectively. In the study of the verbal structures of Manipuri, many derived verb forms have been explored. In the following examples, the underlined verbal roots are derived verbal roots which are termed as complex verbs here.

a. pan- bear fruit
   pan- hit
   pan- rule
   pan- get married
   <u>pannə</u>- supervise, control

b. san- be swift
   san- have a far sight
   <u>sannə</u>- play

c. hən- repeat
   hən- give change after buying something
   hən- be older than somebody
   hən- move back
   <u>hənthə</u>- be of less quality, number
   <u>həndok</u>- translate, vomit, retreat

d. pu- carry
   <u>puthok</u>- discover, invent

e. tha- grow

	tha -	appear examination etc.
	tha-	write, mark
	tha-	describe, mention
	thagət-	appreciate, praise
	thadok-	rinse
f.	oi-	be
	oisin-	heal up, be properly cooked
	oithok-	be possible, etc.

It has been observed that there are two types of verbal forms according to the number of syllables they have as monosyllabic and disyllabic. Monosyllabic roots like **pan-**, **san-**, **hən-**, **pu-**, **tha-**, **oi-** are simple roots (roots which are not themselves based on any more elementary roots – Mathews, 1974:40) whereas the underlined roots like **pannə-**'supervise, control', **sannə-**'play', **hənthə-**'be of less quality, number', **həndok-** 'translate, vomit, retreat', **puthok-** 'discover', **thagət-**'praise', **thadok-**'rinse', **oisin-**'heal up, be properly cooked' are complex roots [which are morphologically derived from the bases like **pan-**, **san-**, **hən-**, **pu- tha-**, **oi-**, etc. (Mathews, 1974: 40)]. The derived or complex verbal stems have a different meaning from the bases. They cannot get the desired meaning until and unless the derivational elements are attached to them. These derived verbal stems have the same status as a verb as simple verbs do. Although they allow morpheme cuts, they will be treated as a single unit and there will be no morpheme cutting within the syllables throughout the study. Instead of writing **san-nə-**, it will not use the hyphen that is used to demarcate the morphemes and will be written as **sannə-**. These complex verbs also undergo the morphological process like derivation and inflection as simple verbs do which will be studied in the following chapters.

7. **sannə-** 'play'
   əŋaŋ-siŋ kaŋɟəi sannə-ri
   child-PL hockey play-PROG-SAM
   'Children are playing hockey'

8. **pathə-** 'spill down'
   səŋgom-du pathə-re
   milk-DEM spill down-PERF-SAM
   'The milk has spilled down'

9. **ceksin-** 'be careful'
   məhak-ti thəbək təu-bə-də jam-nə ceksil-li
   he-PART work do-NMZ-LOC much-ADV careful-SAM
   'He is very careful in doing a work'

A complex verb stem is formed when the root is preceded or followed by a derivational affix. The derivation involved here is class-maintaining derivation which produces a derived form of the same class as the underlying form (Robins, 1980:241). The process of derivation does not change the word class. For instance, **khən-** 'think' is a verbal root and **-nə** 'reciprocal' is added to form **khənnə-** 'discuss' which is again a verbal form. But when **-pə ~ bə** 'nominalizer' is added to a verbal form like **ca-** 'eat', it becomes a nominal form like **ca-bə** 'to eat/eating'. Similarly, when **-nə** 'adverbial' is added to a verbal root like **təp-** 'be slow', it becomes **təp-nə** 'slowly'. Adjectives are also formed by prefixing ə- to a derived nominal form like **phə-bə** 'good' and become **ə-phə-bə lairik** 'good book'. The derivation involved in the formation of nominal, adverbials and adjectives are class-changing derivations, which produce a derived form of another class (Robins, 1980: 241).

Both class-maintaining and class-changing derived forms are also found in English. Some of the class-maintaining derived verbs are formed by prefixing re-, un-, dis, out-, over-, etc.

re- 'again' as in **readmit**, **reappear**, **resurface**, **remarry**, **reappoint**, **reassemble**, etc.

dis- 'the negative or opposite of' as in **disagree, disapprove, disconnect, disinfect, dismount** etc.

un- 'thc opposite or reverse of a process' as in **unlock**, **undo**, **unfold, unbalance**, etc.

out- 'to a greater extent than, great or better than' as in **outdo, outface, outfit, outlast, outgrow, outcast**, etc.

over 'to excess, to much; more than usual' as in **overload, overplay, overwork, overwrite**, etc.

Some of the class-changing derivations are:

Noun > Adjective — beauty > beautiful, nation > national, fame > famous, drama > dramatic, etc.

Verb > Noun — go > gait, act > actor, utter > utterance, elect > election, appoint > appointment, etc.

Noun > Verb — victim > victimize, nation > nationalize, notice > notify, justice > justify, etc.

Adjective > Verb — simple > simplify, short > shorten, popular > popularize, etc

The affixes involved in complex verbal forms, may, sometimes, divert from their actual functions. For instance, **-nə** is a reciprocal suffix involving two or more arguments while carrying out an action as in **khətnə-** 'quarrel', **loinə-** 'accompany with' as in the following sentences:

10. **khətnə**- 'quarrel'
mǝhǝiroi ǝni-du khǝtnǝ-ri
student two-DEM quarrel-PROG-SAM
'The two students are quarrelling with each other'

11. **loinə**- 'accompany with'
əphəbə mi-gə loinə-u
goọd man-ASS accompany with-COM
'Make company with good people'

The verb **khətnə**- 'quarrel' in (10) involves two persons as actors. The verb in (11) **loinə**- 'accompany with' carries two arguments as the meaning demands. It involves more than one person *i.e.* 'with whom to accompany with'. The use of this reciprocal -**nə** has become more grammaticalized and may be extended to other uses where the arguments carried by the verbs may not be persons.

12. **kannə**- 'be useful'
lairik əsi əi-ŋon-də kannə-i
book this I-DIR-DAT useful-SAM
'This book is useful to me'

13. **hotnə**- 'make an effort'
əi cəhi əni-də ph.d. loi-nə-bə hotnə-ri
I year two-LOC Ph.D. finish-PUR-NMZ make an effort-PROG-SAM
'I am making an effort to finish Ph.D. in two years'

The verb in (12) **kannə**- 'be useful' does not necessarily involve two persons as its arguments. Instead, it carries two arguments: one, a person and another, a thing. However, the object **lairik** 'book' may be replaced by a person and in such situations, the verb **kannə**- carries two persons as its arguments. The verb of (13), **hotnə**- 'make an effort' carries a person as an actor and a goal.

Structurally, complex verbs may be classified into two as

(i) Disyllabic complex verbs and
(ii) Polysyllabic complex verbs.

Disyllabic Complex Verbs: The complex verbs are formed by adding affixes to a simple verbal root which are monosyllabic in nature. The affixes that are used to derive class-maintaining complex verbs are: **ja**-, -**nə**, -**khət**, -**thə**, -**sin**, -**thok**, -**khai**, -**thek**, -**thət**, etc.

Disyllabic Complex Verbs with *ja*-: The prefix is used only with verbs of sleeping. The number of verbs that can take prefix **ja**- is limited.

jakai-	wake up, get up (from sleep)
jarek-	stay, rest at night (at somebody's place)
jahəu-	rise, awake (from sleep)
jata-	sleep
jaon-	turning and tossing

14. **jahəu-** 'arise'
pabuŋ jahəu-də-ri
father arise-NEG-PROG-SAM
'Father has not arisen yet'

15. **jaon-** 'toss and turn'
ənabə maikəi-də jaon-gənu
pain side-LOC toss and turn-PROH
'Don't turn to the pain affected side'

The verbs **jakai**-'wake up, get up (from sleep)', **jarek**-'stay, rest at night (at somebody's place)' and **jata**-'sleep' are rather literary and they are not commonly used in day-to-day life. However, **jakairol** 'morning prayer' is a newly coined term by All India Radio, Imphal and has become very popular. It is a programme of songs in prayer to God and comes as an opening programme of the day. It was formerly called **'vandana'** (vandana:) which is a loan word of Sanskrit meaning 'prayer'.

Disyllabic Complex Verbs with *-nə*: Generally, the suffix **-nə** serves as reciprocal when attached to verbal roots. By reciprocal, it does not necessarily mean two persons being involved in an action as in **khətn**ə- 'quarrel', **khənn**ə- 'discuss', **ləkn**ə- 'mock at', etc. (as mentioned above). Sometimes, it may involve things rather than persons as found in **hotn**ə- 'make an effort', **kann**ə- 'be useful', **lakn**ə- 'try hard'or 'torture'. As a result of **-nə** 'reciprocal' becoming more grammaticalized, the use of this suffix has been extended.

ciŋnə-	hesitate
nəinə-	discuss
pəknə-	congenial, suitable
oinə-	have a tiff
həinə-	be accustomed to
cennə-	be involved with
lennə-	flaunt, vaunt
jeknə-	have enmity
mannə-	be similar
khennə-	be different
cənnə-	be fitted
lətnə-	refuse, unaccept, etc.

16. **pannə-** 'supervise, control'
əŋaŋ-siŋ laŋ-də-nə-bə pannə-u
child-PL noise-NEG-PUR-NMZ control-COM
'Control these children (not to make noise)'

17. **tainə-** 'blame'
thəbək həi-tə-rəgə khutlai-də tainə-gənu
work experience-NEG-CPART tool-DAT blame-PROH
'Don't blame the tools when you are not experienced in the work'

18. **konnə-** 'be enough'
ca kəp əni-də cini caməc əmə-nə konnə-de
tea cup two-LOC sugar spoon one-NOM enough-NEG-SAM
'A spoon of sugar is not enough for two cups of tea'

19. **təmnə-** 'be haunted'
məphəm-si təmnə-i
place-DEM haunted-SAM
'This place is haunted'

Disyllabic Complex Verbs with *-khət*: The suffixation of **-khət** to a verbal root denotes upward directional, starting of an action or intensifier, etc. In case of complex verbs with **-khət**, the meaning may be otherwise.

səugət-	help, support
sugət-	grimace
ləukhət-	take up a project or programme
thukkət-	become nervous
liŋkhət-	establish, set up
kupkhət-	recoup
həugət-	help somebody to get up
thaŋgət-	raise (hands)
thagət-	support a candidate in election, etc.

20. **pakhət-** 'be nervous'
pulis u-bə-də huranbə-du pakhət-ləm-mi
police see-NMZ-LOC thief-DEM nervous-COMP-SAM
'The thief got nervous at the sight of police'

21. **onkhət-** 'give a counter statement (specially against elders)'
əhən-gi cin-thək-tə onkhət-kənu
elder-GEN mouth-up-LOC give a counter statement-PROH
'Don't give counter statement against elders'

22. **caukhət-** 'be developed, civilized'

a. mənipur-gi mənuŋ hən-ɟin-bə məphəm-siŋ-də ləmbi thoŋ-gi
Manipur-GEN inner deep-IN-NMZ place-PL-LOC path bridge-GEN

phibəm cau-khət-tə-ri (-tri)
condition develop-NEG-PROG-SAM
'The conditions of roads and bridges in remote areas of Manipur are not developed'

b. noŋcup-lom-gi mi-siŋ-di jam-nə caukhət-le
western-side-GEN people-PL-PART much-ADV civilize-PERF-SAM
'People of western countries are very civilized'

The directional meaning of **-khət** has been extended since **liŋkhət-**, set up', **kupkhət-** 'recoup', **ləukhət-**' take up a project or programme', **thagət-**'praise', etc. do not carry the meaning of directional.
Note: **-gət** follows morphemes beginning with aspirated voiceless stop sounds /**ph**/, /**th**/, /**kh**/ and fricative sounds /**h**/, /**s**/ and end with voiced sounds.

Disyllabic Complex verbs with -*th*ə: Generally, the suffixation of -**th**ə to a verbal root gives the meaning of downward directional or continuation of an action. In case of complex verbs with -**th**ə, the meaning may, sometimes, be diverted from directionals.

centhə-	cause infamy
lekthə-	faint
citthə-	be left out
thinthə-	be late
cokthə-	be tired
pathə-	over flow, spill down
nonthə-	bow down
hathə-	gush out
nanthə-	slip, slide down
pəŋthə-	be paralyzed, be hypnotized
tətthə-	become weak
lukthə-	bow down
litthə-	escape, fall down from a hole, etc.

23. **wanth**ə- 'become unconscious'

əwabə pau ədu ta-bə-də nupi ədu wanthə-khi
sad news that hear-NMZ-LOC woman that unconscious-DEF-SAM
'The woman became unconscious to hear the sad news'

24. **kinthə**-'fall down, crumble, collapse'
juhar-ha-bə-də jum əjambə kinthə-re
earthquake-NMZ-LOC house almost crumble-PERF-SAM
'Many houses have crumbled down in the earthquake'

25. **putthə**-'sink, lag behind'

a. əi-gi khoŋ-si ləikhom-də putthə-re
I-GEN leg-DEM mud-LOC sink-PERF-SAM
'My leg sank into the mud'

b. na-ru-bə-dəgi əi para jam-nə putthə-re
ill-DEIC-NMZ-ABL I lesson much-ADV lag behind-PERF-SAM
'I have lagged behind in many lessons due to illness'

26. **thadə**-'drop, give vote, invest money'

a. phi-du ləibak-tə thadə-gənu
cloth-DEM floor-LOC drop-PROH
'Don't drop the cloth on the floor'

b. nəŋ kəna-də bhot thadə-gəni
you who-DAT vote cast vote-NREAL
'To whom will you cast your vote?'

c. proɟek-si-də nəŋ-nə sen thadə-bə-ra
project-DEM-LOC you-NOM money invest-NMZ-INTR
'Do you invest money in this project?'

citthə- 'be left out', **thinthə**- 'be late', **cokthə**- 'be tired', **pəŋthə**- 'be paralyzed, be hypnotized', **tətthə**- 'become weak' **hənthə**-'reduce', **putthə**-'sink, lag behind', **thadə**- 'drop, give vote, invest money'do not indicate directional meaning. **wanthə**- 'become unconscious', on the other hand, indicates directionality to some extent, as to become unconscious means to fall down, lie down, etc.

Note: -**də** comes after morphemes which begin with /**th**/ and ends with vowel sounds.

Disyllabic Complex Verbs with *-sin*: The General function of -**sin** is also directional indicating inward only. But in case of complex verbs with -**sin**, the meaning may be otherwise.

loisin-	make clean (of an area), keep things in proper place
tusin-	fall, stumble
tasin-	make clean of an area, place
ləisin-	become darker (of colour or complexion)

insin- instigate
səŋjin- shift something to make empty
maithoŋ laŋsin- become pensive
laksin- guess
phəkcin- become dull, etc.

27. **ceksin**- 'be careful'
likli-du kai-gəni, ceksil-lu
glass-DEM break-NREAL careful-COM
'Be careful! the glass may break'

28. **tuŋsin**- 'save (money)'
tuŋ-gi jeŋ-ləgə pəisa khərə tuŋsil-lu
future-GEN look-CPART money some save-COM
'Save some money for the future'

29. **hotcin**- 'run into, join'

a. əaŋ khətnə-rək-pə-dəgi mə-ma-du imuŋ-də
child quarrel-DEIC-NMZ-ABL 3PP-mother-DEM inside the house-LOC

hotcin-khə-re
run into-DEF-PERF-SAM
'The mother ran into the house as the children began to fight or quarrel'

b. mirep oi-gədəbə khərə-di sarkar pai-bə parti-də
candidate be-to be some-PART government take-NMZ party-LOC

hotcin-nə-re
join-REC-PERF-SAM
'Some aspirant candidates joined the ruling party'

30. **oisin**- 'healing up, (of curry) be properly cooked'

a. əsokpə-si numit ni-ni hum-ni-də oisil-lə-ni (oisin-lə-ni)
wound-DEM day two-day three-day-LOC heal up-PROS-NREAL
'The wound will heal up in two or three days'

Note: ni in the above sentence is a contracted form of non-realized **-kəni (-gəni)** (see **5.3**).

b. ensaŋ-si oisin-də-ri (-dri)
curry-DEM properly cook-NEG-PROG-SAM
'The curry is not yet properly cooked'

ceksin-'be careful', **oisin**-'healing up, (of curry) be properly cooked' **maithoŋ laŋsin**- 'become pensive' and **phəkcin**- 'become dull', do not indicate any directional meaning.

Note: -cin follows morphemes that begin with fricative sounds and end with voiceless, unaspirated stop sounds. **-ɟin** comes after morphemes which begin with fricative sounds and end with voiced sounds. –**sin** occurs elsewhere.

Disyllabic Complex Verb with -thok: The suffix **-thok** is generally attached to verbal roots to denote outward directional and completeness of an action. In this context the suffixation may not give directional meaning.

paŋthok-	celebrate, perform
həndok-	retreat, go backward, translate, vomit
thadok-	rinse
lauthok-	announce
ləithok-	evade from work, duty
səndok-	broadcast, telecast
hundok-	cast off, forsake, reject
səudok-	melt
thadok-	release
nanthok-	escape
puthok-	discover, invent
pauthok-	spread slender news
ləuthok-	remove, etc.

31. **kətthok-** 'sacrifice'
pauna brəɟəbasi-nə mə-rəibak-ki-dəmək mə-thəwai kətthok-khi
Paona Brajabasi-NOM 3PP-land-GEN-for 3PP-soul sacrifice-DEF-SAM
'Paona Brajabasi sacrificed his life for the sake of his motherland'

32. **cauthok-** 'be proud'
əpəŋbə mi-tə-nə cauthok-i
foolish man-only-NOM proud-SAM
'Only the fools are proud'

33. **həudok-** 'introduce'
səgol kaŋɟəi haibə məsannə-si mənipur-dəgi həudok-khi
polo connector play-DEM Manipur-ABL introduce-DEF-SAM
'The game of polo was introduced from Manipur'

34. **jəithok-** 'postpone'
ŋəsi həu-gədəbə thaurəm –du numit məŋa-ni jəithok-le
today start-to be programme-DEM day five-day postpone-PERF-SAM

'The programme which was to be held from today has been postponed for five days'

The verbs **kətthok**-'sacrifice', **cauthok**-'be proud', **həudok**-'introduce', **pauthok**- 'spread slender news' do not give any directional meaning at all. But the other verbs **nanthok**-'escape', **puthok**-'discover', **jəithok**-'postpone' give a derived meaning of **-thok** in the sense that they have a directional meaning in the underlying structure. **nanthok**- means to come out from the hand of police. **puthok**- means to find a place for the first time and let it know to others and lastly, **jəithok**- derives the meaning from **jəi-thok**- 'hit and repair a dent utensil'. It means to hit from inside to outward direction.

Note: -thok changes to-**dok** when it is preceded by morphemes that begin with fricative sounds and aspirated stop sounds which end with voiced sounds.

Polysyllabic Complex Verbs: Most of the Complex verbs, polysyllabic in nature have **cə**-, **tə**- and -**nə**.

Polysyllabic Complex Verbs with *cə*-: The affixation of **cə**- to certain verbs gives the meaning of a greater degree. It can be attached to verbs like **kuŋ**- 'dense', **nən**- 'press, put something firmly on surface', **nəi**- 'stir, not clear', **məm**- 'be dark, **laŋ**- 'be noisy', **jet**- 'entangle', **mot**- 'be dirty', **pet**- 'be soft', **lam**- 'be hungry', **kn**- 'be hard', etc.

cənənnə-	overlap, be in disorder
cənəinə-	be complicated, complex, confused, intricate
cəməmnə-	be at a fix, at a loss, confused
cəraŋnə-	be noisy, anxious
cəmotnə-	be filthy, soiled, dirty
cəbetnə-	be soft, tender, etc.

35. **cəguŋnə**- 'be dense'.
    ləikon-si-də ləi tha-ri-bə-si cəguŋnə-re
    garden-DEM-LOC flower plant-PROG-NMZ-DEM dense-PERF-SAM
    'Plantation of flowers in this garden is dense'

36. **cəgənnə**- 'be muscular, hard'
    nupi əsi-gi məsək-si cəgənnə-i
    woman that-GEN face-DEM muscular-SAM
    'This woman has a muscular face'

37. **cəjetnə**- 'be controversial'
    nəŋ-gi waphəm-du cəjetnə-ri
    you-GEN matter-DEM controversial-PROG-SAM
    'Your matter is still controversial

38. **cədətnə-** 'be weak'

cəra henbə-dəgi əhəl əsi cədətnə-re
meal fast-NMZ-ABL old man this weak-PERF-SAM
'This old man has become weak due to fasting'

Polysyllabic Complex Verbs with *-tə*: The suffix has an allomorphic variation as **-tə** ~ -**də**. It is attached to certain verbs that denote negative meaning. These negative verbs have no positive counterparts. They always occur in negative environment.

haleŋdə-	be unflinching
thəoidə-	be careless
thəusadə-	neglect, ignore
nacuŋdə-	be careless

39. **usittə-** 'be rude, impolite, disdain'

məhak-nə kənabu-su usitte
he-NOM no one-also distain-SAM
'He distains anybody'

40. **nacəŋdə-** 'be insincere'

əŋaŋ əsi lairik-tə nacəŋde
child this book-LOC insincere-SAM
'This child is insincere in his study'

Polysyllabic Complex Verbs with *-nə*: The suffix **-nə** takes the role of formative suffix in the construction. It may, sometimes, mean reciprocal as studied earlier and sometimes as a formative particle. In case where it cannot mean reciprocal, it may be explained as simply an extended use of the suffix. In such situations the suffix has become more grammaticalized and as a result it started functioning as a formative particle.

laŋtəknə-	be anxious
soŋɟunə-	be weak, feeble
cuŋsinnə-	collaborate, unite
səkcinnə-	adjust an account
mənɟunə-	be slightly old (of a house, cloth)
athomnə-	specially added
	əkəknə- be special
jemməunə-	food poisoning
khujəunə-	be in a haste
thendrəŋnə-	be squat
cəphəmnə-	be hungry, famished, etc.

41. **kəremnə-** 'mock, jest, make fun'
nə-thək-ki əhən-də kəremnə-gənu
2PP-up-GEN elder-DAT mock-PROH
'Don't mock at your elders'

42. **siɟinnə-** 'use'
əi-gi lairik-tu kəna-nə siɟinnə-ri
I-GEN book-DEM who-NOM use-PROG-SAM
'Who is using my book?'

43. **təusinnə-** 'pretend'
nəŋ na-de- hai-bə əi khəŋ-ŋi, təusinnə-gənu
you ill-NEG-SAM connector I know-SAM pretend-PROH
'I know that you are not ill, so don't pretend'

The suffix **-sinnə** can be attached to verbal roots to mean 'pretend' like **sauɟinnə-** 'pretend to be angry' **kəpsinnə-** 'pretend to be crying', **haiɟinnə-** 'pretend to be true', **tasinnə-** 'pretend to be listening', etc.

Note: The conditioning factor of **-sinnə** and **-ɟinnə** is same to **–sin**.

Classification of Complex Verbs: From the semantic point of view, all complex verbs studied above may be grouped into three. They are (i) verbal roots that cannot occur singly, (ii) Verbal roots that have a derived meaning, and (iii) Verbal roots that have slightly different meaning after derivation.

Verbal roots that cannot occur singly: Verbal roots that cannot occur independently without suffixes take a derivational suffix and form a complex verbal root.

san-	>	sannə-	play
kan-	>	kannə-	be useful
khen-	>	khennə-	be different
təm-	>	təmnə-	haunt
lək-	>	ləknə-	tease, mock, jest
lak-	>	laknə-	try hard, torture, give harassment
cai-	>	cainə-	fight
tai-	>	tainə-	blame
pan-	>	pannə-	supervise, control
len-	>	lennə-	flaunt, vaunt
hot-	>	hotnə-	make an effort
oi-	>	oinə-	have a tiff

sin-	>	sinnə-	entrust
sot-	>	sotthə-	lag behind
		sin-	> sinthə- flow
hən-	>	hənthə-	be of less quality
put-	>	putthə-	sink, lag behind
kin-	>	kinthə-	collapse, crumble
oi-	>	oisin-	healing up, be properly cooked'
loi-	>	loisin-	make clear of an area
loi-	>	loinə-	accompany with, associate
si-	>	siɟinnə-	use, utilise
sək-	>	səkcinnə-	adjust an account
cuŋ-	>	cuŋsinnə-	collaborate
tuk-	>	tukthə-	drop, feel discourage, slouch
thin-	>	thindok-	be exhausted, etc.

Verbal roots that have a derived meaning: In this construction, the meaning of a verbal root that can function as a main verb in other sentences is derived to give a new meaning when it is combined with a suffix. After addition of certain suffixes such as **-sin**, **-nə**, **-thok**, **-thə**, **-khət**, etc. to verbal roots, the newly formed verbal roots have an extended meaning. Thus, the meanings before and after suffixation have semantic correlations.

lak-	bind	>	laksin-	guess
ciŋ-	pull	>	ciŋnə-	hesitate, doubt
paŋ-	open eye	>	paŋthok-	celebrate, perform
nəi-	stir	>	nəinə-	discuss
tha-	release	>	thadok-	rinse (the fall tone changes to level)
jek-	paint	>	jeknə-	have enmity
thək-	dazzle	>	thəktok-	reflect
waŋ-	be tall	>	wanthə-	become unconscious (/ŋ changes to /**n**/)
cau-	be big	>	caukhət-	be developed, civilized
tha-	take into account	>	thagət-	praise(the level tone changes to fall)
lak-	snatch	>	lakkhət-	take water from well or pond
on-	turn	>	onkhət-	give a counter statement
cau-	be big	>	cauthok-	be proud
pa-	full to the brim	>	pakhət-	become nervous
nok-	laugh	>	noknə-	mock, jest
ləi-	turn	>	ləithok-	evade from work, etc.

Verbal roots that have slightly different meaning after derivation: Verbs of this type have almost all the same meaning. They retain the meaning of the first verbal root where it can be used as an independent verb in a sentence.

kai-	break	>	kainə-	separate
khai-	cut	>	khainə-	divorce, separate
ca-	fit	>	canə-	be congenial, suitable
cən-	be fitted	>	cənnə-	be fitted to a family or society
tin-	join	>	tinnə-	make friends
tha-	take into account	>	thanə-	praise
theŋ-	touch	>	theŋnə-	meet by chance
man-	resemble	>	mannə-	be similar
siŋ-	mark	>	siŋnə-	challenge, complete contest
on-	change	>	onnə-	exchange
tha-	release	>	thadə-	drop
nəm-	press	>	nəmthə-	supress
nan-	be smooth	>	nanthə-	slip down
nan-	be smooth	>	nanthok-	escape
in-	push	>	insin-	instigate
səŋ-	be free, empty	>	səŋdok-	shift something from
səŋ-	be free empty	>	səŋɟin-	shift something into, etc.

2.3 Compound Verbs

It is a term used widely in descriptive linguistics to refer to a linguistic unit which is composed of elements that function independently in other circumstances (Crystal, 1985:63). Compound verbs in Manipuri may be of two types: (i) nominal + verbal and (ii) Verbal + Verbal Compound. The first type of compounding is called noun incorporation and the latter is called verbal compound.

Noun Incorporation: Incorporation is the compounding of a word (typically a verb or preposition) with another element (typically a noun, pronoun or adverb). The compound serves the combined syntactic function of both elements (Gerdts, 1998: 84). Noun incorporation is the compounding of a noun stem and a verb to yield a complex form that serves as the predicate of a clause. Compare sentences a. where the nominals are the free standing noun phrases, with sentences b. where they are incorporated into the verb stem. There will be no morpheme cutting within the compounded words.

44.	a.	əi	wakhəl	i-raŋ	laŋ-ŋi
		I	mind	RED-restless	restless-SAM
		'I feel anxious or restless'			

b. əi khoiraŋ-ŋi
I anxious-SAM
'I feel anxious'

45. a. phi əsi əi thəwai-nə ta-re
cloth this I soul-NOM like-PERF-SAM
'I like this cloth (very much)'

b. phi əsi əi khoida-re
cloth this I like-PERF-SAM
'I like this cloth (very much)'

46. a. nupa əmə isiŋ-də laksin-khə-re
man one water-LOC drown-DEF-PERF-SAM
'A man has been drowned'

b. nupa əmə iraknə-khə-re
man one drown-DEF-PERF-SAM
'A man has been drowned'

In sentences (a) the verbs undergo morphophonemic changes and have new verb forms in b. The nouns **wakhəl** 'mind' in (44a) and **thəwai** 'soul' in (45a) take their corresponding form **khoi** 'mind, soul' in (44b and 45b). The verb **laŋ-** 'restless' in (44a) changes to **raŋ-** when incorporated with **khoi-** and forms **khoiraŋ-** 'be anxious' and the verb **ta-** in (45a) changes **da-**. Both **raŋ-** and **da-** are results of intervocalic changes. The noun **isiŋ** 'water' in (46a) takes **-i** only when incorporated with **laksin-**'drown' and finally **lak-** changes **rak-** which is also conditioned by intervocalic changes and finally the verb **iraknə-**'drown' is formed. The noun + verb compound is used to express habitual or general activities or states (Gerdts, 1998: 85).

There are certain restrictions on the nouns that can be incorporated. In Manipuri, nouns that can be skipped down to a simple root can incorporate. Nouns having two syllables do not incorporate as seen in (44b), (45b) and (46b). Similarly, in **nuŋnaŋ-** 'be anxious', **nuŋ-** is the bound nominal root meaning 'inner' (part of the body means 'mind') and **laŋ-** 'be restless' which changes to **naŋ-** which is a morphophonemic change conditioned by the preceding sound. It cannot be **mənuŋlaŋ** (**mə-** is the generalized prefix when used with nominal bound roots and when it is used with verbal bound forms, it is termed as nominalizer prefix). Some restrictions found in noun incorporation in Manipuri are as follows:

(i) *Nouns that arise through nominalizer or generalizer or compounding do not incorporate,*

(ii) *Proper nouns do not incorporate,*

(iii) *Animate nouns do not incorporate*

In some instances, the meaning of these noun + verb compounds may drift from a simple compositional one; that is, they are idiomatic.

47. **laikənnə-** > laina > ənabə/əsokpə kənnə-bə hotnəbə
try to save a wounded, injured or ill person
'take up necessary steps to save one's life'

əsokpə əŋaŋ-du laikənnə-khə-re
wounded child-DEM take up necessary steps to save one's life-PERF-SAM
'Necessary steps were taken up to save the life of the wounded child'

48. **pottha-** > pot thabə
put down, remove a burden or thing
'take rest (of mind, body)

pabuŋ imuŋ-də pottha-ri
father house-LOC take rest-PROG-SAM
'Father is taking rest in the house'

In this sentence, the verb **pottha-** as the lexical meaning is to put down a thing; it does not mean that father is putting down a thing or burden. He is taking rest means he is relaxing his mind and body (after work or tension).

49. **wasək-** > wa səkpə > səri sonbə 'take an oath, promise, swear'
speech sing promise

nəŋ wasək-kənu
you promise-PROH
'(You) don't make a promise'

50. **maithi-** > mai thibə 'get defeated' face ugly
məhak əi-gi khut-tə maithi-re
he I-GEN hand-LOC defeat-PERF-SAM
'He got defeated from me'

Such consideration leads to the conclusion that noun + verb compound in a clause with incorporation is not always a simple paraphrase of the same verb with a free standing noun phrase. Finally, noun incorporations may be grouped into two as (i) Simple noun incorporation and (ii) idiomatic noun incorporation.

Simple Noun Incorporation: The compound forms that do not show any change in meaning, *i.e.* simple compositional compounds are termed as simple noun incorporations.

jumdaŋ- > migi jumdə taŋdunə ləibə take shelter
take shelter in other's house

sagonnə- > sa (həkcaŋgə) konnədunə ləibə associate closely
associate with the body

jumlonnǝ- > jum lonnǝnǝ/thǝŋnǝnǝ lǝibǝ — be a neighbour
houses that are next to each other

sindǝm- > sin/thǝbǝk tǝmbǝ — learn, study something
learn to do something as a profession

khuṭsǝmnǝ- > ǝmǝgǝ ǝmǝgǝ khut sǝmnǝbǝ — collaborate
hand in hand

majoknǝ- > mai oknǝbǝ — face something
be in face to face with something

siŋtha- > mǝsiŋ thabǝ > ǝphǝbǝdǝ thabǝ — praise, take into account
take into account in good terms

nǝmthi- > mǝnǝm thibǝ/hǝinǝdǝbǝ — have an unpleasant smell
smell that is not good

isit- > isiŋ sittokpǝ/lǝuthokpǝ — bale
to take out water from ponds etc.

caŋdǝmnǝ- > ǝphǝ-phǝttǝ caŋ tǝmnǝbǝ — compare
compare merits and demerits of two things

lalhǝu- > lal hǝubǝ (janiŋdǝbǝ utpǝ) — revolt, protest
start a revolution to protest

51. **khunda-** > khundǝ tabǝ /lǝibǝ — 'settle'
live/settle in a village

meetǝi-siŋ-nǝ tǝmpak-tǝ knunda-i
Meetei-PL-NOM valley-LOC settle-SAM

Meeteis settle in valleys (in Manipur)'

52. **warepnǝ-** > wa lepnǝbǝ — 'resolve'
fix something

ekadǝmik kaunsil-nǝ pǝrikhja mǝtǝm ca-nǝ
academic council-NOM examination in time-ADV

haidok-nǝ-bǝ warepnǝ-khǝ-re
result out-PUR-NMZ resolve-DEF-PERF-SAM
'Academic Council resolved to give out results of examinations in time'

53. **ləmɟiŋ-** > ləmbi ciŋbə/takpə 'lead or guide'
lead to a path or something

əi-khoi-gi khoŋcət ədu məhak-nə ləmɟiŋ-gəni
I-PL-GEN journey that he-NOM lead-NREAL
'He will lead our journey'

54. **ləllon-** > ləl onbə > pəisa onbə/tanbə 'do business'
asset exchange change into money

məhak thau ləllol-li
he oil deal in-SAM
'He deals in oil'

55. **məntiknə-** > məməl tiknəbə/ŋaŋnəbə 'bargain'
bargain a price

həndəkti əikhoi məntiknə-rə-gum-si
this time I-PL bargain-PROS-NEG-SUG
'Let us not bargain this time (not like we did before)'

Idiomatic Noun Incorporation: In such type of constructions, the meaning of the compound form is diverted from the lexical meaning. In other words, the meaning is idiomatic.

laijeŋ > laina jeŋbə > ənabə phənəbə təubə
diagnose a disease undergo treatment of disease

ləita- > ləidə tabə > wakhəl təŋ tabə
fall on the ground settle, be peaceful get peace of mind

noŋga- > thəwainə noŋ/məthəktə kabə die, expire
(of soul) to go up (after death)

khoithumnə > khoi/thəmoi/thəwainə penbəməkhəi haubə be very tasty
tasty enough to satisfy the soul

khunthok- > ənəubə ləm əmədə khun tabə settle
settle in a new place

wajen- > əcum əran bicar təubə give judgement
justify what is wrong or right

56. **niŋhənnə-** > wakhəl məniŋlomdə hənbə 'feel discourage'
(of mind) to go backward

mi-gi wa ta-rəgə niŋhənnə-gənu, nəŋ-nə
man-GEN speech hear-CPART discourage-PROH you-NOM

hotnə-gə-də-bə ədum hotnə-u
try-POT-SPE-NMZ still try-COM
'Don't listen to others and feel discouraged. Instead (you) keep trying your best'

57. **khoŋgoinə-** >
məralgidəmək khoŋdə koinə pudunə ikaibə pibə 'give insult in public'
give insult by making someone go round on foot as a punishment

ləmcət cum-də-bə nupa-du mijam maŋ-də khoŋgoinə-khə-re
character straight-NEG-NMZ man-DEM public in front-LOC insult-DEF PERF-SAM
'The man with loose character was insulted in public'

58. **potloi-** > pot loisinbə > həkcaŋ loisinbə 'cremate/bury'
sirəbə mətuŋdə həkcaŋ məi thabə/phumbə
cremate or bury a body after death

məsək khəŋdəbə əsibə-du potloi-də-ri (-dri)
3PP-face know-NEG-NMZ dead body-DEM cremate-NEG-PROG-SAM
'The unidentified dead body has not yet been cremated'

The verbs given in the above examples are idiomatic in the sense that they do not mean the lexical meaning only. In idiomatic noun incorporations, one cannot get the meaning easily from the compound words, that is to say, the lexical meaning is not enough and cannot be analysable as simple noun incorporations do. In such cases, there is always an extra meaning or deep meaning. For instance, in **khoŋgoinə-** the lexical meaning is to take round by going on foot. The underlying meaning here is to insult in public. The verb **wajen-** has its lexical meaning as **wa** 'speech' and **jen-** 'distribute'. However, it does not simply mean to distribute the speech. The idiomatic meaning that the verb gives is to justify or find out who is wrong and who is right and give judgement.

Verbal Compounds: Traditionally, a compound verb is supposed to exhibit functional unity. It contains one and only one 'major' verb or pole. The vector is a minor verb in that it is (i) formally attached (it must occur immediately after the pole, (ii) semantically heteronomous (used as a vector, it does not have the autonomous meaning it has in other sentences where it is used as a pole), (iii) grammatically subservient (it may not independently govern complements or modifiers of its own) (Dasgupta, 1989). These vectors constitute a small class of typically motion verbs like go, sit, come, give, take, etc. (Bhat, 2002). Examples in Hindi:

59. a. *laRka: baRa: ho gaya:*
'The boy got big/grew up'

b. *laRka baRa: hua:*
'The boy got big/grew up'

60. a. *usne ca:i pi: li:*
'He drank tea'

b. *usne ca:i piya:*
'He drank tea'

In (59a), ***ho gaya:*** is a verb compound where ***ho*** is the main or polar verb and ***gaya:*** is the vector verb which takes the verbal suffixes. Similarly, in sentence (60a), ***pi: li:*** is the verb compound of which ***pi:*** is the main or polar verb and ***li:*** is the vector verb with the verbal suffixes. On the other hand, the verbs ***hua:*** in (59b) and ***piya:*** in (60b) are the main verbs without any compounding.

Such types of compound verbs are found in Bengali, Marathi and many other Indian languages. It is one of the hallmarks of the South-Asian Linguistic area (c.f. Masica, 1976) and has been a topic of debate in traditional as well as modern linguistic descriptions. It has been variously referred to by different scholars as modified verbal expression. (PÓZKA, 1967, 1986, Singh, 1998), explicator compound verb (Masica, 1992), serial or compound verb (Kachru, 1979, Kachru and Pandhare Pande, 1980, Fedson, 1985, Pandhari Pande, 1990), verbal expression (Nespital, 1997) (Prashant Pardeshi, 2003: 19).

Some scholars treat **-thok** and **-niŋ** as vector verbs and the combination of a verbal root and one of the two suffixes as compound verbs. But there are problems regarding vector verbs as to whether they are to be treated as vector or suffixes. They can occur as main verbs in the following sentences:

61. **niŋ**- 'wish'
əi ph.d təu-ge niŋ-ŋi
I Ph.D do-INT wish-SAM
'I wish to do Ph.D.'

62. **thok**- 'go out'
məhak jum-dəgi həuɟik-tə thok-khi
he house-ABL now-only go out-DEF-SAM
'He has just gone out of the house'

Inspite of being main verbs, they can generally be attached to other verbs. **niŋ**- 'wish' can occur with dynamic verbs and certain stative verbs as **waŋ**- 'be tall', **khəŋ**- 'know', **pa**- 'be slim', **noi**- 'be fat', etc. **thok**- 'out' can be attached to action verbs, process verbs and certain state verbs like **ŋəu**- 'be fair', **noi**- 'be fat', **cau**- 'be big', **lau**- 'be wide', etc.

Stative Verbs + **niŋ**-

ŋəu-niŋ- wish to become fair

waŋ-niŋ- wish to become tall
khəŋ-ni- wish to become skilful or experienced
cau-niŋ- wish to become big or great
sau-niŋ- wish to be angry or feel angry, etc.

Stative Verbs + **thok-**

ŋəu-thok- become fairer
cau-thok- become bigger
pak-thok- become wider
nəu-thok- become younger
noi-thok- become fatter, etc.

As a result of the fact that one of the constituent elements of such compounds had gradually lost its identity as an independent root element, it might have attained the status of an affix (Bhat, 1986: 128). It may be said that the verbs have been grammaticalized and are discussed under grammaticalized suffixes in (**4.2**). There are reasons for not treating **niŋ**- and **thok**- as vectors as the conditions cannot be applied in Manipuri. First, vector verbs lose their lexical meaning when they are attached to a main verb. But in case of Manipuri, they retain their meaning when attached to a main verb. Hence, they will not be treated as vector verbs in the present study. Instead, they will come under verbal suffixes because of their nature of free occurrence with many verbs.

Another reason for not considering **niŋ**- as a vector verb is that the occurrence of a verbal root + **niŋ**- can be interrupted by the suffixes, for, once a compound form is established, the compound word remains as a compact form and it does not entertain any kind of interruption (may be of suffixes) within the word. In support of this reason, examples are illustrated below:

ca-niŋ-	root + niŋ-	wish to eat
ca-hən-niŋ-	root + suffix + niŋ	wish to let somebody eat
ca-ɟə-niŋ-	root + suffix + niŋ	wish to eat (polite form)
ca-khət-niŋ-	root + suffix + niŋ	wish to start eating
ca-thok-niŋ-	root + suffix + niŋ	wish to complete the action of eating
ca-sin-niŋ-	root + suffix + niŋ	wish to eat more when the stomach is full
ca-bi-niŋ-	root + suffix + niŋ	wish to eat (on somebody's request)
ca-həu-niŋ-	root + suffix + niŋ	wish to eat before doing something
ca-thə-niŋ-	root + suffix + niŋ	wish to continue eating
ca-minnə-niŋ-	root+suffix+suffix+niŋ	wish to eat together
ca-hən-ɟə-niŋ-	root+suffix+suffix+niŋ	wish to let somebody eat (polite form), etc.

Regarding -**thok**, it can be stated that no insertion cannot take place between the root and -**thok** because it comes closest to the root and that is why Shobhana (1997:204) described it as one of the first level derivative suffixes. It has also undergone the same process of grammaticalization and becomes highly productive in the sense that it can go with all types of verbs. It has four different functions (see **4.2**). Thus, it can be concluded that -**thok** and -**niŋ** are no more verbal roots and the combination of a verbal root and -**niŋ** and -**thok** should not be treated as verbal compounds.

Regarding compound verbs in Manipuri, different linguists propose their own arguments. It would be worth to be discussed in this context. Bhat and Ningomba (1986) Bhat and Ningomba (1986) treat -**thok** and -**niŋ** as vector verbs and the combination of a verbal root and one of the two suffixes as compound verbs.

Bidyarani (2000: 54-56), while discussing compound verbs, did not make the point clear. It is confusing and misleading as well as she contradicts herself. She defines Manipuri compound verbs as follows:

> *In Manipuri compound verbs are formed by combination of two or more roots and they must be ended by aspect markers or modality. Compound verbs are very limited in number. They are formed by the suffixation of* **-thok** *or* **-niŋ** *with a verbal root and they must be ended by the aspect markers i.e. even in the compound verb, one aspect marker is necessary to be added.*

In the first sentence she says compound verbs are formed by the combination of two or more roots while in the third sentence she says – they are formed by the suffixation of -**thok** and -**niŋ** with a verbal root. The definition given in the first sentence is correct. However, she did not make it clear that -**thok** and -**niŋ** are to be treated as verbal roots or suffixes. To make the point clear consider the following definition given by Bhat (1986:128).

> *If two or more rather independent linguistic elements are joined together to form a word, we call it compounding whereas if a dependent element (affix) is attached to an independent one, we call it affixation'.*

Further they point out the deference between the two as follows:

> *One interesting difference between affixation and compounding is that in the case of compound words, we generally find it possible or even necessary to establish very rich underlying structures of which only a very small truncated part is overtly retained by the compound word; whereas in the case of composite words derived through affixation, we do not generally find any need to establish underlying structure which are different from the structures that actually occurs in the composite words themselves.*

(The above statement is qouted from Bhat and Ningomba (1986). Still, they are also of the opinion that **-niŋ** and **–thok** are vector verbs).

In suppliment to the above statements one more point that is necessary to be added here is that a compound word (the combination of two linguistic elements) is a compact word. Once two roots or words are compounded the form is established as a free word. Hence, no insertion or any kind of interference is allowed within the compounded form. But in case of **-niŋ** any suffix can be inserted between the verbal root and the suffix. This can be seen in the study of compound verbs by N. Loken Singh (1997:50) as:

Root + suffix(eɜ) + Root + suffix(es)

həŋ + hən + ɟə + niŋ + mən + khə + re
'have too much intention to be asked'

jeŋ + hən + ɟə + niŋ + ləm + de
'had no intention too much to be seen'

hai + hən + ɟə + niŋ + ləm + mi
'had intention to let him to request' and so on.

It can be seen that many suffixes are inserted between the roots **həŋ**- 'ask' and **niŋ**- 'intention' **jeŋ**- 'look' and **niŋ**- 'intention' and **hai**- 'say' and **niŋ**- 'intention'. This evidence easily proves that **niŋ**- is not a verbal root here. In other words, it can be said that the verbal root **niŋ**- 'wish' has undergone a historical and semantic process known as grammaticalization and it has developed into a suffix and it has the essential property of an affix that it is highly productive.

Apart from this, Manipuri verbal structure shows another verbal compounding known as coordinate verbal compound.

Coordinate Verbal Compound: In coordinate verbal compounds, the second verb is semantically autonomous, *i.e.* it carries its full lexical meaning. Both the verbs are the head of the compound and they serve as a regular verb in the language.

coiɟainə-	>	coi- be loose	+	cai- scatter	be in disorder
khebat-	>	khet- scrape	+	phat- give way	lacerate
toŋganə-	>	toŋ- high	+	ka- raise	be slim, slender
khajaknə-	>	kha- bitter	+	jak- salty	be salty
pokkhai-	>	pop- enlarge	+	kai- break	burst, explode

səŋmunnəbə-	>	səŋ- green		mun- ripe	(of fruits) which is fully matured and is about to be ripe
phumbəŋnə-	>	phum bury	+	pəŋ- fool	nonplus
lu-hen-	>	lu- neat/clean	+	hen- excel	neat and tidy
noi-pen-	>	noi- fat	+	pen- satisfy	be stout, plump
maŋ-tak-	>	maŋ- lose	+	tak- damage	go to ruins
koidanə-	>	koi- round	+	ta- fall	be round (especially of face)
ŋaucətnə-	>	ŋau- Mad	+	cət- go	go stray
thoicətnə-	>	thoi- excel	+	cət- go	be proud

63. **koiraunə-** > **koi-** 'round' and **lau-** 'big' 'be of big and round (eyes)'
(/l/ changes to /r/ intervocally)
nupi-si-gi mə-mit koiraunə-i
woman-DEM-GEN 3PP-eye big and round-SAM
'This woman has big and round eyes'

64. **phopcaunə-** > **pop-** 'swell' and **cau-** 'big' 'big and stout'
/p/ of **pop** changes to /**ph**/ when compounded
əŋaŋ əsi mə-sa phopcaunə-i
child this 3PP-body big and stout-SAM
'This child has a big and stout body'

65. **temkhai-** > **tem-** 'level' and **khai-** 'cut' 'make level or to surface'
ləipuŋ əsi temkhai-ju
mound this level-COM
'Level this mound'

66. **satkai-** > **sat-** 'bloom' and **kai-** 'break' 'be in (full) bloom'
gulab əsi satkai-re
rose this bloom-PERF-SAM

'This rose is in (full) bloom'

67. **pomsatnə**- > **pom**- 'which is still in bud' and **sat**- 'bloom (of a flower) '
'not yet in (full) bloom but going to be bloomed in a short time'
thəmbal əsi pomsatnə-ri
lotus this not yet (full) bloom-PROG-SAM
'This lotus is not yet in (full) bloom'

68. **caphat**- > **ca**- 'eat' and **pat**- 'ulcer' 'have an ulcer'
əi-gi khoŋ-sa karək-tə caphat-le
I-GEN leg-toe between-LOC ulcer-PERF-SAM
'I have an ulcer between my toes'

Note: /p/ of **pat**- changes to **/ph/** of **phat**.

69. **nolluk**- > **non**- 'bow down' and **luk-'** hang down (of head)' 'be humble'
nupa-məca əsi nolluk-i
man-small this humble-SAM
'This boy is humble'

Note: /n/ of **non**- changes to **/l/** when followed by **luk-**

Sometimes, the combination of two verbal roots may give a single meaning in the gloss, but still, they have two root meanings in the underlying structure as seen just above in (69). The root meanings may be retained in the gloss also.

In English, verbal compounds are introduced into the language indirectly through nominal compounds. Most of them can be shown to derive from nominal compounds through back formation (Adams, 1973; Bauer, 1983).

Nominal compounds	**Verbal compounds**
globe-trotter	globe-trot
air-conditioner	air-conditioned
double-header	double-head
sleep-walking	sleep-walk

Compound verb is also found in Warumuru language (a Pama-Nyungan language) where a preverb (which form an open class whose members have a status inDEMerminate between being free and bound) is compounded with a verb. The compounded form denotes medium, direction, manner, result, quantifier, etc. Lahu verbs, whether Vact's or Vadj's, may participate in compounds by single juxtaposition. The syntactic behaviour of these compounds is in all essentials identical to that of monomorphemic V_h's (*i.e.* they function a single word) (Matisoff,

1973:197) Lahu has four types of compound verbs: V free + V free, V free V bound, V bound + V bound and V bound + V free/V bound.

2.4 N + V Construction

It refers to a larger construction of Manipuri verbs. It can be divided into two from the functional point of view as: (i) Noun dependent and (ii) Noun independent.

Noun Dependent or Clitics + Verb: In this type of construction, the noun is always dependent on the verb. It cannot occur as a free form elsewhere in a sentence. Hence, it is always attached to a verb and the combined form serves as a main verb in a sentence. On the other hand, the verb itself cannot give the desired meaning without the combination of the noun.

	ta-	reduce, fall
	məjeŋ ta-	reduce
	ne ta-	subside, settle, get peace of mind
	men ta-	know the certainty, confirm
	khoŋgun ta-	be obedient
	məmut ta-	be minute
	mənam ta-	(of hair) be smooth and shinning
	məham ta-	decrease, be useless, futile
	təp ta-	be exhausted, very tired
	təŋ ta-	be fixed, definite, settle
laŋ-	be of different colours, be brindled, dappled, spotted	
	ikhəu laŋ-	be thirsty
	həkcik laŋ-	take fresh air
	məkhe laŋ-	amuse
	meləi laŋ-	behave in a way that is not desirable
ca-	eat	
	khudoŋ ca-	be opportune
	tan ca-	be opportune
cam-	wash	
	paŋthok cam-	be negligent
thi-	be ugly	
	khudi thi-	stumble
	nuŋsa thi-	be anxious, restless

Note: The word **nuŋsa** in **nuŋsa thi-** does not have a semantic correlation with **nuŋsa** 'sunlight'

It comes from **nuŋsa swar** 'breath'.

pha-	catch	
	kaŋdoŋ pha-	(of plants, animals) be grown
	həijiŋ pha-	(of fruit) be fully matured or developed
	sarep pha-	be matured, fully grown
	məpuŋ mərəi pha-	be matured
kai-	break	
	məraŋ kai-	be in plenty
cum-	right	
	mərik cum-	be comprehensive
sən-	spread	
	səra sən-	be open to all
thoŋ-	carry on shoulder, back, head etc.	
	sədəu thoŋ-	exhaust, be fatigue
jeŋ-	look	
	cəgəu jeŋ-	sit idly while others are working

70. **thi-** 'be ugly, not good'
nəŋ-gi khut-i thi
you-GEN handwriting ugly-SAM
'Your handwriting is not good'

71. **khudi thi-** 'stumble'
əi nuŋ-də khudi thi-re
I stone-LOC stumble-PERF-SAM
'I have stumbled over a stone'

72. **tu-** 'fall'
noŋ nuŋsit-nə u jam-nə tu-re
rain wind-NOM tree much-ADV fall-PERF-SAM
'Many trees fell in the storm'

73. **tora-tu-** 'devastate, fall in a mass'
laicət əmə-dəgi imuŋ-si-gi mi pumnəmək tora-tu-re
epidemic one-ABL family-DEM-GEN man every fall in mass-PERF-SAM

'All the members of this family fell ill due to an epidemic'

In (70), the verb **thi-** means 'be ugly, not good'. But in (71), when it goes with a nominal form **khudi-** the meaning changes automatically. It denotes another meaning 'stumble'. The same condition is found in (72) and (73) where the verb **tu-** 'fall' alone, cannot give the desired meaning of **tora-tu-** in (73) which means 'devastate or fall in a mass'. In this case, the meaning is not totally changed as found in (70) and (71); the meaning is expanded, *i.e.*, from 'fall' to 'fall in a mass' or 'destroy or devastate'. In other words, the meaning of the single verbs may be changed, but in some cases, it may be retained as in **ta-** 'reduce' and **məjeŋ ta-** 'reduce'.

74. **wajoŋ cadə-** 'be naughty, destitute of common sense'
    nupa-məca əsi wajoŋ ca-de
    man-small this naughty-NEG-SAM
    'The boy is naughty'
75. **mərəi mun-** 'be comprehensive'
    ma-nə-bu təu-rəbədi thəbək-si mərəi mun-gəni
    he-NOM-ACC do-if work-DEM comprehensive-NREAL
    'The work will be comprehensive when he does it'

The first words that come along with the verbs are nominals according to the function in the sentence. For instance, **məjeŋ** in **məjeŋ ta-**'reduce', **coŋləm** in **coŋləm cadə-** 'be naughty, destitute of common sense', **torot** in **torot khoda-nə-** 'be on speaking terms with, be familiar with', **kaŋkhoŋ** (not 'wheel') in **kaŋkhoŋ cai-** 'be in a state of chaos, be in disorder', **mitsen** in **mitsen khaŋ-** 'have a vigil', etc. are nominals and they cannot stand as a free noun and they are always attached to a verb. Such nominals are termed as clitics. Consider the circumstances under which they are called clitics.

(i) They do not have an independent status of a free form *e.g.*, in **khudi thi-** 'stumble' **khudi** cannot stand as a free form.

(ii) They are always attached to a host (in Manipuri, they are attached on the right. Hence they are called pro-clitics). **khudi** being a dependent word is attached to **thi-**.

(iii) They give a meaning only when they are attached to a verb although they cannot constitute a free word. So, they are called verbal clitics, *e.g.* **khudi** alone cannot constitute a meaning of its own and it gets its meaning only when it is combined with **thi-** > **khudi thi-** 'stumble'.

Clitics, in English, constitute a prosodic unit which denotes any prosodically weak (unaccented) element (Halpern, 2002). Reduced auxiliaries and pronouns in English are often cited as examples of clitics; they lack stress and are pronounced as a single unit with the preceding word. Cliticization, found in the phonological domain has been termed as simple clitics (Zwicky, 1977). Reduced auxiliaries and weak pronouns in English are simple clitics.

76. *She'll go there.*
77. *They've come back.*
78. *Give'em the books.*

In contrast to this prosodic definition of the clitic, special clitic refers to placement of weak pronouns in French, Greek, Macedonian and Albanian languages Halpern, 1998). The type of clitics found in Manipuri is verbal clitic since it is attached to the verb as its host, *e.g.* in **khudi thi-**, the clitic **khudi** is attached to the verb **thi-**. Such type of clitics is termed as special clitics and the distributions of special clitics (as cited by Anderson, 1992) are:

[a] *The clitic is located in the scope of some syntactic constituent (S, VP, NP, etc.) probably only X^{mas} but perhaps e.g. V as well which constitute its domain.*

[b] *The clitic is located by reference to the (first vs. last vs. head element of the constituent in which it appears.*

[c] *The clitic (precedes vs. follows) this reference point.*

In Manipuri, there is no certain rule that clitic should appear adjacent to its host (a verb) as found in other languages. Other words may intervene between a clitic and a verb, but still, it does not disturb the meaning of the verb (as a whole *i.e.* clitic + verb).

79. **ənəm kən-** 'be adamant'

a. əŋaŋ-si ənəm kəl-li
child-DEM adamant -SAM
'The child is adamant'

b. əŋaŋ-si ənəm jam-nə kəl-li
child-DEM much-ADV adamant-SAM
'The child is very adamant'

c. əŋaŋ-si ənəm pəŋ-kən-də kəl-li
child-DEM RED- adamant -LOC-SAM
'The child is very adamant'

The meaning of both the clitic and verb functioning as a main verb in sentences (79a-c) do not change in spite of the insertion of **jam-nə** in sentence (b) and **pəŋ-kən-də** in (c). In other words, the meaning remains unchanged in all the sentences. The insertion is enabled by the verb form as it can take a modifier **jam-nə** and can undergo the process of reduplication **pəŋ-kən-də**.

There is also a larger construction of clitic where more than one form is involved.

80. **ənəm əha cu-** 'be dull'
əŋaŋ-si ənəm-əha cu-re
child-DEM dull-PERF-SAM
'The child has become dull'

81. **cərək cəhiŋ nai-** 'be vague, uncertain'
kərigumbə thəbək əmə təu-bə mətəm-də cərək cəhiŋ nai-hən-gənu

something work one do-NMZ time-LOC vague-CAUS-PROH
'Don't be vague in doing something (do it smoothly)'

Some more examples are given below:

turəi irəi cen-	have obstacles
məron məraŋ tak-	sustain a loss of one's belongings
məŋəm san-	have progress in doing something
ikai seŋgoi haŋ-	feel shame
huiŋək jenək ca-	be nervous, hesitate
inak khun-	be well to do, rich
təksi son-	utter in despair
ikai khumnə-	give/show respect, honour (**ikai**- is not 'shame' here)
sərək si-	interval
pabot lon-	grow thickly
thuk lau-	tingle
srit nan-	be smooth
som tan-	plough a field for the first time in a year
moŋ hadə-	be gentle

From the above examples, it may be concluded that clitics occur only once. Once a clitic is found attached to a verb it cannot take another verb as its host, *e.g.* the clitic **inak-** in **inak khun**- cannot take another verb. In the above examples, some verbs are found to have reduplicated forms. They are discussed in section **2.5** of this chapter.

Noun Independent + Verb: It refers to a larger construction of Manipuri verbs. In this type of construction, a nominal free form is attached to a verbal form to derive a new verb in the language. The free form can function as a free noun elsewhere in other sentences. On the other hand, the verb itself, when occurred alone, gives a different meaning but when it is combined with a nominal free form, it gives a meaning which may be quite different, derived meaning or slightly changed or retained.

cen- order a thing

khurəu	lock on	>	khurəu cen-	hindrance
laina	disease	>	laina cen-	suffer from a disease
pap	sin	>	pap cen-	be sinful
ərthə	meaning	>	ərthə cen-	be meaningful
ləihau	soil	>	ləihau cen-	be fertile
məhu	poison	>	məhu cen-	be poisonous

thaŋ- carry

ləicin	cloud	>	ləicin thaŋ-	be cloudy
nura	grime	>	nura thaŋ-	covered with grime

su- pound

siŋɟu	vegetable mixture	>	siŋɟu su-	prepare vegetable mixture

tha- hit

usa	tree branch	>	usa tha-	cut branches of big trees

cən- be fitted

hakam	yawn	>	hakam cən-	yawn
mənuŋ	inner	>	mənuŋ cən-	include
paukhoŋ	riddle	>	paukhoŋ cən-	make riddle
siŋ	firewood	>	siŋ cən-	collect firewood
miŋ	name	>	miŋ cən-	

ka- climb

ləinin	moisture	>	ləinin ka-	be damp, humid
kokphai	fungus	>	kokphai ka-	be mouldy

sa- hot

nuŋsa	sunlight	>	nuŋsa sa-	be sunny

hun- throw

jenniŋ	bud	>	jenniŋ hun-	sprout

laŋ- be of multicolour

urum	shade	>	urum laŋ-	be shady
ləi	flower	>	ləi laŋ-	offer flower
məisa	heat	>	məisa laŋ-	get the heat/ be in indistress
isəu	hot blood	>	isəu laŋ-	be grouchy
səktəm	role	>	səktəm laŋ-	take the role of

khən- screen, shade

hakthi	sneeze	>	hakthi khən-	sneeze

82. **ja-** 'agree'
əi nəŋ-nə hai-bə-du ja-re
I you-NOM say-NMZ-DEM agree-PERF-SAM
'I agree with you'

83. **səruk** 'share'
əi-gi səruk pi-ro
I-GEN share give-COM
'Give me my share'

84. **səruk thuŋ-** 'get or receive one's share'
nəŋ-gi saruk thuŋ-lə-bə-ra?
you-GEN share get-PERF-NMZ-INTR
'Have you got your share?'

85. **səruk ja-** 'participate, join, take part'
nss kep-tə əi-su səruk ja-gəni
NSS camp-LOC I-also participate-NREAL
'I shall participate in the NSS camp'

In (83), the noun **səruk** 'share' when combined with the verb **ja-** 'agree' a new verb is formed, where the meaning of 'agree' is not seen. But in (84) both the meanings of **səruk** and **thuŋ**-are retained. Another example of meaning-change is given here.

86. **ta-** 'fall'
khau-du məkha-də ta-re
bag-DEM down-LOC fall-PERF-SAM
'The bag fell on the ground'

87. **məka** 'leaf (of spinach, mustard, arum plant etc.)'
əi həŋgam məka jam-nə hek-e
I mustard leaf much-ADV pluck-PERF-SAM
'I have plucked many mustard leaves'

88. **məka ta-** 'sprouting (of spinach, mustard, arum plant etc.)'
həŋgam-si məka ta-re
mustard-DEM leaf sprout-PERF-SAM
'The mustard plant has sprouted many leaves'

The occurrence of the verbal form **məka ta-** 'sprout' may be intervened by words like verbal modifier or reduplication as found in the case of clitics (79a-c).

2.5 Reduplication

Reduplication is the morphological phenomenon in which some morphological material is repeated with a single form, for lexical or grammatical purposes. It is a common phenomenon in the languages of the world, taking a variety of forms and serving a variety of purposes (Trask, 1993). Reduplication stands for all or a part of lexical item carrying a semantic modification (Abbi, 1992: 12).

There are many forms of reduplication like noun reduplication, adjective reduplication, adverb reduplication, etc. But the present study aims at the verbal reduplication only *i.e.*, reduplication involving verbs and it can be classified into two as reduplicated verb 1 and reduplicated verb 2. A tree diagram showing a detailed classification of reduplication is given as follows:

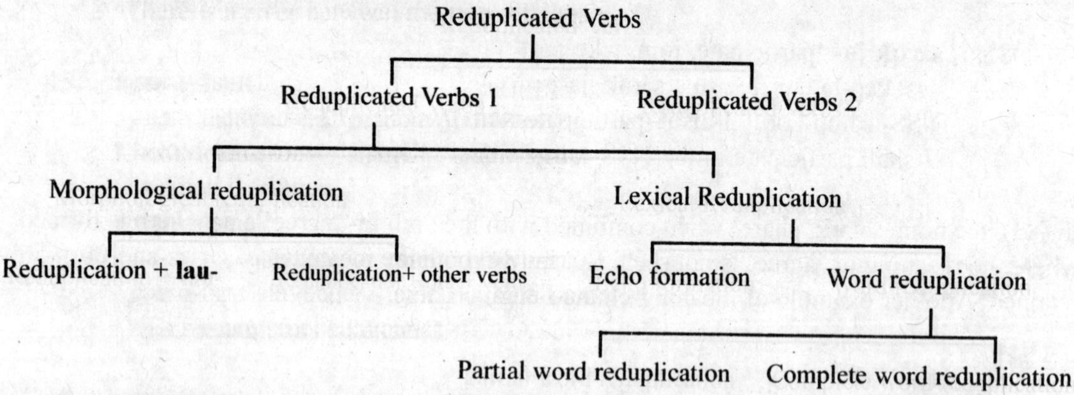

Reduplicated Verb 1: Under this group, verbal reduplication may be classified further into two: (i) morphological reduplication and (ii) lexical reduplication.

Morphological reduplication: It refers to the repeated form of iterated syllables which constitute a word. The syllable when isolated, does not offer any meaning but when it is repeated it gives a meaning. The entire repeated construction works as a morpheme and they are called expressive. Indian expressive manifests feelings, sensations, perceptions, pertaining to five senses, manner of an action and disorderliness. All these relate to the ability of perception of the speaker in a cultural specific environment (Abbi, 1994: 14). Onomatopoeic constructions, imitative, certain instances of sound symbolism, mimic words are all examples of morphological reduplication as the entire repeated structure represents a morpheme or a word and they do not allow morpheme cuts within the word.

Morphological reduplication in the present study, deals with the reduplicated form + a verbal form which functions like any regular verb and contributes in the lexicon of the language. They may be grouped into two as: (i) reduplicated form + **lau**- and reduplicated form with other verbs.

Reduplicated form with lau-: It refers to the minimally meaningful and segmentally indivisible morphemes which are constituted of iterated syllables.

kəp kəp lau-	not strong, not properly fixed
ɟəu ɟəu lau-	be rough
mi mi lau-	having low tone
səubiŋ səubiŋ lau-	be tensed, nervous
səu səu lau-	be whimsical, shrewd, capricious
heŋo heŋo lau-	be childish, inactive, womanly
bup bup lau-	be plump
seŋ seŋ lau-	have a shrill voice
təbəŋ təbəŋ lau-	be innocent
nap nap lau-	be supple
swai swai lau-	be crispy
kudruk kədrak lau-	be uneven (of a surface, face of something)
tət tət lau-	not crispy
sot sot lau-	be soggy

89. **thuk thuk lau**- 'having a vomiting tendency'
ŋəsi-di   əi   thuk thuk lau-i
today-DEM   I   have a vomiting tendency-SAM
'I have a vomiting tendency today'

90. **hop hop lau**- 'be loose'
phurit-si   əi-ŋon-də   hop hop lau-i
shirt-DEM   I-DIR-DAT   loose-SAM
'This shirt is loose to me'

91. **heŋo heŋo lau**- 'be inactive'
thəbək-tu   jaŋ-sil-lu,   heŋo heŋo lau-gənu
work-DEM   fast-IN-COM   inactive-PROH
'Speed up the work, don't be inactive'

92. **swai swai lau**- 'be crispy'
biskit-si   swai swai lau-i
biscuit-DEM   crispy-SAM
'The biscuit is crispy'

In (89), the verb **thuk thuk lau**- means 'having a tendency of vomiting'. The reduplicated form **thuk thuk** cannot stand alone as a free word without the verb **lau-**. It cannot get an entry in the lexicon of Manipuri language, since it is a morphological reduplication and such type of reduplication needs a verb to get the status of a meaningful word. In short, morphological reduplication is incomplete in itself to reach at the stage of full-fledged words and get an entry in the lexicon of the language. Similarly, in (90) **hop hop lau**- 'be loose'; **hop hop** is not a word until it is immediately followed by a verb **lau-**.

Reduplicated form with other verbs: In this type of construction, the occurrences of the reduplicated forms are not restricted as found in **lau**-. However, the reduplicated construction decides to occur with a certain verb only. For instance, the reduplicated form **təgət təgət** takes the verb **tek**- 'fresh' only.

kaphəi kaphəi cət-	toddle
khjau khjau kəŋ-	dry quickly
təp təp ta-	drip
tər tər ciŋsin-	shudder
təram təram ok-	give a warm welcome
thəro thəro on-	roll
ŋrəŋ ŋrəŋ ŋəŋ-	thunder
prok prok cak-	be impatient, burn
gri gri tək-	insist
murum murum son-	murmur
musuk musuk ŋaŋnə-	gossip
cibon cibon ŋaŋnə-	gossip
ninphuŋ ninphuŋ ta-	hear something that is not yet confirmed
munə munə yeŋ-	peer, peep
lipət lipət cət-	go to and fro
huru huru ləi-	whirl
ɟwai ɟwai ta-	(of hair) be straight and fall freely
phi phi kam-	be very angry
hik hik kəp-	sob
phoŋ phoŋ sa-	be very hot
liri liri hum-	(of wind) blow gently
breŋ breŋ ŋaŋ-	speak fluently
bruŋ bruŋ səu-	boil
prik prik səu-	increase, have so many in number of its kind
ɕru ɕru nəi-	torture, insist
khu khu kam-	be very angry
thik thik nok-	giggle
laŋkək laŋkək cu-	rain sparsely
khro khro khot-	scratch, be very impatient
tek tek təu-	do something for the time being

93. **təgət təgət tek**- 'be very fresh'
kobi əsi təgət təgət tek-i
cabbage this very fresh-SAM
'The cabbage is very fresh'

94. **thərak thərak jan-** 'be overhang, flaccid, dangle'
phi-siŋ-si phijankhok-tə thərak thərak jal-le
cloth-PL-DEM cloth line-LOC dangle-PERF-SAM
'The clothes dangled on the cloth line'

95. **ŋahəu ŋahəu cət-** 'stroll'
əhəl əni-du səmudrə məpan-də ŋahəu ŋahəu cət-li
old man two-DEM sea shore-LOC stroll-SAM
'The two old men stroll along the sea beach'

96. **thək thək nik-** 'tremble with fear, shiver with cold'
əŋaŋ-si iŋ-bə-nə thək thək nik-e
child-DEM cold-NMZ-CAUS shake-PERF-SAM
'The child is shivering with cold'

It may be noted here that the perfective suffix **-e** is used to indicate a progressive action with process verbs. The action of shaking is still going on. But when asked a question like this: **əŋaŋ-du həuȷik phaubə nik-li-bə-ra**? 'Is the child still shivering with cold?'; then, the answer may be like this: **hoi, nik-i** 'Yes he is still shivering'. Similarly, when a process verb like **sat-** 'bloom' one may say **ləi əmə sat-le** 'A flower is blooming' not **ləi əmə sat-li** 'A flower is blooming'. The reason behind the progressive meaning of the perfective suffix with process verbs is the semantic component of the perfective suffix -e which indicates the present relevance of an action that has been started in the past.

In the examples given above, the reduplicated forms like **thərak thərak** in (94) goes only with the verb **jan-** 'hang' and it indicates an action of dangling. The reduplicated form **ŋahəu ŋahəu** in (95) associates only with **cət-** 'go' and it indicates an action of going and lastly, **thək thək** in (96) takes the verb **nik-** 'shiver' and gives the meaning 'shiver with cold'. From the analysis, it can be concluded that the reduplicated verbs function as adverbial to the adjacent verbs in one sense.

Lexical reduplication: It may be studied under two heads *viz*. echo formation and word reduplication.

Echo formation: Echo words refer to a situation where the second word in the paired construction does not have any meaning of its own; when it is attached to the first word, an idea of generality is obtained (Yashawanta, 1998: 194).

phəireŋ tureŋ cət-	go in an improper way
turoi ŋamloi cət-	toddle
seran turan təu-	do in a wrong way
məphəm məraŋ khəŋdə-	be in a state of confusion
məmi sami u-	not to see clearly, blur
coitrəŋ patrəŋ khən-	have misconception

97. **əwat əpa ləitə-** 'be well-to-do'
mə-khoi-gi imuŋ-di əwat əpa ləi-te
he-PL-GEN family-DEM well-to-do-NEG-SAM
'Their family is a well to do family'

98. **kithi kirum təu-** 'be timid'
kithi kirum təu-gənu, nəŋ-nə həŋ-niŋ-bə məkhəi həŋ-ŋu
timid-PROH you-NOM ask-wish-NMZ-all ask-COM
'Don't be timid, ask whatever you wish'

In (97) **əwat əpa**, the word **əwat** means 'lack, run short'. The second word **əpa** does not have a meaning, *i.e.*, it is an echo word. Similarly in **kithi kirum**, **kithi** means 'fear' and **kirum** is an echo word. There is no restriction in the reduplication of the first or the second syllable of the first word.

Word Reduplication: It refers to the total or partial bimodal reduplication, meaning thereby repetition of the base of the word or of the stem. Reduplication can be of either a syllable or a larger constituent of a word or of the whole word (Abbi, 1992: 25). It may be partial or complete.

Partial Reduplication: It refers to the paired construction in which the second word is not an exact repetition of the first but is similar or related to the first either on the semantic or phonetic level (Abbi, 1980: 7).

99. **tathok tasin təu-** 'consult'
nəŋ-gi waphəm-du məhak-kə tathok tasin təu-nə-ru
you-GEN matter-DEM he-ASS consult-REC-DEIC-COM
'Go and consult your problems with him'

100. **micəŋ mikhai nai-** 'be partial'
əŋaŋ-siŋ-də micəŋ mikhai nai-gənu
child-PL-DAT partial-PROH
'Do not be partial towards the children'

101. **mijok mican phə-** 'be cordial'
nupi-du mijok mican phə-i
woman-DEM cordial-SAM
'The woman is cordial'

102. **misək mimai jeŋ-** 'do the act of favouritism/be partial'
satrə-siŋ-də misək mimai jeŋ-gənu
student-PL-DAT partial-PROH
'Do not be partial towards the students'

The partial reduplications in the given examples are **tathok tasin** in (99) where the two words are meaningful *i.e.*'hear one another', **micəŋ mikhai** in (100) is also meaningful – **micəŋ** means 'favour, take side (to somebody) and **mikhai** means **mi** 'man' and **khai-** 'separate'. **mijok mican** in (101) means **mijok** > **mi** 'man' **jok-** 'bring up' and **mican** > **mi** 'man' **can-** 'love'. Finally, **misək mimai** in (102) means **misək** 'particular man' and **mimai** > **mi** 'man', **mai** 'face'. Although these partial reduplications are meaningful, they cannot stand alone and constitute a word without the verbs.

Difference between echo formation and partial reduplication: In an echo formation, the first word is always meaningful and the following word is meaningless and echoes the first word. Thus, the combination serves as a lexical item. For example, in **isiŋ maisiŋ, isiŋ** means 'water' whereas **maisiŋ** has no meaning. Similarly in **kithi kirum**, the first word is **kithi** 'fear' and **kirum** has no meaning even though the root **ki-** is repeated. On the other hand, the repeated words in partial reduplication are meaningful. But the following word is not an exact repetition of the first word (the exact repetition of the first word is called complete reduplication and it will come next to partial reduplication).

Complete Word Reduplication: It refers to the phenomenon when a single word or clause is repeated once in the same sentence without any phonological or morphological variations (Yashawanta, 1998:190).

103. **məroŋ məroŋ loŋ-** 'have many branches'
usa-si məroN məroŋ loŋ-ŋi
branch-DEM have many branches-SAM
'This big branch has many small branches'

104. **əon əon ca-** 'be opportunist'
əŋaŋ-nə əon əon ca-gənu
child-NOM opportunist-PROH
'You are a child, so don't be an opportunist'

105. **məreŋ məreŋ cət-** 'be restless, eager to do something, movement of an insect etc.'
əi thəbək-tu həu-niŋ-bə-nə məreŋ məreŋ cət-le
I work-DEM start-wish-NMZ-NOM restless-PERF-SAM
'I am restless to start the work/I am very eager to start the work'

The examples of complete word reduplication just given above are **məroŋ məroŋ** in (103) where both words are meaningful, **məroŋ** > **mə**-nominalizer prefix, **loŋ-** 'grow branches' **əon əon** in sentence (104) can be analysed as ə- formative prefix, **on-** 'turn'. **məreŋ məreŋ** in sentence (105) is also **mə-** nominalizer prefix, **leŋ-** 'move'. Finally, these complete word reduplications take certain verbs to become a full-fledged word since they are incomplete (even if they are meaningful).

Difference between Morphological Reduplication and Complete Word Reduplication:

Both reduplications have similar constructions. In morphological reduplication, the first form is repeated exactly but they are not meaningful words and cannot be analysed. They cannot have morpheme cut as the whole part is a morpheme. But in complete word reduplication, the reduplicated forms are meaningful and they can be analysed further as seen just above. For instance, in **phak phak nok**- 'laugh freely, laugh aloud' **phak phak** is a morphological reduplication since it has no meaning without the verb, whereas in **məcoi məcoi ta**- 'be in pieces', **məcoi məcoi** can be analysed as **mə**- nominalized prefix, **coi**- 'separate, make small pieces from a bigger thing'. One should not be confused with these two types of reduplications as they have the same surface structure.

Reduplicated Verbs 2: In this type of construction, verbal suffixes are attached directly to the reduplicated forms and a verbal paradigm is formed.

horo həra-	be careless
təha təha-	be hasty
tərau tərau-	be loose, wide
khirum khirum-	have mild fever
məraŋ turaŋ-	have many colours, be of multicolour
məriŋ məraŋ-	be odd, unusual, eccentric, strange
təgup təreŋ-	twinkle
khoidriŋ khoidraŋ-	be zigzag
khaibuŋ khaibuŋnə-	be separated
cikkhon naukhon-	be caring
cəraŋ khoiraŋnə-	be restless
pomtha həithanə-	be plump
nuŋsuk nuŋɟanə-	be broody
kəllək kənɟau-	be envious
tuson manson-	be timid, cow
nokrem haigremnə-	be frivolous
kərem kəthainə-	make fun
lairə cudətnə-	be indigent
urau thərau-	make noise
cinda paudanə-	be argue
iru maithəɟə-	take bath
haiŋəm təuŋəmdə-	be over smart
əpha əpunnə-	feel not free
təbəŋ təbəŋ-	be innocent
məsen məraŋ-	be, blur, etc.

106. **niŋkok niŋkok-** 'feel hesitant, be anxious'
thəbək-tu təu-bə-də əi niŋkok niŋkok- i
work-DEM do-NMZ-LOC I hesitate-SAM
I feel hesitant while doing the work'

107. **musi musi-** 'be dim, dull, darkish, indistinct'
thauməi-gi məŋal-si musi musi-re
lamp-GEN light-DEM dim-PERF-SAM
'The light of the lamp is dim'

108. **uri wauri-** '(of weather) be dull'
ŋəsi-di uri wauri
today-DEM dull-SAM
'Today, the weather is dull'

109. **tiŋək maiŋəknə-** 'be shocked, amazed (when something unexpected happens)'
oɟa-nə cəi-bə-du-də əŋaŋ-du tiŋək maiŋəknə-re
teacher-NOM scold-NMZ-DEM-LOC child-DEM surprise-PERF-SAM
'The child was shocked when the teacher scolded him (when he did not expect it)'

110. **tuson manson-** 'be timid'
əŋaŋ-si məjam-nə cəi-mən-bə-dəgi tuson mansol-le
child-DEM many-NOM scold-EXC-NMZ-ABL timid-PERF-SAM
'The child has become timid due to excessive scoldings'

From the examples given above, it can be seen that reduplicated verb forms function like a simple verbal root and take the verbal suffixes directly. Such type of form is found frequently in the language.

In this chapter Manipuri verbs have been classified into five groups on structural level. The next chapter is an attempt to give the semantic classification of verbs into action, stative and process. It examines the syntactic structure as well as the semantic component of the verbs.

CHAPTER

3

SEMANTIC CLASSIFICATION OF MANIPURI VERBS

Verb plays a very important role in a sentence. It is generally inflected for tense, aspect, mood, gender, number, person, etc. With the help of verbs one can express a situation, a quality of somebody or something, an event or a happening. Accordingly, the role of verbs in the semantic level is also different. Some verbs may be action-oriented while some show a state, quality or feeling. On further analysis, some verbs may have agents while some do not have and some verbs may be changing or unchanging. There are also some verbs which may involve duration while some do not. Such verbs are always in the midway of classification and they make a group of their own which compel the study to go into a deeper level.

Perception of a language by the speech community is very important and it should always be kept in mind while working on a particular language as language is perceived in different ways by different speech communities. Language exists in the culture and society of the speech community. The social and cultural variation makes a language different from others. This difference is clearly seen in the lexicon of the language. For instance, a particular Manipuri verb may not have its equivalent word in English. This is true for the latter also. The verb **seŋ-** and **maŋ-** are antonyms. In English it is translated by Khelchandra (2004) and Imoba (2004) as 'pure' and 'impure'. The meaning given in English is inadequate. In one sense, it is correct as to mean 'This gold is pure' **səna əsi seŋ-ŋi/səna əsi əseŋbəni**. But in case of the English sentence ***This gold is impure/ not pure*** may not mean **səna əsi əmaŋbəni/ maŋŋi** in Manipuri. This is because the scope of the meaning of these two words occurs in the culture of Manipur society. Of course, it has the relevant word in Hindi as **pavitra** and **apavitra** which mean 'holy' and 'unholy' in English. The meaning of the word **holy** given by Oxford Advanced Learners' English Dictionary (5th Edition) is as follows: 1(a) associated with God or with religion; of God: the Holy Bible/Scriptures. (b) regarded as sacred; consecrated: holy ground, holy water (*i.e.* water blessed by a priest); a holy war (*i.e.* one fought to defend what is sacred); Islam's holiest shrine. 2. devoted to the service of God; pure in the moral and spiritual sense; a holy man; live a holy life. The use of the word 'holy' is extended somewhat to the society of Manipur. It may also mean a cloth which is washed and to be used for religious purposes, to take bath before praying to God, or cooking in the kitchen, etc. Cleaned utensils are also considered to be **seŋ-** 'clean' whereas utensils in which somebody has eaten and the left over are considered to be **maŋ-** 'unclean'. In one sense, **seŋ-** may mean 'good' and **maŋ-** 'not good' *e.g.* **pukcel seŋ-** 'be honest', **məbuk maŋ-** 'be dishonest'. This shows that the perception of a language is controlled by the particular culture of the speech community and every language has a unique feature thus making it inappropriate to apply the norm of a language to another, say to Manipuri.

Study of Manipuri verbs on semantic level has already been done by many linguists like Madhubala (1979), unpublished Ph.D. thesis; Nonigopal (1987) unpublished Ph.D. thesis; Ch. Yashawanta (2000); Bhat and Ningomba (1997); Bidyarani (2002), unpublished Ph.D. thesis. The classification given by them is mainly based on root level analysis as action, state and process. According to Bhat and Ningomba, the class of state verbs includes (i) a large number of monosyllabic roots that translate as adjectives in English and other familiar languages (ii) roots that indicate states of affairs (like *know*) (iii) roots that denote spatial and temporal locations, and (iv) roots that denote adverbial notions. Following Dixon (1982), they subgroup the adjectival state verbs into seven different semantic groups as: (i) Dimension verbs (ii) Physical property verbs (iii) Colour verbs (iv) Human propensity verbs (v) Age verbs (vi) Value verbs (vii) Speed verbs; and furthermore, according to Dixon (1991), put another three in addition to the list as: (viii) Difficulty verbs (ix) Qualification verbs (x) Similarity verbs. Apart from this, Bhat and Ningomba further discovered four more sub-groups and added to the list as: (xi) Locational verbs (xii) Temporal verbs (xiii) Quantifying verbs and (xiv) Modal and epistemic verbs thereby giving a total of fourteen different verbs in Manipuri language so far. Thus, the analysis of state verbs is very detailed on root level. Madhubala (1979) discussed this area involving valency pattern which does not help much in the differentiating factors. Process and action verbs were also described further.

Linguists have hitherto broadly divided verbs into stative and dynamic. As mentioned above stative verbs are translatable as adjective in English and they are verbs of state or quality or cognition (Bhat and Ningomba, 1997). Dynamic verb can be classified into two: action verbs and process verbs. On syntactic level, verbs that can go with progressive aspect as *he is running* and command as *run*! are termed as dynamic verbs. On the contrary, verbs that cannot go with progressive aspect and imperative command are termed as stative verbs. On semantic level, they express states of affairs rather than action, *i.e.* the expression of relational processes (*e.g. be*, *belong to*, *involve*, *seem*) or of inactive perceptual cognitive processes (*e.g. know*, *mean*, *realize*, *suppose*) (Crystal, 1985). The incompatibility of a stative verb with progressive aspect and imperative command is a semantic problem not a syntactic one (which will be discussed later). The semantic component of the verb decides the ability of a verb to go with a particular aspect or mood in sentence level. John Lyons (1965: 325) classifies verbs as progressive and non-progressive. Progressive verbs are action verbs while non-progressive verbs always referring to the state of affairs rather than actions, events or processes are termed as stative verbs. While discussing progressive aspect he claims that the most common function of the progressive is to indicate duration and it is quite natural for stative verbs not to combine with progressive. His argument is that the implication of duration is already contained in the general meaning of the verbs. The sense of duration is an integral part of the lexical meaning of the verb, and there is, for this reason, no need for progressive form to indicate duration (Palmer, 1974: 73). Kate (2000: 156) quotes Jesperson (1932:178-180) regarding the canonical reading of progressive as a temporal frame: the progressive reports the time of an event or situation as a temporal frame containing another time. Another way of describing the reading is to say that the progressive takes us inside the duration of a reported event to where the event is in progress.

The temporal frame reading is typical of the progressive with event verbs. State verbs generally have a temporal frame reading in the non-progressive, as illustrated below:

1 a. *Generally when Lucas arrives home it is dark.*

b. *When Lucas opened the door the light was on.*

In sentence (1a), the state of darkness surrounds the time of Lucas' arrival and it is already dark before he arrives. In sentence (1b) the state of the light's being on surrounds the time of opening the door. 'The progressive forms occur only with dynamic verbs *i.e.* with verbs that show qualities capable of change as opposed to state verbs which show qualities not capable of change'.

Quirk *et al*. (1985:198) explained the situation as state verb meanings are inimical to the idea that some phenomenon is 'in progress'. States are 'like parted' in that every segment of a state has the same character as any other segment: no progress is made.

Coming to imperative, it is a universal fact that command involves two persons: a person who is giving the command and another to whom the command is given and this person is second person 'you' which occur almost covertly in sentences. The semantic component of a command is to ask somebody (second person) to carry out an action. State verbs which refer to a state, condition or quality cannot go with command that is to say one cannot ask somebody to be tall, to be cold, to hope etc. There is no question of carrying out an action with state verbs except for certain verbs like *be wise*, *don't be silly*, *be a good boy*, etc. which come under controllable state verbs (Bhat and Ningomba, 1997: 156).

Kapoor (1985: 36-37) discussed the Punjabi verbs under three heads *viz*., (i) State (2) Happening/Activity (3) Actions. He claims that all the predications are about states or changes in state. Thus *kətab* p^h*əti hoi* 'The book is torn' is a statement of state of things in the real world; (2) *kətab* p^h*t gəi* 'The book got torn' is a statement of change in the state of the 'book' from being intact to being torn; and (3) *one kətab* p^h*ari/*p^h*arditti* is also a statement of change in the state of the book with the difference that the agency of this change also gets explicit mention. He further gives a rule to examine the verbs, *e.g.* for stative verbs – verb root plus *hona* or one of its alternant; for happening or activity verbs – verb root plus *ho ȷana* or one of its equivalents and for action verbs – by one of the *karna do* forms of the verbs (Kapil, 1985: 39). Madhubala (1979) defines state verbs as referring to states or conditions. She further divides state verbs into five sub-classes which are based on argument structure or valency pattern. According to Nonigopal (1987), verbal roots that express the meaning of an action, a process, motion, etc. are grouped under dynamic verbs and verbal roots that express the meaning of a state, quality, quantity, etc. come under the category of stative verbs. Again, Bidyarani (2002) observed that action verbs are attributing action of verb to person or thing where it proceeds *i.e.* process of acting and further they denote controllable events whereas process verbs are changing verbs that have duration and they denote only non-controllable events. Contrasting to the above two types, state verbs denote a state of affair, which hold between two referents by virtue of their intrinsic nature and also include verbs of inert cognition. Regarding process verbs, Bhat and Ningomba (1997: 161-164) observed that process verbs represent only non-volitional events, they take themes and not actors. Even animate beings can only function as their themes as they would have no control over the processes.

All the earlier works carried out by different scholars mainly focus on root level analysis. There are many other criteria for the semantic classification of verbs. This chapter attempts to bring out those criteria and analyse the verbs through various dimensions. There are some verbs which are always in the midway of the classification. They are termed as 'stance' by Quirk *et al.* (1985: 205-206). They are characterized by their ability to be used both in action and state; and sometimes as action and process.

2. a. *John lives in London.*
   b. *John is living in London*

3. a. *The statue stands at the city gate.*
   b. *Tom is standing in the bus stand.*

Sentences (2a) and (3a) indicate permanent state while sentences (2b) and (3b) denote a temporary state. Hence the verbs *lives* and *stands* in sentences (2a) and (3a) are stative while *is living* and *is standing* in sentences (2b) and (3b) are action verbs. This type of overlapping happens in case of Manipuri verbs also which will be discussed later in sub-section (**3.3**). From the illustrations given above, one cannot easily decide the verb class by simply looking at the base form. It needs a thorough study of the semantic entailment of the verbal structure as well as the sentence structure.

Another important area of verb analysis is suffixes. Both verbal roots and suffixes are bound forms in Manipuri. Verbal roots become verbs only when inflectional suffixes are attached to them. There are also selectional restrictions in the combination of verbal roots and verbal suffixes. Some verbs may take certain suffixes while some may have restrictions in using it. This restriction is purely based on semantic level and addition of particular suffixes to particular verbs cause change of verb classes also. Hence, suffixes take a major part in the semantic classification of verbs which will be studied under the following sub-sections.

3.1 Contrastive Features

Verbs, according to their semantic properties, may broadly be studied under two groups on the basis of their contrastive features although there are three classes of verbs *viz* Action, State and Process. The two of them share one or the other property. For instance, state and process verbs share one common feature *i.e.* non-agentive while action and process share the feature 'verbs of changing'. These changing verbs come under one head named dynamic verbs. In a language like English, verbs may be grouped into progressive and non-progressive. This feature may not be a classificatory factor for Manipuri verbs, as in Manipuri, some stative verbs, not all, can go with progressive aspect. Verbs, concerning the common feature they share, may have the following semantic features.

Stative verbs versus Non-Stative verbs: Verbs fall under either of the two categories: (i) Stative verbs that refer to state or conditions of the referent and (ii) non-stative verbs that refer to action and process on the other hand (as both of them share one common feature *i.e.* non-stativity). The notion of 'agency' is used to sub-divide non-stative verbs into 'non-agentive' and 'agentive' (Kapil, 1985:39).

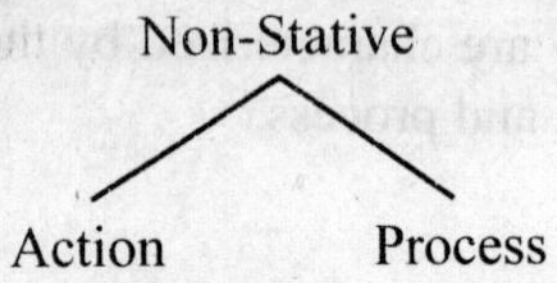

Changing verbs versus Non-Changing verbs: Verbs, according to their meaning, may be studied under the heads 'changing verbs' and 'non-changing verbs'. State verbs like *know*, *exist* and *be verbs* which express equality, membership, existence, attribution, location, possession, etc. indicates an unchanged mode. Accordingly, stative verbs are grouped under the head 'non-changing verbs'. On the other hand, verbs like *drink*, *come*, *grow*, *bloom*, *die*, etc. show some mode of changing by the virtue of which process and action verbs are categorized under the head 'changing verbs'.

In the present section, action and process verbs are grouped under the same category. This shows that both of them share the features of non-stativity and changing. In the same way, state and process verbs also share one common feature, *i.e.* non-agentivity, as discussed in the subsequent section.

Agentive verbs versus Non-Agentive verbs: The notion of agentivity is one of the most important features that help in the study of dynamic verbs to classify them into action and process verbs. Action verbs are those that are carried out by animate agents meanwhile state and process verbs do not take an agent but the theme as their subject. The notion of agentivity entails intentional and controllable acts. On the contrary, the notion of non-agentive verbs like state and process entails unintentional and uncontrollable actions (see **3.4** for agentivity). However, there are some controllable state verbs like **noi**- 'be fat' and **phəɟə**- 'be beautiful'. It would be worth to mention that there is no common feature shared by action and state verbs.

3.2 Semantic Classes of Verbs

Manipuri verbs can be grouped into three classes namely

(i) Action verbs,

(ii) State verbs and

(iii) Process verbs.

Action Verbs: Action verbs refer to actions. They are agentive as well as changing verbs. All action verbs are controllable verbs and always need agents to carry out the actions. These verbs can successfully go through the test 'What does X do?' They can occur freely with all verbal suffixes except adverbial suffixes denoting degree which are a specific feature of state verbs. The suffixes are **-sin**, **-səŋ**, **-droŋ**, **-throk**, etc. (see **4.2**). Furthermore, action verbs may be studied under the following heads: (i) Directional versus non-Directional, (ii) Durative versus Punctual and (iii) Destructive versus non-Destructive.

Directional versus Non-Directional verbs: Verbs which can generally take the four directional markers are termed as directional verbs. There are certain verbs which cannot go with the directional markers. Such verbs come under the head 'non-directional verbs'.

Directional Action Verbs: There are four directional suffixes namely **-sin** 'inward directional', **-thok** 'outward directional', **-khət** 'upward directional' and **-thə** 'downward directional'. Verbs that can occur with these four suffixes may be termed as Directional Action Verbs. There are some specific action verbs which essentially take **–sin** and these groups of verbs make a contrast with verbs which usually take **-thok** as in **khum-ɟin-** 'cover something' and **haŋ-dok-** 'open'**.** Similarly, the verbs of upward movement which take **-khət** are contrasted with the verbs of downward movement, *i.e.*, the verbs with **-thə** like in **lep-khət-** 'stand up' and **phəm-thə-** 'sit down'.

Verbs which take *-sin* and *–thok*

thup-cin-	fold	pha-ɟin-	take someone under arrest
haŋ-dok-	open	hap-cin-	put something inside box, bag, etc.
tha-dok-	release	juŋ-sin	erect something
lon-sin-	close	səttok-	remove/ take out
tiŋ-thok-	stretch	khum-ɟin-	cover something
in-sin-	insert	ta-sin-	collect or gather
cai-thok-	scatter	phum-ɟin-	bury something
ləu-thok-	take out	cəŋ-sin-	enter, advance
hən-dok-	retreat	mit ui-sin-	close eye
sət-tok-	take out	paŋ-thok-	open eye
hən-dok-	dig out, etc.		

4. a. **khum-jin-** 'cover'

isiŋ hap-pə kon-siŋ-du məkhum khum-ɟil-lu
water keep-NMZ container-PL-DEM lid cover-IN-COM
'Cover the water containers with the lids'

b. **haŋ-dok-** 'open'

nuŋsit nuŋsa cəŋ-nə-bə thoŋ thoŋnau-siŋ-du haŋ-dok-u
wind sunlight enter-PUR-NMZ door window-PL-DEM open-OUT-COM

'Keep the doors and windows open to let in fresh air and sunlight'

Verbs which take *-khət* and *-thə*

khun-gət-	pick up	tha-də-	drop
lep-khət-	stand up	phəm-thə-	sit down
hen-gət-	exceed	hən-thə-	reduce
ka-khət-	climb up	kum-thə-	get down
həu-gət-	get up/wake up	hip-thə-	lie down
hai-gət-	price hike	ta-thə-	reduce
lon-khət-	pile up	ləu-thə-	take down, etc.

5a. **khun-gət-** 'pick up'
tebəl məkha-dəgi ce-du khun-gət-lu
table under-ABL paper-DEM pick up-COM
'Pick up the paper lying under the table'

b. **tha-də-** 'drop'
phi-du məkha-də thadə-gənu
cloth-DEM down-LOC drop-PROH
'Don't drop the cloth on the floor'

Verbs which can take all the four directional markers

hun-	throw	kap-	shoot
ləŋ-	throw	jeŋ-	look
pu-	carry	kəu-	call
in-	push	thaŋ-	carry
ciŋ-	drag	hon-	carry
cen-	run	hai-	swing
coŋ-	jump	kam-	blow
pi-	give	ləu-	take
thəu-	drive	pai-	fly, etc.

6. **cen-**

a. **cen-sin-** 'run inside'
huranbə-du pulis u-bə-də imuŋ-də cen-sin-khə-re
thief-DEM police see-NMZ-LOC inside the house-LOC run IN-DEF-PERF-SAM
'The thief ran inside the house on seeing the police'

b. **cen-thok-** 'run outside'
həudoŋ-du imuŋ-dəgi cen-thok-khə-re
cat-DEM inside the house-ABL run OUT-DEF-PERF-SAM
'The cat ran out of the house'

c. **cen-khət** 'run up'
əŋaŋ-du siri-də cen-khət-khə-re
child-DEM stair-LOC run-UP-DEF-PERF-SAM
'The child ran up the stair'

d. **cen-thə-** 'run down'
cinŋkaroi-siŋ-du ciŋ-dəgi cen-thə-rək-i
climbers-PL-DEM hill-ABL run-DOWN-DEIC-SAM
'The climbers run down the hill'

The above examples show that the verb **cen-** can occur with all the directional markers. Similarly, verbs like **pai-** 'fly', **hon-** 'carry', **ciŋ-** 'drag', etc. can be used in the same pattern.

Non-Directional Action Verbs: These verbs cannot occur with the directional suffixes. They do not indicate a specific direction.

phu-	beat	ta-	listen
hai-	say	cəi-	rebuke
nok-	laugh	jat-	cut
kəp-	cry	cik-	bite
sək-	sing	khin-	place
həu-	start	həŋ-	ask
sannə-	play	khum-	give answer, reply, respond
hot-	scratch	phəu-	keep in the sun
hotnə-	try	tək-	grind
ŋai-	wait	səŋ-	keep on guard, etc.

7. **ŋai-** 'wait'
əi ma-bu puŋ məa phaubə ŋai-gəni
I he-ACC hour five till wait-NREAL
'I will wait for him till 5 o'clock'

8. **khin-** 'place'
gəmla-du sumaŋ-də khil-lu
flower pot-DEM lawn-LOC place-COM
'Place the flower pot in the lawn'

Durative versus Non-Durative (Punctual) verbs: In this section, verbs which can take duration in performing an action are contrasted with momentary verbs.

Durative Verbs: Durativity is also another feature of action verbs which distinguishes actions that are capable of having duration from those that do not have. Since durative situation types take place over a (normally limited) period of time, they characteristically combine with progressive.

əurai-	read, rehearse	su-	wash
lon-	knit	sa-	build
ca-	eat	sem-	repair, prepare
thoŋ-	cook	jek-	paint
sit-	sweep	hək-	carve
iruɟə-	take bath	phi sa-	weave
khənnə-	discuss	phen-	scour
jok-	bring up	nai-	wait
i-	write	sok-	fetch, draw water from river, pond
su-	wash	loi-	domesticate animal
sannə-	play	pottha-	take rest
pannə-	take care	jetnə-	argue, etc.

Since durative verbs occur along a time span they are capable of going with **-khət** 'start' as a suffix. Another reading of 'start' is expressed by using the verb **həu-** 'start' in the sentence. In this construction, the main verb becomes nominalized and the verb **həu-** bears the aspect and mood markers and this type of construction is possible for all types of verbs. Although **həu-** is capable of going with all types of verbs there is a restriction for **-khət** 'start'. It goes only with durative verbs and addition of the suffix means starting of an action (see **4.2**). An interesting point to be noted here is that there is a third way of expressing 'start' apart from **-khət** suffixation and use of **həu-**. In this type of construction **-khət** is directly attached to the verb **həu-**.

9. **thoŋ-** 'cook'

a. əi cak thoŋ-gət-le
I rice cook-UP-PERF-SAM
'I have started cooking'

b. əi cak thoŋ-bə həu-re
I rice cook-NMZ start-PERF-SAM
'I have started cooking'

c. əi cak thoŋ-bə həu-gət-le
I rice cook-NMZ start-UP-PERF-SAM
'I have started cooking'

The three types of sentences express the starting of an action while the main concern is the suffixation of **-khət** to the verb. The suffix has three allomorphic variations as **-kət** ~ **khət**, ~ **-gət**. **-kət** occurs in verbal bases that begin with aspirated sounds/**ph**/, /**th**/, /**kh**/, /**h**/, /**s**/ and end in voiceless sounds. **-gət** comes after verbal bases that begin with aspirated sounds and end in voiced sounds as found in **thoŋ**- 'cook', **sa**- 'build, construct'. **-khət** occurs elsewhere.

Punctual Verb: Punctual verbs refer to verbs of momentary action. They do not entail duration. They are theoretically incompatible to take progressive aspect: they occur with progressive only through a special interpretation (Quirk ***et al***, 1985: 207-208). Progressive aspect of the punctual verbs means repetition of the action. A list of some punctual verbs is given below:

tha-	hit	(mit) paŋ-thok-	open eye
kau-	kick	khubaknə tha-	slap
coŋ-	jump	(mit)ui-sin-	close eye
sok-	touch	(mit)kup-	blink
thadə-	drop	phəm-thə-	sit down
ləŋ-	throw	lepkhət-	stand up
thəm-	plac	jot-	swallow
thin-	knock	ŋək-nom-	nod
thom-	hit, etc.		

10. **ŋək nom**- 'nod'

a. nupi-du-nə wahə-du-gi paukhum oi-nə ŋək nom-mi
woman-DEM-NOM question-DEM-GEN reply be-ADV nod-SAM
'The woman nods her head as a reply to the question'

b. nupi-du-nə wari-du ta-nə ta-nə ŋək nom-mi (-li)
woman-DEM-NOM story-DEM listen-ADV listen-ADV nod-PROG SAM
'The woman is nodding her head while listening to the story'

11. **coŋ**- 'jump'

a. əŋaŋ-du-nə khoŋban-du coŋ-ŋi
child-DEM-NOM trench-DEM jump-SAM
'The child jumps across the trench'

b. əŋaŋ-siŋ-nə khoŋ-ban-du coŋ-ŋi (-li)
child-PL-NOM trench -DEM jump-PROG-SAM
'Children are jumping across the trench'

Sentences of group (a) denote momentary actions. But in group (b) sentences, the verbs refer to repetition of the actions and as a result, they take progressive aspect. In sentence (10a) the action of nodding occurs only once while it is repeated in (b). In sentence (11a) the action of jumping is carried out by a boy while in (b) it is repeated by many boys. Thus, it can be concluded that the repetition of an action may involve more than one actor or an actor may repeat the action. In such situations, progressive aspect is used to denote repetition of an action while the general function of progressive aspect is to show continuation.

Destructive Verbs: Verbs which can occur with destructive suffixes are discussed under the head: destructive verbs. There are some action verbs which have the destructive nature inherently. They usually take the three destructive suffixes: **-khai**, **-thət** and **-thek**. Verbs again may be grouped into three according to their semantic nature as verbs which occur with **-khai**, verbs which takes -**thət** and verbs which go with **-thek**.

Verbs which occur with *–khai*

cəp-khai-	crush
su-gai-	pound in order to break
tək-khai-	grind something in order to break
nəi-khai-	make water dirty
sugai-	pound something hard
hən-gai-	pierce/dig out
cik-khai-	bite into pieces
ot-khai-	stir vigorously
nəm-khai-	press hard to break
kau-khai-	kick something in order to break
ləŋ-khai-	throw violently or kick something
met-khai-	squeeze violently, etc.

12. **thugai**- 'break into pieces'
    tombə-nə miŋsel-du thugai-re
    Tomba-NOM mirror-DEM break-PERF-SAM
    'Tomba broke the mirror'

13. **jan-khai**- 'cut into pieces'
    sau-rə-bə nupa-du-nə iŋkhol-gi məna məsiŋ
    angry-PERF-NMZ man-DEM-NOM kitchen garden-GEN vegetable

    pumnəmək jan-khai-khə-re
    all cut-DEST-DEF-PERF-SAM
    'The angry man cut all the vegetables of the kitchen garden into pieces'

Note: The occurrence of the allomorphic variations –**khai~gai~kai** is same to -**khət~gət~kət** in **4.2**

Verbs which go with *-thət*

kək-thət-	cut
thə-dət-	tear something apart
khot-tət-	scratch
ciŋ-thət-	pull hard to break
hek-tət-	pluck
len-thət-	cut into pieces
ləi-thət-	twist something in order to break
khai-dət-	cut into pieces, etc.

14. **thə-dət-** 'tear something apart'
məhak-nə ləŋ-du məjai-də thə-dət-li
he-NOM thread-DEM centre-LOC tear- DEST-SAM
'He tears the thread in the centre'

15. **phoi-dət-** 'uproot'
sumaŋ-də həu-ri-bə napi-siŋ-si phoi-dət-lu
lawn-LOC GROW-PROG-NMZ grass-PL-DEM uproot-DEST-COM
'Uproot all the grasses that are grown in the lawn'

16. **khai-dət-** 'cut into pieces'
sərət-nə mairen-du təkhai ta-nə khai-dət-le
Sarat-NOM pumpkin-DEM half fall-ADV cut-DEST-PERF-SAM
'Sarat has cut the pumpkin into two halves'

Both **thə-dət-** 'tear something apart' and **phoi-dət-** 'uproot' do not need a weapon. **thə-dət-** in (14) indicates to tear the thread by pulling hard while **phoi-dət-**'uproot' in (15) refers to uproot or destroy a plant completely. The verb **khai-dət-** 'cut into pieces' in (16), involves a sharp weapon like a knife to cut the pumpkin into two pieces.
Note: For the occurrence of the allomorphic variations –**thət~dət~tət** see **4.2**

Verbs that go with *-thek*

ləi-thek-	twist hard in order to break
nəi-thek-	destroy by trampling
thu-dek-	break
nən-thek-	press hard

17. **ləi-thek-** 'twist hard to break'
usa-siŋ-du ləi-thek-kənu
branch-PL-DEM twist-DEST-PROH
'Do not twist the branches'

18. **nəi-thek**- 'destroy by trampling'
həwai pambi-siŋ-du sən-nə nəi- thek -khə-re
bean plant-PL-DEM COW-NOM destroy-DEST-DEF-PERF-SAM
'Cow has destroyed the bean plants'.

Compared to other destructive verbs the combination of **-thek** is very few in number. The verb **ləi-thək**-'twist hard to break' in (17) indicates to twist hard to break the branches with the hand. It does not need a weapon. Similarly all the verbs which go with **-thek** do not involve a weapon.

Stative Verbs: Stative verbs refer to a state or condition which is not likely to change. They denote a condition or state which may be a person, place or thing or whatever at a given time or during a given time interval (Katz, 1972: 302). They are durative verbs and they occupy time and can be said to last for minutes, weeks, years and centuries. In other words, it can be said that a state may be either temporary (of limited duration *e.g. be angry*, *be sick*) or permanent (of relatively long duration *e.g. be tall*, *have blue eye*, *have brown hair*, etc.) or of some intermediate duration (Givon, 1979).

Stative verbs make contrast with action verbs in taking the subject nominals. They take theme which may be animate or inanimate (while action verbs take an agent to perform the action). They are not performing verbs. They also make contrast with dynamic verbs in the sense that they are not changing verbs while action and process are changing verbs. One more point of difference between stative verbs and action verbs is that they are not controllable verbs. They can be divided into verbs of perception or cognition (which refer to things in the mind) or verbs of relation (which describe the relationship between things). Among stative situation types a rough distinction may be drawn between qualities and states. Qualities are relatively permanent and inalienable properties of the subject referent. The primary verbs **be** and **have** are pre-eminently quality-introducing verbs; but they can also introduce the less permanent situation types called state (Quirk ***et al***, 1985: 200).

	Quality		**State**
19 a.	*Mary is Canadian.*	20 a.	*Mary is tired.*
b.	*Mary has blue eyes.*	b.	*Mary has a bad cold.*

Stative verbs cannot normally be used in the continuous (be + ing) forms. The continuation of stative + progressive is very rare in English and they give another reading. With a number of state verbs, however, the progressive form suggests a shortened duration for the state or suggests temporariness (Kate, 2000: 157). This temporariness of the state gives the reading of action verbs (see **3.3**).

As discussed above, progressive aspect has become an important criterion for the classification of verb classes in English while the situation is contrastive in Manipuri. Many stative verbs in Manipuri have a temporal meaning in the sense that the meanings of the verbs of which one can expect a change to take place *e.g.* 'short hair' can be expected to become 'long', 'curly hair' can become 'straight', 'dark skin/complexion' can become 'fair', 'beautiful appearance' may lose its beauty, a 'healthy person' may become 'unhealthy', a 'thin body' may become 'fat', etc. When such situations remain as it is and when no such expectations become realized then, progressive aspect is used to denote that the situation still remains as it is and there is no change. In such situations, the verb in progressive aspect normally takes adverbs like **əsum, ədum** which mean 'still' or **huɟik phaubə** 'till now'. This adverb may be used in covert or overt role in the sentences.

21. **məsa phə-** 'be healthy'
    əŋaŋ-si ədum məsa phə-ri
    child-DEM still healthy-PROG-SAM
    'This child is still healthy'

22. **phəɟə-** 'be beautiful'
    thəɟə-di həuɟik-su phəɟə-ri
    Thaja-DEM now-also beautiful-PROG-SAM
    'Thaja is still beautiful'

The verb **məsa phə-** in (21) implies that the child is as healthy as before and there is no change in his health. The progressive aspect in (22) gives the meaning that the referent is as beautiful as before. The verbs given in the above examples express temporary meaning and they come under the group of state verbs as classified by Quirk ***et al***., (1985: 200). Verbs of qualities, on the other hand, cannot go with progressive aspect *e.g.* one cannot expect a change in the quality of *be tall*, *have blue eyes*, etc. A tall person cannot become short and person with blue eyes cannot become black-eyed. In other words, it can be said that verbs of qualities are relatively permanent and they cannot be expected to change and as a result, they cannot occur with progressive aspect.

Theoretically, all stative verbs are uncontrollable. It shares this property with process verbs and differentiates between stative verbs and action verbs. They are uncontrollable as they do not take an agent. Controllabity is a property of agentive verbs (see **3.1**). All action verbs are agent-oriented verbs and they have control over the situation while stative and process verbs are uncontrollable. Yet there are some stative verbs which are controllable and on this basis they can be divided into controllable and uncontrollable verbs.

Controllable Stative Verbs: Mental situation verbs like **siŋ-** 'be clever' **ki-** 'fear', **pen-** 'satisfy', **nuŋŋai-** 'be happy', **pəŋ-** 'be foolish', **sau-** 'be angry', **niŋhənnə-** 'feel discourage', **thaɟə-** 'belief', **napəl ka-** 'be proud', **ikai-** 'feel shy', **cəm-** 'be simple' and verbs of temporal meaning like **ŋən-** 'be early', **theŋ-** 'be late', **thu-** 'be quick', **təp-** 'be slow, low', etc. are controllable stative verbs. They can occur with imperative which is a property of controllable verbs.

23. **ki-** 'fear'
əcumbə-du khəŋ-bə pam-ləbədi nəŋ kəna-bu-su ki-gənu
truth-DEM know-NMZ like-if you who-ACC-also fear-PROH
'If you want to know the truth do not be afraid of anybody'

24. **napəl ka-** 'be proud'
haknə napəl ka-gənu! wa-ton-nə waŋ-ləgə kwak-nə
much be proud-PROH bamboo-top-NOM tall-CPART crow-NOM

phəmdek-i
sit-SAM
'Don't be so proud! Remember 'Every pride has a fall'

The verbs **ki-**'fear' in (23), **napəl ka-** 'be proud' in (24) are given in the prohibitive meaning as it is quite undesirable for someone to ask somebody to fear, be angry and feel shy in the situations given in the sentences. The situations demand encouragement and it is quite natural to give the prohibitive meaning with the verbs which imply a negative sense.

Non-Controllable Verbs: All the stative verbs excepting the above given types are non-controllable. Verbs like **cau-** 'be big', **saŋ-** 'be long', **waŋ-** 'be tall', **noi-** 'be fat', **pik-** 'be small', **iŋ-** 'be cool', **sa-** 'be hot', **ŋəu-** 'be fair', **cin-** 'be tight', **pək-** 'be suitable', **pet-** 'be soft', **kəŋ-** 'be dry', **thən-** 'be full', **jak-** 'be salty, be deep (of colour)', **lum-** 'be heavy', **kha-** 'be bitter', **hau-** 'be tasty', **lu-** 'be difficult', **nan-** 'be slippery', **then-** 'be shallow', **kheŋ-** 'be bright (of colour), **wau-** 'be light (of colour), **kop-** 'be dent', **lau-** 'be broad', etc. are non-controllable verbs. They are theoretically incapable of occurring in the imperative construction since they have no control over the situation.

Stative verbs have some selectional restrictions with certain verbal suffixes. They are not as versatile as action verbs. They cannot go with suffix **-minnə-** 'together' as found in action verbs like **ca-minnə-** 'eat together', **thək-minnə-** 'drink together', **cət-minnə-** 'go together', etc. One cannot say ***waŋ-minnə-** 'be tall together', ***kəŋ-minnə-** 'be thin together'. The suffix -**minnə** implies associativeness of an action *i.e.* to perform an action together. It involves more than one performer. Since stative verbs are not performing verbs, there is no question of performing an action together with stative verbs.

Benefactive suffix **-pi ~ bi** is another suffix which stative verbs cannot take. It is a grammaticalized suffix which originates from the verb **pi-** 'give' which entails generosity of someone by giving something. The person who receives this generosity is benefited and thus, the suffix gets its name 'benefactive'. Where no action of giving is performed with an agent then, it is quite natural for stative verbs not to take this benefactive suffix **-pi ~ bi**. One can say **təubi-** 'to do something for someone', **pubi-** 'carry something for someone', **thoŋbi-** 'cook for someone'. The verb **-pi** 'give' itself can also take this suffix as in **pibi-** 'give something to someone'. One cannot become fat for someone as ***noibi-**, ***nembi-** 'become short for someone'. Stative verbs which have no control over the events cannot combine with benefactive suffix **-pi ~ bi**. Bhat and Ningomba (1997: 157) have given the statement that benefactive **-bi** when attached to non-controllable state verbs, the meaning conveyed is that the underlying event occurred unexpectedly, *e.g.*

25. *məhak ŋən-bi*
 *he early-*BEN
 'He was early for someone else's sake'

The sentence is ungrammatical and no such combination is found to be used by the native speakers. The grammatical sentence may be as illustrated below:

26. məhak əi-gi-dəmək ŋən-nə həu-gət-li/ lak-i /lak-pi
 he I-GEN-for early-ADV get-up-SAM/come-SAM/come-BEN-SAM
 'He got up early for me' OR 'He came early for me'

Reflexive suffix **-cə ~ ɟə** cannot go with stative verbs. The semantic property of the suffix indicates to perform an action by the self and action verbs like **ca-** 'eat', **thək-** 'drink', **su-** 'work', etc. can have this suffix and form the following words like **caɟə-** 'eat oneself', **thəkcə-** 'drink oneself', **suɟə-** 'do oneself'. But stative verbs like **cau-** 'be big', **saŋ-** 'be long', **pak-** 'be broad', etc. cannot have the following forms like ***cauɟə-** 'be big by itself', ***saŋɟə-** 'be long by itself', ***pakcə-** 'be broad by itself' since a verb which have no control over the event cannot perform an action by itself.

Suggestive suffix **-si** is also another suffix which cannot be attached to stative verbs. **-si** means to suggest someone to perform an action and it is translated in English as 'Let' construction. Thus one can say **ca-si-** 'Let us eat', **thək-si** 'Let us drink', **pa-si** 'Let us read', **cət-si** 'Let us go', etc. But verb forms which have stative plus suggestive **-si** is unnatural like ***ŋəu-si** 'Let us be fair', ***sa-si** 'Let us be hot', ***iŋ-si** 'Let us be cold', etc. But there is one possible way of adding this suffix to stative verbs like **ŋəu-hən-si** 'Let it become white', **sa-hən-si** 'Let it become hot', **i-hən-si** 'Let it become cold'. This construction becomes grammatically as well as semantically approved because of the suffixation of **-hən** 'causative', which brings a change in the meaning of the verb. When **-hən** is added, the verb's meaning is changed and it involves an agent to carry out the action of making someone or something fair or white. There are many suffixes of this type which bring a change in the meaning of the verb classes and it will be discussed in section **3.5.**

Stative verbs cannot take the deictic suffix **-rə** which means come and perform an action at the speaker's place (see **4.2**). It is ungrammatical to combine this suffix with stative verbs. The examples given by Bhat and Ningomba (1997: 188) as **lam-mə-i** 'came here and hungry', **cil-lə-i** 'came here and be busy', **phə-rə-i** 'came here and is good', and **iŋ-ŋə-i** 'came here and feels cold', **cum-mə-i** 'came here and straightened something here', **khoi-rə-i** (river) flows straight and bend here' are some of the examples which native speakers do not use in day-to-day speaking. However, suffix **-lu** and **-lək** can go with stative verbs.

Deictic suffix **-lu** denotes to do an action at some place and return back. Normally, it goes with performing verbs *i.e.* action verbs and it refers to physical displacement which involves volition on the actor's part (see **4.2**). With stative verbs there is no volitionality since they are not performing verbs and they do not have an actor or agent. With action verbs the meaning spreads in the dimension of space but with stative verbs it spreads in time. It gives a contrastive meaning of the situation of the present time with that of the previous time. It can be shown by the following diagram:

Action Verbs -lu (In space dimension)

A B

Stative Verbs V + -lu (In time dimension)

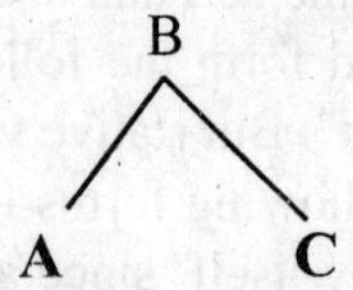

The verb **ca**- 'eat' can have the form **ca-ru-re** 'I have gone there, eaten there and came back'. The action of **ca**- is performed at a place B and returns to place A again and the speaker gives this particular statement at point A. Similarly, when someone says **noi-ru-re** 'he was fat sometime back', he was slim at point A and he became fat at a particular time at point B and now the situation is changed and he has become slim again at point C as he was before at point A. Thus, the figure of the man keeps changing and in both conditions at point A and C, he remained slim. Such verbs, though, they come under stative verbs have a temporary meaning which make contrast with quality verbs like **waŋ**- 'be tall' and one cannot say ***waŋ-ŋu-re** 'he was tall sometime back'. This is because one cannot become short after he was tall. Once a person becomes tall he can never become short *i.e.* the state of being tall can never be changed.

27. **kom**- 'be loose'
phurıt-si əi-ŋon-də kom-mu-re (-lu)
blouse-DEM I-DIR-DAT loose-DEIC-PERF-SAM
'This blouse was loose to me sometime back'

28. **thaɟə**- 'believe'
əi ma-bu thaɟə-ru-re
I he-ACC believe-DEIC-PERF-SAM
'I believed him' (it was wrong to have believed him)

The verb **kom**-'be loose' in (27) refers that the blouse was once fit to the speaker but at a particular time it became loose and now it is loose no more. Similarly, the verb **thaɟə**- 'believe' in (28) means that the speaker did not believe him but at some particular time he believed him and now he does not believe him. In another sense, it may also mean to believe him from the beginning. In the two sentences the verbs show a contrastive situation of the previous time with the present time.

There are some state verbs which do not show the contrastive situation. They simply denote a situation encountered by chance with no intention on the speaker's part.

29. **ta-** 'hear'
mə-khoi-nə ŋaŋ-nə-rəm-bə-du əi-nə ta-ru-re
he-PL-NOM speak-REC-COMP-NMZ-DEM I-NOM hear-DEIC-PERF-SAM
'I happened to hear what they were talking'

30. **theŋnə-** 'meet by chance, encounter'
əi ma-gə ləmbi-də ŋəraŋ theŋnə-ru-i
I he-ASS way-LOC yesterday encounter-DEIC-SAM
'I encountered him on the way yesterday'

The deictic suffix **-lək** is a grammaticalized suffix and it is originated from the verb **lak-** 'come'. As the meaning of the verb implies to come towards the speaker, the underlying meaning of the suffix also implies direction towards the speaker (see **4.2**). The verb **pu-** 'carry' in **purək-i** 'brought here' means to bring something from another place. With action verbs it generally entails space *i.e.* from somewhere or performs an action somewhere rather than here and come towards the speaker. But with non-performing verbs like statives the suffix denotes continuation of a situation from a period of time upto the present time. A temporal adverb is required to show the point of time in every sentence.

31. **noi-** 'be fat'
a. nupi əsi hannə-dəgi noi-rək-i
woman this before-ABL fat-DEIC-SAM
'This woman has been fat since a long time'
b* nupi əsi ŋəraŋ-dəgi noi-rək-i
woman this yesterday-ABL fat-DEIC-SAM
'This woman has been fat since yesterday'

32. **inak-khun-** 'be rich'
a. imuŋ əsi məmaŋ-ŋəi-dəgi inak khul-lək-i
house this ancient time-DUR-ABL rich-DEIC-SAM
'This family has been rich since ancient times'

b.* imuŋ əsi məmaŋ tha-dəgi inak khul-lək-i
house this previous month-ABL rich-DEIC-SAM
'This family has been rich since previous month'

The verb **noi-**'be fat' in (31a) denotes that the woman has been fat since a long time and the sentence is grammatically and semantically acceptable. But in (b) the temporal adverb **ŋəraŋ** 'yesterday' does not give any sense to the sentence. This is because one cannot become fat in an overnight. It takes a long time to become fat. Similarly, it becomes quite nonsense or impractical since it is quite unnatural for someone to become healthy within two or three days. In one sense, it may be sensible to mean to improve one's health after an illness. Otherwise, it takes some time to become healthy, not days. It does not make any sense as the suffix **-lək** implies occurrence of a condition, state or situation since a long time. Of course, one can become rich overnight but in such situations the verb will not take **-lək**. The verb may be in reduplicative form like **khəŋ-khun khun-gət-** 'to become rich suddenly'. Now, consider one more sentence.

33. **son-** 'weak'
nupi-si mə-jum-dəgi mə-sa sol-lək-i
woman-DEM 3PP-house-ABL 3PP-body weak-DEIC-SAM
'This woman has been sick before her marriage'

The literal meaning of the word **məjum-dəgi** 'from her house' refers to place as well as time. But, native speakers perceive this sentence in such a manner – the state of sickness has been inherently acquired by the woman since she was at her parent's home and she still continues to be sick at her husband's house.

There are certain adverbial suffixes which can go with stative verbs only. They are **-drit**, **-droŋ**, **-trik**, **-səŋ**, **-sin**, **-drik**, **-throk**, **-rək**, etc. They intensify the meaning of state verbs. They always occur in reduplicative forms (see **4.2**) 'be rich'

Process Verbs: Process verbs are uncontrollable verbs. They are changing verbs and they do not have an agent. Semantically, animate agents are considered to be agents by linguists. Thus, inanimate forces like wind, storm and other agent-like properties are not considered to be agents (see **3.4**). This is because of the lack of volitionality and control on the part of the inanimate agents. Generally, state verbs as well as process verbs take theme as their subject in a sentence. Sometimes, process verbs may take inanimate agents like wind, storm, rain, etc.

Process verbs may be grouped into two based on the semantic level. Process verbs which have inanimate agent and have another meaning of action verbs *i.e.* which have dual functions come under Group-I. Verbs, which do not have another reading except process meaning, come under Group-II. Verbs of this type usually take perfective suffix **-e** instead of realized suffix **-i**. When they take this suffix **-i** the meaning of the verb changes to stative meaning. This difference is not seen in the verbs of Group-I. The suffixation of **-i** may mean both action and process.

Verbs of Group-I : There are some verbs which may have both action and process meaning. For action verbs there is an agent and for process verbs the agent-like properties may be inanimate forces like wind, storm, rain, etc.

34. **khik-** 'sprinkle'
a. əi-nə ləimai-də isiŋ khik-i
I-NOM floor-LOC water sprinkle-SAM
'I sprinkle water on the floor'

b. həuɟik ŋaihak-ki məmaŋ-də noŋ khik-ləm-mi
now a while-GEN before-LOC rain sprinkle-COMP-SAM
'It drizzled a short while ago'

35. **haŋ**- 'open'

a. əi-nə thoŋ haŋ-ŋi
I-NOM door open-SAM
'I opened the door'

b. nuŋsit-nə thoŋ haŋ-ŋi
wind-NOM door open-SAM
'The wind opens the door'

In the above examples verbs of group (a) denote action meaning as they have an animate agent and they also take aspect marker **-i**. In (34a) the verb takes an animate agent while in (b) the agent is inanimate *i.e.* **noŋ** 'rain'. In (35a) also an animate agent is there to perform the action of opening while in (b) the agent is a natural force doing the same action. The difference seen in the sentences above is 'agent'. Animate agents of sentences (a) have volitionality and control over the act while inanimate agents like natural forces of sentences (b) do not have control over the act as well as they lack volitionality (for more detail see **3.4**). Sentences of group (a) which denote action meaning have the realized suffix **-i** and when they take perfective suffix **-e** the meaning of the verb class do not change and they simply refer to perfective aspect of the actions.

Verbs of Group-II: Verbs of this type do not have another reading as found in Group-I. The meaning shift in the verb classes is caused by the use of different suffixes. These process verbs take perfective suffix **-e** generally to indicate process meaning. But when they take realized aspect marker **-i** the meaning of the verb changes to stative.

36. **sat**- 'bloom'

a. gulab əŋaŋbə-si sat-le
rose red-DEM bloom-PERF-SAM
'This red rose has bloomed'

b. laibreri məmaŋ-də gulab jam-nə sat-li
library in front-LOC rose much-ADV bloom-SAM
'Many roses bloom in front of the library'

37. **pum**- 'be rotten'

a. ensaŋ-si pum-me
curry-DEM rotten-PERF-SAM
'This curry has got rotten'

b. kalen tha-də ensaŋ thu-nə pum-mi
summer month-LOC curry quick-ADV rotten-SAM
'Curry gets rotten quickly in summer'

38. **ken-** 'fall'

a. həinəu əmunbə əmə kel-le
mango ripe one fall-PERF-SAM
'A ripe mango has fallen down'

b. naken tha-də una-siŋ kel-li
autumn month-LOC leaf-PL fall-SAM
'Leaves fall in autumn'

39. **si-** 'die'

a. əi-gi i-ce-du si-re
I-GEN 1PP-sister-DEM die-PERF-SAM
'My sister is dead'

b. lalhəubə-gi iraŋ ləi-bə ləm-də numit khudiŋ-gi
insurgency-GEN problem have-NMZ place-LOC day every-GEN

mi si
people die-SAM
'People die everyday in places having insurgency problem'

40. **həu-** 'grow'

a. əi-nə tha-bə thəbi-du həu-re
I-NOM plant-NMZ cucumber-DEM grow-PERF-SAM
'The cucumber which I have planted has grown'

b. sorok-ki nakəl əni-də u pambi pəreŋ sa-nə həu-i
road-GEN side two-LOC tree plant line make-ADV grow-SAM
'Trees grow parallel on both sides of the road'

Sentences of group (a) in the above examples denote process meaning when they occur with perfective suffix -**e**. Sentences of group (b) indicate a general statement. For instance, the verb **pum-**'be rotten' in (37a) refers to a particular curry while in (b) it refers to all types of curry in general. It can be concluded that process verbs which go with simple aspect marker -**i** denote a state or condition of something (making it a general statement).

Process verbs cannot go with imperative -**u**. The inherent property of the process verb *i.e.* uncontrollablility do not allow the combination of imperative marker. Things happen by itself in process verbs. There is no agent or actor to cause an act. Thus, one cannot command a mango to fall down by itself. Of course, process verbs can take command markers only when a suffix is inserted between the verb and the command suffix **-u**. For instance, **-hən** 'causative' can be inserted between the verb **tau-** 'float' and command marker **-u** to form **tau-həl-lu** 'let it float on water'. Similarly, **kəŋ-həl-lu** 'let it dry (in the sun, or on fire)', **mot-həl-lu** 'let it be dirty', etc. In such constructions the meaning of the verb is shifted to action meaning.

Benefactive **-pi** ~ **bi** which is homophonous with honorific **-pi** ~ **bi** cannot be attached to process verbs. One cannot say ***ken-bi** 'fall for the benefit of someone', ***sat-pi** 'bloom for the benefit of someone'. As process verbs cannot have control over the act as well as no agent is there to perform the act, they cannot take benefactive suffix **-pi** ~ **bi**. Being uncontrollable verbs they cannot take suffixes like **-cə** ~ **-ɟə**, **-niŋ**, **-ke** ~ **-ge**, **-si**, etc.

3.3 Overlapping of Verb Classes

According to the various forms of the verbs found in the syntactic level it may be discussed under the following heads.

Action versus State: There are some verbs which can be used in different situations referring to both actions and states. The verb will remain same in the sentences.

41. **koi-** 'go round'
    a. əi-nə jumbi-si məŋa-rək koi
       I-NOM pillar-DEM five-times go round-SAM
       'I go round this pillar five times'

    b. **koi-** 'have a round shape'
       nupi-du mə-mai koi
       woman-DEM 3PP-face round-SAM
       'The woman has a round face'

42. **mtum ta-** 'to make something round/make a ball of something'
    a. əi-nə jam-du mətum-tai
       I-NOM flour-DEM make a ball-SAM
       'I make a ball of the flour'

    b. **mətum ta-** 'be round, be spherical'
       prithibi mətum ta-i
       earth spherical-SAM
       'The earth is spherical in shape'

43. **tiŋ-** 'stretch something'
    a. əi-nə ləmbi-də thəuri tiŋ-ŋi
       I-NOM road-LOC rope stretch-SAM
       'I stretch a rope on the road'

b. **tiŋ**- 'be straight'
nupa-du mə-jaŋlen tiŋ-ŋi
man-DEM 3PP-back straight-SAM
'The man has a straight back'

44. **khən**- 'intervene, put something between two things'
a. əi-nə phi əaŋbə əni-gi mərək-tə əsəŋbə əmə-nə khəl-li
I-NOM cloth red two-GEN between-LOC green one-NOM put-SAM
'I put a green cloth in between the two red clothes'

b. **khən**- 'intervene, lie between two things'
khun əni-gi mərək-tə turel əmə-nə khəl-li
village two-GEN between-LOC river one-NOM intervene-SAM
'There is a river between the two villages'

45. **nəm**- 'smell'
a. əi-nə thəmbal-du mənəm nəm-mi
I-NOM lotus-DEM smell smell-SAM
'I smell the lotuses'

b. **nəm**- 'smell'
ka-si ɟatikuppi mənəm nəm-mi
room-DEM lavender smell smell-SAM
'This room smells lavender'

46. **seŋ**- 'clean'
a. memi-nə məndir seŋ-ŋi
Memi-NOM temple clean-SAM
'Memi cleans the temple'

b. **seŋ**- 'be clean (of utensils), be washed (of clothes), etc.'
baltin ɔsi seŋ-ŋi
bucket this clean-SAM
'This bucket is clean'

47 **kok**- 'shave, clean'
a. tombə ŋəraŋ mə-koi kok-i
tomba yesterday 3PP-beard cut-SAM
'Tomba shaved yesterday'

b. **kok**- 'be barren'
ciŋmai-si pum-kok kok-i
brow-DEM RED-barren barren-SAM
'This brow is totally barren'

In the above given examples all the (a) type sentences refer to actions rather than state or condition as they are doing verbs. On the other hand, all the (b) type sentences are stative as they denote a state or condition.

Action versus States which refer to the result of the Action: There are certain action verbs in Manipuri which tend to become state verbs. They refer to the result of the actions which remain at the present situation. For instance, **jek-** 'paint' is an action verb which needs an agent or doer to carry out the action of painting. When the action of painting is over it remains at the present situation and it refers to a state that one can say like this *The cover of the book has a picture of flower*.

48. **segai-** 'tear'

a. nupa-məca-du-nə lairik-tu segai
man-small-DEM-NOM book-DEM tear-SAM
'The boy tore the book'

b. **segai-** 'be torn'
lairik-tu segai
book-DEM torn-SAM
'The book is torn'

49 **məpan khop-** 'hem on something'

a. ləta-nə phi-siŋ-du məpan khop-pi
Lata-NOM cloth-PL-DEM border hem-SAM
'Lata hems the clothes'

b. **məpan khop-** 'hem'
phi-siŋ-si loinə məpan khop-pi
cloth-PL-DEM all hem-SAM
'All the clothes are hemmed'

50 **jom-** 'pack something'

a. i-ma-nə phi-siŋ-du jom-mi
my mother-NOM cloth-PL-DEM pack-SAM
'My mother packs the clothes'

b. **jom-** 'be packed'
mithai-du ce əŋaŋbə-nə jom-mi
toffee-DEF paper red-NOM pack-SAM
'The toffee is packed with red paper'

51a. **khən-** 'put on a screen'
əi-nə thoŋnau-du pərda əŋəubə əmə khəl-li
I-NOM window-DEM screen white one screen-SAM
'I put up a white screen on the window'

b. **khən**- 'use a screen'
siloŋ-gi jum-siŋ-di ɟali-gi pərda khəl-li
Shillong-GEN house-PL-DEM net-GEN screen put up-SAM
'The houses of Shillong has netted-screens on the doors and windows'

52a. **lon**- 'embroider'
memə-nə phi lol-li
Mema-NOM cloth embroider-SAM
'Mema embroiders clothes'

b. **lon**- 'be embroidered'
ma-gi phənek məpan-du
she-GEN a traditional dress of Manipuri women border-DEM

lə əmubə-nə lol-li
thread black-NOM embroider-SAM
'The border of her **phanek** is embroidered by black thread'

53a. **la**- 'make noise'
əŋaŋ-siŋ-nə pum-laŋ laŋ-ŋi
child-PL-NOM RED-noise noise-SAM
'Children make much noise'

b. **laŋ**- 'be noisy'
kəithel-də-di mətəm pumnəmək-tə laŋ-ŋi
market-LOC-DEM time all-LOC noisy-SAM
'It is always noisy in the market.

54a. **kup**- 'cover'
tombə-nə jum-thək-tə ɟiŋghə əsəŋbə-nə kup-pi
Tombə-NOM house roof-LOC corrugated iron green-NOM cover-SAM
'Tomba covers the roof the house with green corrugated iron sheet'

b. **kup**- 'be roofed'
jum-du ɟiŋghə əsəŋbə-nə kup-pi
house-DEM corrugated iron sheet green-NOM roof-SAM
'The house is roofed with green corrugated iron sheet'

55a. **jan**- 'hang'
əi-nə heŋgər-də phurit jal-li
I-NOM hanger-LOC shirt hang-SAM
'I hang shirt on hanger'

b. **jan**- 'be hanged'
phurit-siŋ-du heŋgər-də loinə jal-li
shirt-PL-DEM hanger-LOC all hang-SAM
'All the shirts are hanged on the hangers'

56a. **hək-** 'carve'
əŋaŋ-siŋ-nə u-də mə-miŋ hək-i
child-PL-NOM tree-LOC 3PP-name carve-SAM
'Children carve their names on tree'

b. **hək-** 'be carved'
əribə məjek-siŋ-du nuŋ-də hək-i
old script-PL-DEM stone-LOC carve-SAM
'The old scriptures are curved on stones'

All the sentences of group (a) are actions while sentences of group (b) are examples of stative 'be' asserting a property of the referent nouns. 'Book' in (48b), 'clothes' in (49b), 'toffee' in (50b), 'doors and windows' in (51b), 'border of **phənek**' in (52b), 'market' in 53b), 'house' in (54b), 'shirts' in (55b) and 'old scripts' in (56b) are the referent nouns. Their quality or state is referred by the action verbs which result in states. There are some more verbs of this type. Verbs like **khin-** 'place', **tha-** 'plant', **khum-** 'cover', **thet-** 'hang', **ke-** 'put on make-up', **səmbən kha-** 'make fence', **set tha-** 'set designs', **təi-** 'paint', etc. can also become state verbs.

Action versus Process Verbs: The main difference between action and process verbs is that action verb is agent- oriented as seen in the above examples and process verbs refer to events of changing which do not involve an agent. There are some Manipuri verbs which may have both the readings.

57a. **nik-** 'shake'
əi-nə likli-du nik-i
I-NOM bottle-DEM shake-SAM
'I shake the bottle'

b. **nik-** 'shake'
əŋa-du iŋbə-nə nik-i
child-DEM cold-due to shiver-SAM
'The child shivers due to cold'

58a. **uŋ-** 'spin'
əi-nə khuŋ uŋ-ŋi
I-NOM top spin-SAM
'I spin the top'

b. **uŋ-** 'spin'
əi-gi kok-si uŋ-ŋi
I-GEN head-DEM spin-SAM
'My head spins'

59a. **lit**- 'go through'
əi-nə polaŋkhok məkha-də lit-li
I-NOM cloth line under-LOC go through-SAM
'I go through the cloth line'

b. **lit**- 'escape'
laŋ-dəgi ŋa əmə lit-khə-re
net-ABL fish one escape-DEF-PERF-SAM
'A fish has escaped from the net'

60a. **leŋ**- 'move'
nə-sa-du khərə leŋ-ŋu
2PP-body-DEM slightly move-COM
'Move your body slightly'

b. **leŋ**- 'move'
nuŋsit sit-pə-də pambi-siŋ-du leŋ-ŋi
wind blow-NMZ-LOC plant-PL-DEM move-SAM
'The plants move when the wind blows'

61a. **thit**- 'make a mixture of something with water'
əi-nə səŋgom thit-le
I-NOM milk mix with water-PERF-SAM
'I have mixed the milk powder with water'

b. **thit**- 'be slushy'
ləmbi-si ləikhom-nə thit-le
path-DEM mud- NOM slushy-PERF-SAM
'The path has become very slushy'

In the above given examples, verbs of group (a) refer to activities which are carried out by an agent or actor. On the other hand, verbs of group (b) denote process without involving any human agent. There are many more verbs which denote both actions and processes.

Kapil Kapoor (1985:36) observed that even though there are some verbs which are essentially states or processes, the classification of verbs into actions, states and processes is not at all certain. He further quotes from Thomas Montgomery (***Indian Linguistics***, Vol. 50, 1978: 907) that 'it is in fact the uses of the verbs rather than the verbs themselves that are stative' (see **3.1**). This is the main reason why many situations of overlapping happen. One class of verb may be used in another situation as well as they tend to change the classes by other factors also. Quirk ***et al***. (1985: 177) prefer to talk of dynamic and stative meanings, rather than dynamic and state verbs. They give the reason as follows: this is because one verb may shift, in meaning, from one category to another, *e.g. have* may have both stative and dynamic as possess and eat.' In *I have two eyes* the verb has stative meaning and in *I have my lunch at Mr. K's house* the verb has dynamic meaning of *eat*.

In section **3.1** it has been discussed that the distinction is made between action versus state and action versus process. Sentences of group (a) refer to activities which are carried out by an agent or actor. Action verbs take an agent or actor as their subject while state and process verbs take a theme as their subject (Bhat and Ningomba, 1997:193). In sentence (57a) **əi** 'I' is the agent who carries out the activity of shaking the bottle, while in (b), the animate noun **əŋaŋ** 'child' is the theme which undergoes the effect of the action **nik**- 'shake'. Hence, agents become an important criterion for the classification of verbs.

3.4 Agentivity

Kate Kearns (2000: 237-240) suggested a test through which agentivity can be decided. They are (a) volition and control by applying the verb 'persuade', (b) **agentive adverbs** *e.g.* deliberately, carefully, consciously, etc. (c) imperative voice and (d) what X did context. Verbs which can go through this test successfully are action verbs.

Sometimes, inanimate agents or agent-like properties act as agents in sentences. Kate (2000: 240-244) discussed these agent-like properties under the following heads as: natural forces, projectiles, quasi-agentive, etc. Natural forces are autonomous forces like winds, storms, etc. as in *The wind opened the door*. Consider the following examples in Manipuri.

62. **nom**- 'shake'

a. tombə-nə həinəu-du nom-mi
Tomba-NOM mango-DEM shake-SAM
'Tomba shakes the mango tree'

b. nuŋsit-nə həinəu-du nom-mi
wind-NOM mango-DEM shake-SAM
'The wind shakes the mango tree'

The subject **tombə** in (62a) is an animate subject who does the activity of shaking the tree. It entails volition of doing the act. But in (b) the inanimate subject **nuŋsit** 'wind' is an autonomous force as well as it does not have volition and control over the activity as found in the human agent **tombə** in (a) (for more detail see **3.2)**. Inanimate forces are also found in machines which work under their own power, unlike tools which are directly manipulated.

63. **cəpkhai**- 'crush'

a. əi-nə cəmpra-du cəpkhai
I-NOM lemon-DEM crush-SAM
'I crush the lemon'

b. mecin əsi-nə nuŋ cəpkhai
machine this-NOM stone crush-SAM
'This machine crushes stones'

Both **əi** 'I' in (63a) and 'machine' in (b) function as agents in both sentences. But the inanimate agent 'machine' lacks volition and control over the activity. A projectile force is another inanimate agent-like property that is not an autonomous force like wind or storm.

64. **thugai-** 'smash, break'

a. kəplibə əŋaŋ-du-nə redio-du thugai-khə-re
crying child-DEM-NOM radio-DEM smash-DEF-PERF-SAM
'The crying child smashed the radio into pieces'

b. noŋməi məru-du-nə məni-gi ŋəksəm-gi səru thugai-khə-re
gun bullet-DEM-NOM Mani-GEN neck-GEN bone smash-DEF PERF-SAM
'The bullet smashed Mani's collar bone'

In sentence (64b) **noŋməi məru** 'bullet' is a projectile force functioning as an inanimate agent in the sentence. Quasi-agentive is based on the inherent design or construction of instruments as found in the example below:

65. **haŋdok-** 'open'

a. əi-nə so-nə thoŋ haŋdok-i
I-NOM key-INST door open-SAM
'I open the door with a key'

b. so-du-nə thoŋ haŋdok-i
key-DEM-NOM door open-SAM
'The key opened the door'

In sentence (65a) 'the key' is an instrument with which the activity of opening the door is carried out. But in (b) it functions as an inanimate agent in the sentence. The key is an instrument which is designed for a specific purpose of opening a lock.

The inanimate agent-like properties so far discussed do not entail volition and control which are the most important feature of agentivity. Such properties are termed as linguistic agentivity by linguists. They simply perform the activity without any intention and they do not have control over the act. The highest ranking agents are conscious, deliberate, controlling performers of their deeds (Kate, 2000: 243). He observed that agentivity is not a simple unified property, but a cluster of properties which characterize different kinds of agentivity. Finally, he postulated a four-way feature of animate agent as:

1. *Volition – voluntary involvement in an event or state'*
2. *Control over involvement in an event or state'*
3. *Wilful initiator or instigator of an event, and*
4. *Consciousness, sentience, perception.*

For many writers the term 'agent' can apply only if properties in the animate set are present (Kate, 2000: 245). However, volition alone may be considered to be sufficient to make an event with a human protagonist agentive as seen in sentences (a. of 62-65). Action verbs which take an agent refer to this animate agent only.

The second of the four points given above *i.e.* control over involvement in an event or state is also an important factor of agentivity as well as for action verbs. However, this is not as much important as volition since control over an event or state can regularly occur with imperative and this imperative feature can also go with some state verbs which come under controllable verb groups (see **3.2**).

The third property of agentivity is wilful initiator or instigator of an event. It is the agent who willingly initiates an event. Non-agentive forces like natural forces, projectiles also initiate an event but not willingly. The last property is about adverbs. An agent always takes adverbs like 'consciously', 'carefully' and 'deliberately' which other non-agentive forces cannot take.

66a. məhak-nə thəbək-tu ceksin-nə təu-i
he-NOM work-DEM careful-ADV do-SAM
'He does the work carefully'

*b. əŋaŋ-du mə-mai ceksin-nə cau-i
child-DEM 3PP-face careful-ADV big-SAM
'The child's face is carefully big'

*c. nuŋsit-nə ceksin-nə sit-li
wind-NOM careful-ADV blow-SAM
'Wind blows carefully.

The adverb **ceksinnə** 'carefully' can go with animate agent **məhak** 'he' in sentence (66a) and it is grammatically and semantically acceptable. Sentences (b) and (c) are grammatically correct but semantically they are unacceptable. The child's face in sentence (b) cannot become big carefully and the wind in sentence (c) cannot blow carefully. **əŋaŋ** 'child' in sentence (b) cannot become an agent as it functions as a theme in the sentence. The agent-like force **'wind'** in sentence (c) does not have control over the act of blowing and thus, it cannot take the agentive adverb 'carefully'.

3.5 Shifting of verb's meaning from one category to another

There are certain suffixes which play an important role in the analysis of Manipuri verbs. The semantic classification of verbs so far studied would be incomplete without the study of suffixes. The verbs may shift in meaning from one category to another when certain suffixes are attached to them. The change in meaning may be from stative to process, stative to action and very rarely from process to action.

Suffixes *-sin, -thok, -khət, -thə, -hən,* etc.: The directional suffixes **-sin**, **-thok**, **-khət**, -

thə give directional meaning when they go with directional action verbs like **ləŋ**- 'throw', **in**- 'push', **cen**- 'run', **co**- 'jump', **hai**- 'swing', etc. (see **3.2**). When these four suffixes combine with stative verbs, they give another meaning while the directional meaning is somewhat retained. They refer to a change of state of a verb and the process involved in this change gives the verbs a process meaning, sometimes an action meaning. As suggested by Surmangol Sharma (1998:66). The four suffixes **-sin**, **-thok**, **-khət**, **-thə** may be represented as horizontal and verbal planes as follows:

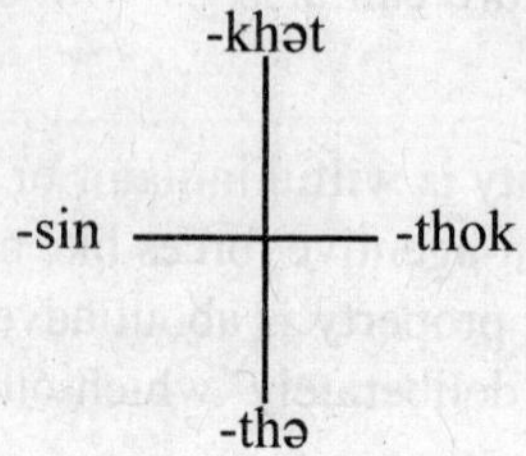

-**khət** and -**thə** represent vertical plane while -**sin** and -**thok** horizontal one. The suffixes show oppositions -**thok** vs -**sin** and -**khət** vs -**thə** by taking the verbs of oppositional pairs such as **ŋu**- 'be white' vs **mu**- 'be dark, black', **cau**- 'be big' vs **pik**- 'be small', **waŋ**- 'be tall' vs **nem**- 'be short', etc. The verbs may be shown with the suffixes as follows:

ŋəu-thok-	become fair	mu-sin-	become dark
cau-thok-	become big	pik-sin-	become small
cau-khət-	increase size	pik-thə-	relatively small
waŋ-khət-	increase height	nem-thə-	reduce height, etc.

Bernd Heine, Ulrike Claudi and Friederike Hünnemeyer (1991:51) quote from Lakoof and Johnson (***Metaphors we live by***, 1980:14-21) that show the distinction **up** versus **down** as their metaphorical vehicle as:

Happy is up; sad is down

Conscious is up; unconscious is down

Health and life are up; sickness and death are down

Having control or force is up; being subject to control is down

More is up; less is down

High status is up; low status is down

Good is up; bad is down

Virtue is up; depravity is down

Rational is up; emotional is down

The addition of the four suffixes to stative verbs may also give a comparative meaning (see **4.2**).

pik-	be small	>	pik-thə-	be relatively small
cau-	be big	>	cau-khət-	be relatively big
məm-	be dull (of colour)	>	məm-sin-	be relatively dim
wau-	be light (of colour)	>	wau-thok-	be relatively light coloured, etc.

The Suffix -*sin*: The suffixation of **-sin** to stative verbs indicate a change of state and it gives a process meaning. Sometimes, it gives a change of meaning from stative to action.

kəŋ-	be thin	>	kəŋ-sin-	become thin
cəp-	be lean	>	cəp-sin-	become lean
məm-	be dark	>	məm-sin-	become dark
pəŋ-	be foolish	>	pəŋ-sin-	become foolish
pət-	be rotten	>	pət-sin-	become rotten
nəŋ-	be thick	>	nəŋ-sin-	become thick
khu-	be narrow	>	khu-ɟin-	become narrow
mu-	be black	>	mu-sin-	become black
nək-	be near	>	nək-sin-	become near
pik-	be small	>	pik-sin-	become small
ten-	be short	>	ten-sin-	become short, etc.

67. **kəŋ-** 'be thin'

a. əŋaŋ-si mə-jaŋ kəŋ-ŋi
child-DEM 3PP-back thin-SAM
'This child is thin'

b. əŋaŋ-si mə-jaŋ kəŋ-sil-le
child-DEM 3PP-back thin-IN-PERF-SAM
'This child has become thin'

68. **pik-** 'be small'

a. redio əsi pik-i
radio this small-SAM
'This radio is small'

b. həinəu əsi pik-sil-le
mango this small-IN-PERF-SAM
'This mango has become relatively small (as compared to last year)'

69. **khu-** 'be narrow'

a. ləmbi əsi khu-i
path this narrow-SAM
'This path is narrow'

b. ləmbi əsi khu-ɟil-le
path this narrow-IN-PERF-SAM
'This path becomes narrower'

Sentences of group (a) denote a situation or condition of something while sentences of group (b) show a change in meaning. Sentence (67b) indicates that the child was not thin before, but now he has become thin means that a change in the state of the child's health has taken place. Sentence (68b) means that the mango was not small last year but the size of the mango has reduced. The verb **khu-ɟin-** 'become narrower' in (69b) also denotes a change in the state of the path that it was not narrow before but now it becomes narrower due to some reasons. Hence, the stative verbs which have **-sin** ~ **ɟin** in the above examples express a process meaning.

There are some stative verbs which tend to change to action meaning. They can take imperative marker as well as an agent.

lik-	be miserly	>	lik-sin-	spend as little money as possible
tuŋ-	store or	>	tuŋ-sin	deposit, reserve remain stagnant
səŋ-	be free	>	səŋ-ɟin-	to shift a content to another container
thəŋ-	lend money/ before or after	>	thəŋ-ɟin-	blame, give responsibility be in a position
səm-	be short	>	səm-ɟin-	make a process/journey short
khəŋ-	know	>	khəŋ-ɟin-	know for the future
həi-	know, have knowledge of something	>	həi-ɟin-	know, have knowledge of something, etc.

70. **tuŋ**- 'store or remain stagnant'

a. əkutpə məphəm-si-də isiŋ khə-rə tuŋ-ŋi
low place-DEM-LOC water some store-SAM
'Some water is stored in this low area'

b. əi tha khudiŋ-gi pəisa khərə khərə tuŋ-sil-li
I month every-GEN money some some deposit-IN-SAM
'I deposit / save some money every month'

71. **səm**- 'be short'

a. əwaŋ-lom-də cət-pə ləmbi əsi-nə səm-mi
north-direction-LOC go-NMZ road this-CONT short-SAM
'The road which goes to the north is short'

b. nəŋ-gi wari-du khərə səm-ɟil-lu
you-GEN story-DEM some short-IN-COM
'Shorten your story'

72. **həi**- 'know, have knowledge of something'

a. məhak thaŋ hai-nə-bə həi
he sword swing-REC-NMZ know-SAM
'He knows the art of fencing'

b. phi lon-bə-su həi-ɟil-lu, kannə-rək-kəni
cloth embroider-NMZ-also know-IN-COM useful-DEIC-NREAL
'Know/learn the art of embroidery, it may be useful in future'

Sentences of group (a) refer to stative meaning while group (b) sentences refer to action reading.

There are two verbs which change meaning from process to action when **-sin** is attached to them.

loi-	finish	>	loi-sin-	make an area clean
phun-	be full	>	phun-ɟin-	to fill a pit

73. **loi**- 'finish'

a. i cak thoŋ-bə loi-re
I rice cook-NMZ finish-PERF-SAM
'I have finished cooking'

b. cak thoŋ-bə loi-rəgə cakkhum-maŋ-du loi-sil-ləm-mu
rice cook-NMZ finish-CPART kitchen-DEM make it clean-COMP-COM
'Clean the kitchen (properly) when you finish cooking'

74. **phun**- 'be blocked'

a. toti paip əsi phul-le
tap pipe this block-PERF-SAM
'This pipe is blocked'

b. kom əsi phun-ɟil-lu
pit this fill-IN-COM
'Fill this pit'

The verb **loi-sin**-'clean' in (73b) and **phun-ɟin**-'fill' in (74b) denote action meanings since they involve agents to perform the acts of cleaning and filling.

There is also a verb of action meaning which shifts to process meaning when **-sin** is attached to it.

ciŋ- pull > ciŋ-sin- contract

75. **ciŋ**- 'pull'

a. əŋaŋ-gi səm-du ciŋ-gənu
child-GEN hair-DEM pull-PROH
'Do not pull the hair of the child'

b. phi əsi su-rəgə ciŋ-sin-gəni
cloth this wash-CPART contract-IN-NREAL
'This cloth will get contracted after wash'

The Suffix *-thok*: When the suffix **-thok** is attached to stative verbs it gives a change in meaning to process and action. It can also be suffixed to process verbs to give action meaning. Following is a list of stative verbs which change to process meaning.

noi-	be fat	>	noi-thok-	become fat
cau-	be big	>	cau-thok-	become big
ŋəu-	be fair	>	ŋəu-thok-	become fair
pak-	be broad	>	pak-thok-	become broad
hoŋ-	be cheap	>	hoŋ-dok-	become cheap
thap-	be far	>	thap-tok-	become far
wau-	be of light colour	>	wau-thok-	be of relatively light colour
lau-	be broad	>	lau-thok-	become broad
saŋ-	be long	>	saŋ-dok-	become long
ŋaŋ-	be red	>	ŋaŋ-thok-	be of relatively red colour, etc.

76. **ŋəu**- 'be fair'

a. əŋaŋ əsi ŋəu-i
child this fair-SAM
'This child is fair'

b nəŋ-gi kucu ŋəu-thok-e
you-GEN complexion fair-OUT-PERF-SAM
'Your complexion has become fairer'

77. **hoŋ**- 'be cheap'

a. həuɟik kəithel-də kobi jam-nə hoŋ-ŋi
now market-LOC cabbage much-ADV cheap-SAM
'Nowadays cabbage is very cheap in the market'

b. khamen-gi məməl khərə hoŋ-dok-e
brinjal-GEN price some cheap-OUT-PERF-SAM
'The price/rate of brinjal has become cheaper'

The verbs of group (b) sentences in the above given examples denote a change of state and the change refers to process meaning.

Some stative verbs give action meaning when **-thok** is added to them.

lai-	be easy	>	lai-thok-	take easy
pen-	satisfy	>	pen-thok-	try to satisfy
nuŋŋai-	be happy	>	nuŋŋai-thok-	try to be happy
nan-	be slippery	>	nan-thok-	escape
kon-	be bend	>	kon-thok-	bend
sən-	be spread	>	sən-dok-	spread
mən-	be old	>	mən-thok-	(of dress) use as casual

ho-	be hollow	>	ho-dok-	inform in advance
cəm-	be simple	>	cəm-thok-	act to be simple
səŋ-	be free	>	səŋ-dok-	make empty
cum-	be correct	>	cum-thok-	make correction
lap-	be far	>	lap-thok-	make distance, etc.

78. **mən**- 'old'

a. əi-gi phurit-si məl-li
I-GEN shirt-DEM old-SAM
'My shirt is old'

b. phurit-tu mən-thok-kənu
shirt-DEM old-OUT-PROH
'Do not use the shirt casually'

79. **cum**- 'be correct'

a. ma-gi paukhum-si cum-mi
he-GEN answer-DEM correct-SAM
'His answer is correct'

b. oɟa-nə əŋkə əsi cum-thok-i
teacher-NOM sum this correct-OUT-SAM
'Teacher corrects the sum'

80. **lap**- 'be far'

a. əi-khoi-gi jum-dəgi koleɟ-si jam-nə lap-pi
I-PL-GEN house-ABL college-DEF much-ADV far-SAM
'This college is very far from our house'

b. əi memə-dəgi lap-thok-e
I Mema-ABL far-OUT-PERF-SAM
'I have made a distance from Mema'

The verb **mən-thok-**'use casually' takes a command marker like any action verb. **lap-thok-** 'make a distance' and **cum-thok-**'correct' imply action meaning with an agent. All the sentences of group (a) denote stative meaning whereas group (b) sentences give action reading.

-**thok** has the same function with process verbs also in the sense that it entails volitionality and the verb resulting from the suffixation of -**thok** gives action meaning.

si-	die	>	si-dok-	die for a purpose
kau-	forget	>	kau-thok-	forget intentionally
loi-	finish	>	loi-thok-	finish intentionally
tum-	sleep	>	tum-thok-	'sleep purposefully,etc.

81. **si-** 'die'

a. ənabə-du ŋəraŋ si-re
patient-DEM yesterday die-PERF-SAM
'The patient died yesterday'

b. thaŋgal menɟor-nə mə-rəibak-ki dəmək si-dok-khi
Thangal Menjor-NOM 3PP-motherland-GEN for die-OUT-DEF-SAM

'Thangal Menjor sacrificed his life for his motherland'

82. **kau-** 'forget'

a. əi məhak-nə ŋəraŋ hai-rəm-bə-du kau-re
I he-NOM yesterday say-DEIC-NMZ-DEM forget-PERF-SAM
'I forgot what he told me yesterday'

b. nuŋŋai-tə-bə thəudok-siŋ-du kau-thok-khə-ro
happy-NEG-NMZ event-PL-DEM forget-OUT-DEF-COM
'Forget the unfortunate events'

83. **loi-** 'finish'

a. əi phi su-bə loi-re
I cloth wash-NMZ finish-PERF-SAM
'I have finished washing'

b. thau-du ŋəsi loinə loi-thok-kum-si,
oil-DEM today all finish- OUT-NEG-SUG
'Let's not finish all the oil today (let's save some for later use)'

The above examples show the difference in meaning in the pairs of sentences. Group (a) sentences indicate process meaning while sentences of group (b) refer to action meaning as the verbs imply volitionality and they show controllable acts. The verb **si-dok-** in (81b) has an agent who did the action intentionally.

The Suffix *-khət*: The suffixation of **-khət** to a verb may bring a change in meaning from stative to process, stative to action. Following is a list of some stative verbs which change to process meaning when **-khət** is added to them.

cau- be big > cau-khət- develop, become fat
noi- be fat > noi-khət- become fat
waŋ- be tall > waŋ-khət- become tall
tek- be fresh > tek-khət- become fresh
kən- be hard, strong > kən-khət- become hard, strong
toŋ- be high (of ground) > toŋ-khət- become high
kəu- be short (of dress) > kəu-khət- become short

then-	be shallow	>	then-gət-	become shallow
hen-	be more	>	hen-gət-	become more/increase, etc.

84. **waŋ**- 'be tall'

a. u əsi jam-ɲə waŋ-ŋi
tree this much-ADV tall-SAM
'This tree is very tall'

b. əŋaŋ əsi jam-nə waŋ-khət-le
child this much-ADV tall-UP-PERF-SAM
'This child has become very tall'

85. **kən**- 'be strong'

a. nupa-du mə-sa kəl-li
man-DEM 3PP-body strong-SAM
'The man is strong'

b. əŋa-du lajeŋ-bə-dəgi mə-sa kən-khət-le
child-DEM treatment-NMZ-ABL 3PP-body strong-UP-PERF-SAM
'The child has gained strength after treatment'

86. **hen**- 'be more in number or quantity'

a. mə-khoi-gi imuŋ-də sel tan-bə mi-dəgi
3PP-PL-GEN family-LOC money earn-NMZ man-ABL

cə-bi-nə-bə mi-nə hel-li
eat-BEN-PUR-NMZ man-CMP more-SAM
'In his family, number of persons without earning is more than those who are earning'

b. əŋaŋ əmə lak-pə-dəgi mə-khoi-gi mi-siŋ hen-gət-le
child one come-NMZ-ABL 3PP-PL-GEN man-number more-UP-PERF-SAM
'The number of his family members has increased since the coming of a child'

The verb **waŋ**-'be tall' of sentence (84a) denotes stative meaning while **waŋ-khət-** 'become tall' in (b) refers to a process meaning *i.e.* a change has taken place. Similarly, all the verbs of group (a) refer to stative meaning while sentences of group (b) mean process of the verb.

There are some stative verbs which can function as action verbs when **-khət** is attached to them. They are few in number.

pan-	have, fix	>	pan-khət-	assemble
sau-	be angry	>	sau-gət-	get angry suddenly
phiŋ-	be hot-blooded/rash	>	phiŋ-gət-	have short-temper

87. **pan**- 'have or possess'

a. əi-gi mit əni pal-li
I-GEN eye two have-SAM
'I have two eyes'

b. anən-nə telibhiɟən əmə pan-khət-le
Anand-NOM television one fix-UP-PERF-SAM
'Anand has assembled a television'

88. **phiŋ**- 'be rash'

a. nupa əsi phiŋ-ŋi
man this rash-SAM
'This man is rash'

b. phiŋ-gət-kənu! ma-gi wa-si han-nə ta-khi-si
become rash-PROH he-GEN speech-DEM first-ADV listen-DEF-SUG-SAM
'Don't act rashly! Let us listen to him first'

The verbs **pan-khət-**'assemble' **phiŋ-gət-**'act rashly' in sentences (b) give action meaning.

The Suffix *–th*ə: The suffixation of –**th**ə to a stative verb may give process meaning. Sometimes it also gives action meaning.

nəŋ-	be poor	>	nəŋ-thə-	become poor
pəŋ-	be foolish or blunt	>	pəŋ-thə-	becomenumb orfaint
lum-	be heavy	>	lum-thə-	become heavy
lu-	be deep	>	lu-thə-	become deep
pət-	be rotten	>	pət-thə-	become exhausted
con-	be long	>	con-thə-	become long
iŋ-	be cold	>	iŋ-thə-	become cool
saŋ-	be long	>	saŋ-thə-	become long
tən-	be lazy	>	tən-thə-	become lazy
son-	be weak	>	son-thə-	become weak
pum-	be rotten	>	pum-thə-	become rotten, etc.

89. **iŋ**- 'be cold'

a. siloŋ-di ənəmbə mətəm-də iŋ-ŋi
Shillong-DEM almost time-LOC cold-SAM
'It is cold in Shillong almost all the time'

b. ŋuŋdaŋwairəm-si-də khərə iŋ-thə-rək-e
afternoon-DEM-LOC some become-cold-DEIC-PERF-SAM
'It is becoming cool in the afternoon'

90. **son**- 'be weak'

a. əhəl-si jam-nə sol-li
old man-DEM much-ADV weak-SAM
'This old man is very weak'

b. kalen-də-di i-sa-si jam-nə son-thə-i
summer-LOC-PART 1PP-body-DEM much-ADV weak-become-SAM
'I become very weak in summer'

The verbs which have **-th** in sentences (b) denote a process meaning while (a) group sentences refer to stative meaning.

Sometimes some stative verbs may give action meaning when **-thə** is attached to them.

təp-	be slow	>	təp-thə-	make slow
nan-	be slppery	>	nan-thə-	slip
pak-	be broad	>	pak-thə-	make low, bend down on the floor, be on one's hands and knees

91. **təp**- 'be slow'

a. nupi əsi cət-pə-də təp-pi
woman this go-NMZ-LOC slow-SAM
'This woman is slow in walking'

b. əi thəbək-si khərə təp-thə-rə-ge
I work-DEM some slow-DOWN-PROS-INT
'I intend to delay this work'

92. **pak**- 'be wide'

a. ləmbi əsi jam-nə pak-i
road this much-ADV wide-SAM
'This road is very wide'

b. noŋməi kap-nə-rək-pə-du-də mi punməmək pak-thə-rəm-mi
gun fire-REC-DEIC-NMZ-DEM-LOC man all wide-DOWN-DEIC-SAM
'When the gunfire took place people got down on the floor'

93. **nan**- 'be slippery'

a. ləimai əsi isiŋ cot-ləbədi jam-nə nal-li
floor this water wet-if much-ADV slippery-SAM
'This ground is very slippery when it is wet'

b. əŋaŋ-siŋ-nə park-tə nanthəbi-də nan-thə-i
child-PL-NOM park-LOC slide-LOC slip-DOWN-SAM
'Children slip on the slides at the park'

Sentences of group (b) in the above given example denote action meaning as they are agent-oriented verbs while sentences of group (a) refer to stative meaning.

The Causative Suffix *-hən*: The addition of this suffix to stative and process verbs gives a change in the meaning of the verbs. It means to make somebody to do something and it is the agent who is making to do something or make something happen. The verb **mu-** 'be black' is a stative verb but when **-hən** is attached to it the verb form **mu-hən** 'make something black' entails an agent to carry out the action of making something black.

hau-	be tasty	>	hau-hən-	make something tasty
phəɟə-	be beautiful	>	phəɟə-hən-	make beautiful
kannə-	be useful	>	kannə-hən-	make something useful
ŋəu-	be white	>	ŋəu-hən-	make something white
cot-	be wet	>	cot-hən -	make something wet
ləŋ-	be bright'	>	ləŋ-hən-	make something bright
pet-	be soft	>	pet-hən-	make something soft
kən-	be hard	>	kəl-hən-	make something hard
ten-	be short	>	tel-hən-	make something short
cin-	be tight	>	cil-hən-	make something tight
kəu-	be short	>	kəu-hən-	make something short, etc.

94. **kəŋ-** 'be dry'

a. pukhri əsi kəŋ-ŋi
pond this dry-SAM
'This pond is dry'

b. phi-siŋ-si əi-nə kəŋ-həl-le
cloth-PL-DEM I-NOM dry-CAUS-PERF-SAM
'I have made these clothes dry'

95 **saŋ-** 'be long'

a. ləirək əsi jam nə saŋ-ŋi
lane this much-ADV long-SAM
'This lane is very long'

b. əi-gi səm-si saŋ-həl-lə-ge
I-GEN hair-DEM long-CAUS-PROS-INT
'Make your hair long'

96 **nan-** 'be clean/neat and tidy'

a. Ciil-gi kempəs-tu jam-nə nal-li
C.I.I.L.-GEN campus-DEM much-ADV clean-SAM
'The campus of C.I.I.L. is very clean'

b. əi-nə ka əsi nal-həl-le
I-NOM room this neat-CAUS-PERF-SAM
'I have cleaned this room'

Some process verbs like **ken**- 'fall' can take the causative suffix **-hən** as **kel-hən-** 'make something fall' which gives an action reading.

si-	die	>	si-hən-	make somebody/something die
tek-	break	>	tek-hən-	make something break
kai-	break	>	kai-hən-	make something break
tət-	break	>	tət-hən-	make something break
pət-	be rotten	>	pət-hən-	make something rotten
pum-	be rotten	>	pum-hən-	make something rotten
phəm-	curdle	>	phəm-hən-	make something curdle/somebody seat
səu-	boil	>	səu-hən-	make something boil
mot-	be dirty	>	mot-hən-	make something/somebody dirty
tu-	tall	>	tu-hən-	make somebody/something fall, etc.

97. **ken**- 'fall'

a. u-si una kel-le
tree-DEM leaf fall-PERF-SAM
'The leaves fall from this tree'

b. əi-nə cət-thok-tə-riŋəi-də una əkən-bə-siŋ-du kel-həl-li
I-NOM go-OUT-NEG-SPFD-LOC leaf dry-NMZ-PL-DEM fall-CAUS-SAM
'I make dry leaves fall before going out'

98. **phəm**- 'curdle'

a. kalen-də səŋgom thu-nə phəm-mi
summer-LOC milk quick-ADV curdle-SAM
'Milk gets curdled quickly in summer'

b. səŋgom-du əi-nə cəphu əmə-də phəm-həl-le
milk-DEM I-NOM pot one-LOC curdle-CAUS-PERF-SAM
'I have made the milk curdled in a pot'

It is the causative suffix **-hən** which brings a change in the meaning of the verbs making them action verbs.

The Perfective Suffix ***–le*** **(lə+i)**: This perfective suffix **-le** also plays an important role in the shifting of vebal categories. The function of this suffix in general, is to show completeness of an action. But when it is added to a stative verb it gives another meaning. The verb does not remain as stative anymore when **-lə** follows it. For instance, the verb **mu**- 'be black' is a stative verb and **mu-re** gives a change in the meaning of the stative verb to process meaning as 'It has become black'.

99. **mu**- 'be black'

a. satin əsi mu-i
umbrella this black-SAM
'This umbrella is black'

b. caŋ nai-nə thau təi-bə-dəgi əi-gi səm-si mu-re
regular-ADV hair oil apply-NMZ-ABL I-GEN hair-DEM black PERF-SAM
'My hair has become black due to regular application of hair oil'

100 **kom-** 'be loose'

a. kisi əsi kom-mi
knot this loose-SAM
'This knot is loose'

b. əi-gi khudop-si kom-me
I-GEN ring-DEM loose-PERF-SAM
'My ring has become loose'

101 **mək-** '(of colour) be dull'

a. nəŋ-gi phurit məcu-du mək-i
you-GEN shirt colour-DEM dull-SAM
'The colour of your shirt is dull'

b. kori cəphu-si mək-e
copper pot-DEM dull-PERF-SAM
'This copper pot has become dull'

The verb **mu-re** 'has become black' in (99b) implies that it was not black before, but now it has become black. It shows a change in meaning from stative **mu-**black' to **mu-re**. The verb **kom-me** in sentence (100b) also implies that it was not loose before, but now it has become loose and is no more fitting to the referent. The verb **mək-e** in sentence (101b) shows a change in meaning that the pot was not dull before, but now it has become dull and is no more bright as before. The change in the meaning of the verbal categories from stative to process is brought by the suffixation of perfective suffix **-le**.

In this chapter, Manipuri verbs have been semantically classified. In the chapter that follows, verbal derivative affixes are alanysed with mainly focussing on the grammaticalized and non-grammaticalized suffixes, deictic suffixes and multi-functional suffixes.

CHAPTER

4

DERIVATIVE AFFIXES

Verbal derivative affixes in Manipuri may be studied under two groups as verbal derivative prefixes and verbal derivative suffixes. Verbal prefixes are very few in number while suffixes are large in number. They take a major part in the functioning of the language since Manipuri verbal roots are bound and they take the help of the suffixes to become free words.

4.1 Prefixes

In the analysis of verbal affixes in Manipuri one interesting fact that emerges in the scene is grammaticalization. The by now classic definition of the term 'grammaticalization' was provided by Jerry Kurylowicz [(1965) 1975: 52]: 'Grammaticalization consists in the increase of the range of a morpheme advancing from a lexical to a grammatical or from a less grammatical to a more grammatical status, e.g. from a derivative formant to an inflectional one' (Bernd *et al.*, 1991: 3). Grammaticalization is inherently a diachronic concept. It refers to a historical semantic process whereby a 'root morpheme with a full lexical meaning assumes a more abstract functional or grammatical meaning' (Matisoff, Areal and Universal Dimensions of grammaticalization in Labu, Vol. 1, cited in Bernd *et al.*, 1991).

Many linguists accept the notion 'what-today-are-affixes-were-once independent words' proposed by George Vonder Gabetentz (1901: 250-251) (Bernd *et al.*, 1991: 8). The free form gradually loses its identity and it might have attained the status of an affix. In other words, grammaticalization is a process through which a lexical item develops into a grammatical item. In this process, the meaning of the lexical item may be lost completely and sometimes, it becomes hard to trace the origin of the grammatical item.

Grammaticalized Prefixes *pəŋ-, pum-, khəŋ-, koi-*: The affixation of the prefixes demands the verbal roots to be reduplicated.

pəŋ-: It is derived from the verb **pəŋ-** 'be foolish'. The addition of this prefix to a verbal root gives the meaning 'to do something carelessly or foolishly or without any good reason'. It may sometimes mean recurrence of an action which is indicated by the suffix **-tə ~ də**. In negative environments (which will be discussed just after this sub-section) the suffix is dropped.

1. **ca**- 'eat'
   məhak-ti əphəŋ əphəŋ-bə pəŋ-ca-də ca-i
   he-PART get get-NMZ RED-eat-only eat-SAM
   'He eats whatever he gets (less caring about diet)'

2. **cət**- 'go'
   məhak-ti pəŋ-cət-tə cət-li
   he-PART RED-go-only go-SAM
   'He strays (anywhere) without any purpose'

The suffix **pəŋ**- has another variation **puŋ**- which is used in spoken form only. **pəŋ**- is retained in the written texts while **pu**- is not used in texts.

pəŋ-ca-də ca-i ~ puŋ-ca-də ca-i	eats anything/carelessly
pə-cəi-də cə-i ~ puŋ-cəi-də cə-i	scolds somebody purposelessly
pə-lak-tə lak-i ~ puŋ-lak-tə lak-i	comes habitually without any reason
pə-pa-də pa-i ~ puŋ-pa-də pa-i	reads anything
pə-tum-də tum-mi ~ puŋ-tum-də tum-mi	sleeps almost all the time
pə-hə-də hərau-i ~ puŋ-hə-də hərau-i	is happy foolishly/unreasonably
pə-ke-də ke ~ puŋ-ke-də ke	puts on make-up all the time or without any reason
pə-thək-tə thək-i ~ puŋ-thək-tə thək-i	drinks heavily without any control
pə-sau-də sau-i ~ puŋ-sau-də sau-i	gets angry on petty matters

The prefixation of **pəŋ**- to a verbal root can occur in negative environment also where it means not much, not frequently'.

3. **nop**- 'be weak'
   ma-gə jeŋnə-bə-də nəŋ-su pəŋ-nop nop-te
   he-ASS compare-NMZ-LOC you-also RED-weak weak-NEG-SAM
   'You are not too weak compared to him'

4. **ŋaŋ**- 'talk, give comment'
   məhak-ti mi-gi mərəm-də pəŋ-ŋaŋ ŋaŋ-de
   he-PART man-GEN about-LOC RED-talk talk-NEG-SAM
   'He does not talk much' or 'He hardly gives any comment about others'

pum-: It is originated from the nominal bound root **-pum** 'whole'. The prefixation of **pum**- to a verbal root gives the meaning 'completely'. The prefix has also two variant forms as **pum**- and **puŋ**-. The first variant form **pum**- is used in written form while **puŋ**- is found in spoken form only. It is homophonous with **puŋ**- a variant of **pəŋ**-.

5. **tət**- 'break, torn'
phi-si pum-tət tət-le
cloth-DEM RED-torn torn-PERF-SAM
'This cloth is completely torn'

6. **cot**- 'be wet'
əi noŋ-nə pum-cot cot-le
I rain-NOM RED-wet wet-PERF-SAM
'I am completely drenched in the rain'

The verbs **tət**-'break, torn' in (5) is a process verb while **cot**-'be wet' in (6) is a stative verb. The prefix **pum**- cannot go with action verbs.

pum-cəm cəm-mi ~ puŋ-cəm cəm-mi	is completely tasteless
pum-cai cai-re ~ puŋ-cai cai-re	is completely untidy
pum-ŋau ŋau-re ~ puŋ-ŋau ŋau-re	has gone completely mad
pum-pen pen-le ~ puŋ-pen pen-le	is completely satisfied
pum-haŋ haŋ-Ne ~ puŋ-haŋ haŋ-Ne	is completely empty
pum-pət pət-le ~ puŋ-pət pət-le	is completely rotten
pum-lep lep-pe ~ puŋ-lep lep-pe	has completcly stopped
pum-mot mot-le ~ puŋ-mot mot-le	is completely dirty
pum-tot tot-sin-nə-re ~ puŋ-tot tot-sin-nə-re	is completely mixed up
pum-top top-pi ~ puŋ-top top-pi	is completely different
pum-lak lak-sil-le ~ puŋ-lak lak-sil-le	is completely under control, etc.

The occurrence of **pum-** with action verbs would be ungrammatical.

*pum-ca ca-re	has completely eaten
*pum-cen cel-le	has completely run
*pum-pa pa-re	has completely read

It may be noted that the homophonous prefix **puŋ**- can occur with stative verbs. The interesting fact that may be observed here is that the prefix **puŋ**- which occur in negative environment is derived from the verbal root **pəŋ**- 'be foolish' while the other prefix occurred in positive environment is derived from the nominal bound root **-pum** 'whole'.

khəŋ-: It is derived from the verb **khəŋ**- 'startle'. When it is attached to a verbal root it gives the meaning of 'suddenness'. Most frequently, it occurs with action and process verbs. It can also occur with process verbs (which changes from stative) very rarely in a comparative environment.

***khəŋ-* with action verbs**

7. **thadok**- 'release'
əi-nə thəuri-du khəŋ-tha tha-dok-i
I-NOM rope-DEM RED-release release-OUT-SAM
'I release the rope suddenly'

8. **nok**- 'laugh'
nupi-du khəŋ-nok nok-khət-lək-i
woman-DEM RED-laugh laugh-START-DEIC-SAM
'The woman started to laugh suddenly'

***khəŋ*- with process verbs**

9. **lep**- 'stop'
ləmbi-də gari-du khəŋ-lep lep-khə-re
way-LOC vehicle-DEM RED-stop stop-DEF-PERF-SAM
'The vehicle stopped suddenly on the way'

10. **ta**- 'fall'
lairik-tu əi-gi khut-təgi khəŋ-ta ta-khə-re
book-DEM I-GEN hand-ABL RED-fall fall-DEF-PERF-SAM
'The book suddenly fell off my hand'

There are also some process verbs which have been originated from stative verbs (see **3.5** and **4.2**). They can also take this prefix but in certain contexts.

11. **iŋsin**- 'become cold'
khəŋ-iŋ iŋ-sil-lək-i
RED-cold cold-IN-DEIC-SAM
'It becomes cold suddenly'

12. **piksin**- 'become small'
mɑ gə jeŋnə-bə-də nəŋ khəŋ-pik pik-sin-khə-re
he-ASS compare-NMZ-LOC you RED-small small-IN-DEF-PERF- SAM
'You become relatively small when compared to him'

In (11) the verb **iŋ-sin**-'become cold' with the reduplicative prefix **khəŋ**- 'suddenly' implies that there is a reference on which the speaker presupposes a situation which might be cool or hot and compared to it there is a sudden change of climate. The occurrence of **khəŋ**- with the verb **pik-sin**-'become small' in sentence (12) implies that with reference to a bigger man the referent becomes relatively small. In other words, it shows a comparison between two persons of different heights.

The prefix **khəŋ**- has semantic restriction with stative verbs. This is because something or somebody cannot acquire a quality suddenly *e.g.* somebody or something cannot become big or small, tall or short instantly. Of course, there are some stative verbs which are temporal in nature *e.g.* **kəŋ-** 'be dry', **phə-** 'be cured of an illness'. They can take the prefix **khəŋ-**.

13. **phə-** 'be cured of an illness/get relief from pain'

a. hidak əsi ca-bə-dəgi əi kok cik-pə khəŋ-phə phə-re
medicine this eat-NMZ-ABL I headache RED-cure cure-PERF-SAM
'I have got relief from headache suddenly after taking this medicine'

b. pau-du ta-bə-də mə-ma-du ənabə khəŋ-phə
news-DEM hear-NMZ-LOC 3PP-mother-DEM illness RED-relieve

phə-re
relieve- PERF-SAM
'The mother was relieved from anxiety instantly on hearing the good news'

14. **kəŋ-** 'be dry'
ləimai-də ta-bə petrol-du khəŋ-kəŋ kəŋ-khə-re
floor-LOC fall-NMZ petrol-DEM RED-dry dry-DEF-PERF-SAM
'The petrol on the floor has dried up instantly'

Both sentences (13a and b) show happenings which take place suddenly due to some cause. But the degree of suddenness is slightly different. In (a) the referent gets relief from headache quickly after taking medicine but not instantly. In other words, the relief from headache may take place after a few minutes, *i.e.* the reaction/effect of the medicine does not work instantly. On the other hand, the relief, which the mother gets from anxiety in (b), comes instantly when she heard the good news. In both cases, the prefixation of **khəŋ-** is acceptable. An event or happening may take place within a short time and beyond one's expectation and in such situations the adverb **jamnə thunə** 'very soon' is used.

15. **kəŋ-** 'be dry'
pukhri-si jam-nə thu-nə kəŋ-ŋi
pond-DEM much-ADV quick-ADV dry up-SAM
'The pond dries up quickly'

16. **cau-** 'be big, grow'
əŋaŋ-si jam-nə thu-nə cau-i
child-DEM much-ADV quick-ADV big-SAM
'The child grows up quickly (unusually)'

koi-: It is derived from the verbal root **koi-** 'go or move round'. When attached to a verbal root it gives the meaning of 'around, everywhere, without purpose or aimlessly'.

koi-raŋ laŋ-ŋi	make noise without rhyme and reason
koi-rau lau-i	shout indiscriminately/without rhyme and reason
koi-thi thi	search/look for in every possible way
koi-sen sen-nə-i	take care of (someone) in every possible way
koi-rot lot-li	hide in every possible place
koi-tan tan-nə-i	chase every where
koi-khom khom-mi	collect from everywhere

17. **pu-** 'carry'
    ma-nə cət-pə-də əŋaŋ-du koi-pu pu-i
    he-NOM go-NMZ-LOC child-DEM RED-carry carry-SAM
    'He carries the child with him wherever he goes'

18. **cen-** 'run'
    əŋaŋ-du sumaŋ-də koi-cen cel-li
    child-DEM lawn-LOC RED-run run-SAM
    'The child runs around in the lawn'

It may be noted that **koi-** cannot occur with stative verbs because of the semantic constraint of the prefix, *e.g.*

*koi-thum thum-mi	around + sweet
*koi-nuŋ nusi	around + love

Non-grammaticalized prefixes *i*-, *tə*-, *suk*-: The non-grammatizalized prefixes that are involved in the process of reduplication of Manipuri verbs are as follows:

Prefix *i*-: The prefix **i-** when attached to a verbal root gives the meaning 'general, anything, almost'.

19. **ja-** 'agree/accept'
    əi-di i-ja ja-i
    I-PART RED-agree agree-SAM
    'I agree with anything'

20. **segai-** 'be torn'
    phi-si i-se segai-re
    cloth-DEM RED-torn torn-PERF-SAM
    'The cloth is almost torn'

Another function of the prefix **i-** is to show superlative degree with stative verbs where the comparison is among similar category and the noun phrase of the sentence takes **-nə** 'comparative marker'.

21. **nem**- 'be short'
əŋaŋ əsi-nə i-nem nem-mi
child this-CMP RED-short short-SAM
'This child is the shortest (among the boys)'

22. **wa**- 'be tired'
əi ŋəsi-nə i-wa wa-i
I today-CMP RED-tired tired-SAM
'I feel most tired today (compared to other days)'

The prefix **i**- can also occur in negative environment where it gives the meaning of 'not much'. It may be noted that the first syllable of a verb in case of disyllabic or polysyllabic verbs reduplicate, *e.g.* in **segai**- in sentence (20).

23. **ca**- 'eat'
məhak-ti həi i-ca ca-de
he-PART fruit RED-eat eat-NEG-SAM
'He does not eat fruit much'

24. **pen**- 'be satisfied'
əi ma-gi thəbək-si i-pen pen-de
I he-GEN work-DEM RED-satisfy satisfy-NEG-SAM
'I am not much satisfied with his work'

Prefix *tə*-: The prefixation of **tə**- to some stative verbs gives the meaning of a greater degree. When the verb is reduplicated the prefix **tə**- occurs two times unlike the other reduplicative prefixes.

25. **nəu**- 'be fresh/look young'
nupi-məca əsi tə-nəu tə-nəu-ri
woman-small this RED-young RED-young-PROG-SAM
'This girl is still very young'

26. **seŋ**- 'be real/be confirmed'
ma-gi mə-ma ləi-tə-re hai-bə-si tə-seŋ
he-GEN 3PP-mother be-NEG-PERF-SAM connector RED-confirm

tə-seŋ-ŋe
RED-confirm-PERF-SAM
'It has been confirmed that his mother has expired'

Prefix *suk*-: The prefix **suk**- always occurs in a negative environment and it means 'never'. It can occur with all classes of verbs: action, stative and process.

27. **lak**- 'come'
məhak ŋəraŋ məphəm əsi-də suk-lak lak-te
he yesterday place this-LOC RED-come come-NEG-SAM
'He never came here yesterday'

28. **pan**- 'bear fruit'
həinəu pambi əsi həinəu suk-pan pan-de
mango tree this mango RED-bear bear-NEG-SAM
'This mango tree never bears fruit'

4.2 Suffixes

Derivative suffixes that are attached to verbal roots may be classified into two: grammaticalized suffixes and non-grammaticalized suffixes.

Grammaticalized Suffixes: There are twelve grammaticalized suffixes established in the Manipuri language. Four of them are restricted in the sense that they can occur with certain verb groups only while the remaining eight suffixes are non-restricted *i.e.* they can occur freely with any type of verb.

Restricted grammaticalized suffixes *-thət, -thek, -khai, -hət*: The restricted grammaticalized suffixes are derived from destructive verbs and addition of these suffixes gives the meaning 'to do something forcefully in order to destroy'. Sometimes, the meaning of destruction is not seen in some cases.

The verbal roots from which the destructive suffixes are originated are **thət**- 'pluck' > -**tht**, **thek**- 'break' > -**thek**, **khai**- 'cut' > -**khai** and **hat**- 'kill' > -**hət**. The verbal roots to which the first three destructive suffixes are to be attached may be analysed from three points of view by the binary feature as (i) ± Agentive, (ii) ± Force and (3) ± Separation.

± Agentive: Almost all the verbal roots, which can take the destructive suffixes, are action verbs (see **3.2**). Hence, they are agentive (see **3.4**) *i.e.*, + Agentive. However, there are some process verbs which can take the destructive suffixes as shown below:

niŋkhai-	shatter
cekkhai-	crack
khamdek-	scar/burn
satkai-	bloom
ciŋkhai-	crack
pokkhai-	burst
cathət-	have ulcer, etc.

± Force: The application of force while performing an act varies according to the acts. For instance, tearing off a paper **segai**- takes less force than tearing off a thick paper or cloth.

Similarly, the amount of force applied in performing the act **sik-tət-** 'pinch' is much less than that of **nəi-thət-** 'squeeze/crush'. The verbs which are – Agentive are – Force.

± **Separation**: The action of the destructive verbs may result in separation or sometimes not. But the normal shape of the objects is broken. The verb **jan-thət-** 'cut apart', **thudek-** 'break a stick', **thugai-** 'break glass', **cik-thət-** 'bite', **cəp-thət-** 'cut with scissors', **soi-dət-** 'cut with knife', **segai-** 'tear apart', etc. are verbs that result in separation by cutting with a sharp weapon or by biting with teeth and by hitting on a hard surface. On the other hand, verbs like **ciŋ-thət-** 'pull hard to break', **ləi-thət-** 'twist hard to break', **ləi-thek-** 'twist hard', **net-thət-** 'trample', etc. do not give the result of separation. They simply give a broken shape of the thing to which the above actions are applied. In other words, it can be said that destructive suffixes may or may not retain their original meaning when they are attached to different action verbs as they have undergone the process of gramaticalization. The loss of meaning, if there is, may be partial or complete.

Suffix *-thət*: It is originated from the verb **thət-** 'pluck'. When it is attached to destructive verbs, it gives the meaning 'to destroy by cutting sharply or pluck by breaking' (Madhubala, 1997). The suffix has three phonologically conditioned allomorphs as **-tət** ~ **dət** ~ **thət**. **-tət** occurs after a verbal root which begins with fricative and aspirated stop sounds and end in a voiceless sound *e.g.* **phuk-tət-** 'pull out', **khot-tət-** 'scratch', **set-tət-** 'tear apart', **hut-tət-** 'bore a hole', etc. **-dət** occurs in the same situation but the final sound of the verbal root is voiced *e.g.* **soi-dət-** 'cut apart', **phan-dət-** 'mow', **su-dət-** 'pound', **thom-dət-** 'hit hard'. **-thət** occurs elsewhere *e.g.* **ciŋ-thət-** 'pull hard to break' **ləi-thət-** 'twist hard to break', **cəp-thət-** 'cut apart with scissors', etc.

29. **phuk-tət-** 'pull out'
napi-siŋ-du loi-nə phuk-tət-lu
grass-PL-DEM finish-ADV pull-DEST-COM
'Pull out all the grass (to make the area clean)'

30. **phu-dət-** 'beat'
huranbə-du mi-jam-nə phu-dət-le
thief-DEM man-many-NOM beat-DEST-PERF-SAM
'The thief was beaten by the people'

31. **khai-dət-** 'cut'
mairen-si əi-nə khai-dət-le
pumpkin-DEM I-NOM cut-DEST-PERF-SAM
'I have cut this pumpkin apart'

The verb **phuk-tət-** 'pull out' in (29) results in separation when the destructive suffix is attached to it. The meaning of the verb implies that an agent carries out the action of separating the plant from the soil and it also implies force. The verb **phu-dət-**'beat' in (30) implies an agent and force is applied in the act of beating but it does not result in separation. The verb

khai-dət-'cut apart' in (31) implies an agent and necessary force applied to cut apart the pumpkin and finally it results in separation. Verbs like **mut-thət-** 'extinguish' may mean both burning fire and an electric current. It needs an agent in both types of action and it finally results in separation in the sense that a burning fire is stopped and an electric current is cut off. But the force applied in the actions is different. In case of power cut, no force is used while in extinguishing a fire like burning of a house, necessary force is applied. However, in case of putting off a small fire like burning of firewood used for cooking does not need much force. Another verb **ca-thət** - 'have ulcer' in *I have mouth ulcer* may give a different meaning from others in the sense that it lacks an agent (an animate agent see **3.4**) it does not result in separation but the normal shape of the lip is broken. On the other hand, **net-thət** - 'trample' implies an agent but it does apply force in the sense that the child trampled the flower without notice while playing and the act of trampling may or may not result in separation. It depends on the weight of the child and the type of thing as well.

Suffix ***-thek***: The suffix is derived from the destructive verb **thek-** 'break a stick with hands'. The addition of this suffix to destructive verbs implies to do something hard in order to break or destry the normal shape of something. The suffix has also three phonologically conditioned allomorphs as **-tek ~ dek ~ thek** and the conditioning factor is same with **-thət**. Verbs which take **-tek** are **phuk-tek-** 'pull out', **thup-tek-** 'fold improperly'. They are very few in number. Verbs with **-dek** are **thudek-** 'break', **su-dek-** 'pound', **kham-dek-** 'scar', **phu-dek-** 'beat to break', etc. Verbs with **-thek** are **nəm-thek-** 'press hard', **ciŋ-thek-** 'pull hard to break', **ləi-thek-** 'twist hard to break', **nən-thek-** 'press hard', **kau-thek-** 'kick hard', etc.

32. **ciŋ-thek-** 'pull hard'
uri-si əŋaŋ-nə ciŋ-thek-e
creeper-DEM child-NOM pull-DEST-PERF-SAM
'The child pulled the creeper'

33. **ləi- thek-** 'twist'
tu-sin-bə-də əi-gi khoŋ ləi-thek-e
fall-IN-NMZ-CAUS I-GEN leg twist-DEST-PERF-SAM
'My leg got twisted when I stumbled'

34. **nəi- thek-** 'stir'
iŋkhol-gi məna-məsiŋ-si sən-nə nəi-thek-e
kitchen garden-GEN vegetable-DEM COW-NOM stir-DEST-PERF-SAM
'The vegetables in the kitchen garden have been trampled by the cow'

The verb **ciŋ-thek-**'pull hard', **ləi-thek-**'twist' and **nəi-thek-** 'stir', are all agentive and force is applied but they do not result in separation. The normal shape of the referent nouns e.g. creeper in (32), leg in (33), and vegetables/plants in (34) are broken. On the other hand, **kham-dek-** 'have scar mark after a burn' is not agentive.

Suffix ***-khai***: The destructive suffix **-khai** is originated from the verbal root **khai-** 'cut'.

The suffixation of **-khai** to action verbs gives the meaning 'to cut or break something'. It has also three allomorphic variations as **-kai ~ gai ~ khai** and their distribution is also same to **-thət**. Verbs with **-kai** are **sik-kai**- 'pinch', **satkai**- 'bloom'(process verb), **phək-kai**- 'pull apart'. Verbs with **-gai** are **theŋ-gai**- 'collide', **phu-gai**- 'beat', **se-gai**- 'tear apart', **su-gai**- 'pound to break', **ho-gai**- 'scratch', **hən-gai**- 'prick', **kho-gai**- 'scratch', etc. Verbs with **-khai** are **tək-khai**- 'rub hard on a surface', **len-khai**- 'cut with a sharp blade', **təu-khai**- 'dig in the soil', **nəi-khai**- 'stir', etc.

35. **sik-kai**- 'pinch'
    ləisabi-du-nə mə-mai-dəgi uriŋ-siŋ-du sik-kai
    girl-DEM-NOM 3PP-face-ABL pimple-PL-DEM pinch-DEST-SAM
    'The girl pinches the pimples on her face'

36. **su-gai**- 'pound'
    əi-nə morok su-gai-re
    I-NOM chilli pound-DEST-PERF-SAM
    'I have pounded the chilli (and made powder of it)'

37. **ləŋ-khai**- 'throw violently
    nupa-du-nə kon-siŋ-du ləŋ-khai-rəm-mi
    man-DEM-NOM utensil-PL-DEM throw-DEST-COMP-SAM
    'The man threw all the utensils violently'

The verb **sik-kai**- in (35) implies that there is an agent to perform the act of squeezing and no force is applied and the result is also not separation. **su-gai**- 'pound' in (36) implies an agent and necessary force is applied and the action results in separation. **ləŋ-khai**- in (37) has an agent and the action is done violently by applying full force to break. The result may be separation if the utensils are broken and if it is not, then, the result may not be separation. But the thing is not in its place (separated from its own place). It may cause the breaking down of the normal shape of the utensils.

Sufix *-hət*: The suffix **-hət** is derived from the verbal root **hat**- 'kill'. The suffix has restricted use with some verbs and the suffixation of **-hət** to the verbal roots give the meaning of superiority in most cases.

38. **tu-hət**- 'exploit'
    inak khun-bə-nə lairə-bə-bu tu-hət-li
    rich-NMZ-NOM poor-NMZ-ACC fall-SUP-SAM
    'The rich exploits the poor'

39. **nəm-hət**- 'supress'
    tombə-nə əŋaŋ-du-bu ədum nəm-hət-li
    Tomba-NOM child-DEM-ACC always press-SUP-SAM
    'Tomba always suppresses the child'

40. **cəi-hət-** 'scold'
nə-kha tha-bə-siŋ-bu ədum-nə cəi-hət-kənu
2PP-down be-NMZ-PL-ACC like-ADV scold-SUP-PROH
'Do not scold your juniors like that'

The verbs **tu-hət**-'exploit' , **nəm-hət**-'suppress' and **cəi-hət**-'scold' show superiority or power possessed by the agent and exercise it on others. Verbs like **sum-hət**-'keep under spell' and **ka-hət**- 'become dark due to exposure to sunlight' also imply the meaning of superiority indirectly.

Non-restricted grammatilized suffixes-*kən, -lək, -thok, -pi, -mən, -həu, -niŋ, -təu*: There are eight non-restricted grammaticalized suffixes in Manipuri which are derived from verbal roots. They are non-restricted in the sense that they can be attached to any class of verb. They are **-kən** 'habitual', **-lək** 'deictic', **-thok** 'outward', **-pi** 'benefactive', **-mən** 'excessive', **-həu** 'inceptive', **-niŋ** 'wish', and **-təu** 'do'.

Suffix *-kən*: The suffix **-kən** is originated from the verb **kən-** 'be strong, be good in doing something' and in course of time, it has developed into a grammaticalized suffix and the meaning changes to habitual. The suffix has two variations **-kən ~ gən**. **-kən** occurs after unaspirated voiceless stops /**p**/, /**t**/, /**k**/ and **-gən** occurs elsewhere. **-kən ~ gən** changes to **-kəl ~ gəl** when followed by /**l**/.

41. **ŋaŋ- gən** 'be talkative'
ma-di wa ŋaŋ-gəl-li
he-PART speech talk-HAB-SAM
'He is talkative'

42. **ŋəŋ- gən** 'hum usually'
ma-di cak thoŋ-bə-də isəi ŋəŋ-gəl-li
he-PART rice cook-NMZ-LOC song hum-HAB-SAM
'She usually hums songs while cooking'

43. **soi- gən** 'make mistake usually'
ma-nə təu-bə thəbək-ti soi-gəl-li
he-NOM do-NMZ work-PART mistake-HAB-SAM
'He usually makes mistakes'

The verbs **ŋaŋ- gən-** 'be talkative', **ŋəŋ- gən-** 'hum usually' and **soi-gən-** 'make mistake usually'show habitual act or event. On the other hand, the suffixation of **-kən ~ gən** to stative and process verbs like **kai-gən**- 'be breakable', **həu-gən**-'grow easily', **tek-kən**-'be breakable' and **saŋ-gən**- 'grow quickly'show physical property of the object referred. Verbs like **siŋ-gən**- 'be wise in general', **noi-gən**-'be fat usually', **məkok ləi-gən**-'be brainy usually' refer to a quality which is generally acquired by a group of people. The verb **thum-gən**- 'be flooded usually' refers to a condition which generally occurs in low lying area.

Sufix *-lək*: The suffix **-lək** is originated from the verb **lak-** 'come'. The suffixation of **-lək** to a verbal root involves both space and time in the sense that it implies physical displacement as well as time continuation. Three semantic parameters were suggested by Bhat and Ningomba (1997: 186). The motion orientation of the suffix **-lək** is towards the speaker, the place of occurrence is away from the speaker's place and the relative position of the event precedes the motion. The suffix has five variations as **-lək ~ rək ~ pək ~ mək ~ŋək.**

44. **ləi- rək-** 'buy'
i-ma-nə kəithen-dəgi ŋa ləi-rək-i
1PP-mother-NOM market-ABL fish buy-DEIC-SAM
'My mother bought fish from the market'

45. **jeŋ-ŋək-** 'watch'
əi sinema-si benarəs-tə jeŋ-ŋək-i
I cinema-DEM Benaras-LOC watch-DEIC-SAMßßß
'I have watched the film at Benaras'

46. **pa- rək-** 'read'
əi-di əŋaŋ oi-riŋəi-də wari lairik jam-nə pa-rək-i
I-PART child be-SPFD-LOC story book much-ADV read-DEIC-SAM
'I read many story books in my childhood days'

The verbs **ləi-rək-** 'buy' and **jeŋ-ŋək-** 'watch' imply physical displacement. The action is performed away from the speaker and at some other place. Hence, the actions occurs in space while the verb in **pa-rək-** 'read' implies an action or event that is occurred in a specific time which is away from the present *i.e.* past time.

Suffix *-thok*: The suffix **-thok** is derived from the verbal root **thok-** 'go out'. The meaning of the verb is retained in the suffix while denoting directionals. It generally goes with directional verbs and the suffixation of **-thok** means outward directional. The suffix has three variations as **-tok ~ dok ~ thok**. Verbal roots with **-tok** are **sat-tok-** 'bloom fully', **phat-tok-** 'give way', **khet-tok-** 'scratch out', **sit-tok-** 'spit out', etc. Verbal roots with **-dok** are **səu-dok-** 'melt out', **phau-dok-** 'go through', **san-dok-** 'lend something to others', **khən-dok-** 'select a particular item from a group', **həi-dok-** 'pour out', etc. Verbal roots with **-thok** are **ciŋ-thok-** 'pull out', **in-thok-** 'push out', **ləŋ-thok-** 'throw out', **pu-thok-** 'carry out', **ləu-thok-** 'take out', etc.

47. **ləŋ-thok-** 'throw'
əi-nə phi segai-bə-siŋ-du ləŋ-thok-khə-re
I-NOM cloth tear off-NMZ-PL-DEM throw-OUT-DEF-PERF-SAM
'I have thrown out the torn clothes'

48. **ciŋ-thok-** 'pull out'
əi-nə tebəl-du ciŋ-thok-i
I-NOM table-DEM pull-OUT-SAM
'I pulled out the table'

49. **sət-tok-** 'pull out'
ma-nə tiŋkhəŋ sət-tok-i
he-NOM thorn pull-OUT-SAM
'He pulled out the thorn'

Suffix *-pi*: The suffix is homophonous with **-pi** ~ **bi** 'honorific'. It is derived from the verb **pi**- 'give'. The verb has undergone a process of grammaticalization and it gradually loses its syntactic freedom and develops into a suffix. The semantic structure of **pi**- 'give' is to be generous of doing something. The generosity of the agent is received by someone else and the person who receives the generosity is benefited by the act of giving or doing something and thus, the suffix **-pi** has attained its meaning as 'benefactive'.

50a. əi-nə memə-də lairik əmə pi
I-NOM Mema-DAT book one give-SAM
'I give a book to Mema.'

b. əi-nə lairik əmə ləi-rəgə memə-də pi
I-NOM book one buy-CPART Mema-DAT give-SAM
'I bought a book and gave it to Mema.'

c. əi-nə memə-gidəmək lairik əmə lə-i/ləi-bi
I-NOM Mema-for book one buy-SAM/buy-BEN-SAM
'I buy a book for Mema.'

d. əi-nə memə-gi lairik əmə ləi-bi
I-NOM Mema-GEN book one buy-BEN-SAM
'I buy a book for Mema.'

e. əi-nə memə-gi lairik əmə ləi
I-NOM Mema-for book one buy-SAM
'I buy a book for Mema.'

The first two sentences have **pi**- 'give' as a main verb in the sentences while in (c) the structure of the sentence has been changed. The main verb is **ləi**- 'buy' or **ləi-bi** 'buy for someone'. The noun sequence **-gidəmək** 'for' has shown the benefactive meaning which makes the verb **ləi**- 'buy' enable to stand alone without the benefactive suffix **-pi**. In other words, it can be said that **-pi** ~ **bi** is optional with the beneficiary **-gidəmək**. The suffix **-dəmək** can also be dropped from the sequence **-gidəmək** and only **-gi** is remained in the surface form and in such cases the main verb optionally takes the benefactive suffix **-pi** ~ **bi** as seen in sentence (d. and e.) while keeping the meaning of the sentence intact. Here we are dealing with an instance of grammaticalization whereby a lexical item, the verb 'give' assumes a grammatical meaning, that of expressing a 'prepositional notion', 'for' or 'to' in certain contexts, a process that has occurred in a number of languages worldwide (Bernd, 1991: 2).

The suffix **-pi** has two variations as **-pi** ~ **bi**. **-pi** occurs after unaspirated voiceless stop sounds /**p**/, /**t**/, /**k**/ while **-bi** occurs after voiced sounds.

51. **tak-pi-** 'teach'
    əi-nə əŋaŋ-siŋ-du lairik tak-pi
    I-NOM child-PL-DEM book teach-BEN-SAM
    'I teach the children'

51. **tak-pi-** 'teach'
    əi-nə əŋaŋ-siŋ-du lairik tak-pi
    I-NOM child-PL-DEM book teach-BEN-SAM
    'I teach the children'

52. **khak-pi-** 'keep one's share'
    ensaŋ-du ma-gi khərə khak-pi-ju
    curry-DEM he-GEN some spare-BEN-COM
    'Spare some curry for him'

Extensive use of suffix *-pi ~ bi*: Although the semantic component of **-pi** always denotes to do something good for someone, it fails in some cases. The verb **pi-** 'give' means generosity of someone. But this meaning is sometimes lost when it goes with certain action verbs like **phu-** 'beat', **hat-** 'kill', **net-** 'trample', etc.

53. **phu-bi-** 'beat'
    mə-khoi-nə əŋaŋ-du phu-bi-re
    he-PL-NOM child-DEM beat-BEN-PERF-SAM
    'They beat the child'

54. **hat-pi-** 'kill'
    ma-gi mə-ca-du sək khəŋ-də-bə-siŋ-nə hat-pi-khə-re
    he-GEN 3PP-offspring-DEM face know-NEG-NMZ-PL-NOM kill BEN-DEF-PERF-SAM
    'Some unknown persons killed his son'

The verbs **phu-bi-**'beat' in (53) and **hat-pi-**'kill' in (54) do not necessarily mean benefactive instead of the attachment of the benefative suffix **-pi** ~ **bi**. The reason for the incapability of giving the meaning of generosity is due to the semantic structure of the destructive verbs for one cannot be generous by the above actions. It can be concluded that verbs of destruction cannot give the meaning of generosity and here the mood of the speaker's side can also be examined. The actions above are not necessary and can be avoided. In such cases the suffix **-pi** ~ **bi** is used to show actions which are unwanted.

Another use of the suffix **-pi** ~ **bi** can be seen in the following sentences.

55. **ca-bi-** 'eat'
    əi morok-si ca-bi-ge
    I chilli-DEM eat-BEN-INT
    '(I accept the challenge that) I will eat this chilli'

56. **lek-pi-** 'hold night'
    təmnə-i hai-bə jum-du-də əi əhiŋ lek-pi-ge
    haunt-SAM say-NMZ house-DEM-LOC I night hold-BEN-INT
    '(I accept the challenge that) I will hold night in the haunted house'

The verb **cabi**-'eat' in (55) denotes a challenge from the speaker's side. The speaker is challenging that he can eat the chilli. In the second sentence, the speaker challenges that he can hold a night in the house that is haunted.

Suffix *-mən*: The suffix is originated from the verb **mən**- 'be excessive' which is very rarely used. The suffixation of **-mən** to a verbal root gives the meaning 'to do something excessively or do something out of one's control'.

57. **mən**- 'be excessive'

    a. nəŋ ca-bə-də jam-nə məl-le
       you eat-NMZ-LOC much-ADV excessive-PERF-SAM
       'you are too excessive in eating.'

    b. nəŋ jam-nə ca-məl-le
       you much-ADV eat-EXC-PERF-SAM
       'You are too excessive in eating'

In sentence (a) the verb that carries the aspect marker is **mən**-'be excessive' which changes to **məl**- when followed by **-le**. In (b) the main verb of the sentence is **ca**- which takes the excessive suffix **-mən** as well as the aspect marker. With stative verbs it means 'excess of something'

58. **kui**- 'be long (of time)/take much time'
    nəŋ-nə cak thoŋ-bə-si kui-mən-khə-re
    you-NOM ice cook-NMZ-DEM long-EXC-DEF-PERF-SAM
    'You take much time in cooking (finish it quickly)'

59. **theŋ**- 'be late'
    nəŋ jahəu theŋ-məl-le
    you get up late-EXC-PERF-SAM
    'You get up very late (try to be early)'

Suffix *-həu*: The suffix **-həu** is derived from the verb **həu**- 'start'. It is discussed in detail under the head multifunctional suffixes in the same section.

Suffix *-niŋ*: The suffix **-niŋ** is originated from the verb **niŋ-** 'wish' and the meaning is retained in the suffix also. The suffixation of **-niŋ** to a verb means 'wish to do something or become something' (for more detail of **-niŋ** see **2.3**).

60. **jau-** 'join'
    əi n.c.c. jau-niŋ-ŋi
    I NCC join-wish-SAM
    'I want to join NCC'

61. **waŋ-** 'be tall'
    əi nəŋ-gum-nə waŋ-niŋ-ŋi
    I you-like-CMP tall-wish-SAM
    'I want to be tall like you'

Suffix *-təu*: The suffix is originated from the verbal root **təu-** 'do'. In the sentence level, the suffix is usually followed by **-ri** and **-re**.

62. **təu-** 'do'
    əi thəbək təu-ri
    I work do-PROG-SAM
    'I am working.'

63. əi thəbək təu-gə-dəu-ri
    I work do-POT-do-PROG-SAM
    'I am going to do (some) work.'

In (62) the verb **tu-** 'do' occurs as a main verb in the sentence while in (63) it becomes a grammaticalized suffix. English has also the same situation as given by Palmer (1965:163) as cited by Bernd *et al.*, (1991:46).

a. *Henry is going to town.*
b. *The rain is going to come.*

According to Palmer, the verb 'is going to' in both sentences have considerable differences in meaning that the two meanings are 'synchronically unrelated'. Again, Bernd *et al.*, (1991) quoted Jesperson from A Modern English Grammar on Historical Principles (1911: 217). He described the situation like this – Sentences like (b) have developed historically from sentences like (a) and that before the fifteenth century (b) is unlikely to have been altered. Palmer again give reason about the development of (b) as an instance of grammaticalization: the verb of motion *be going to* occurring in (a) has given rise to a future tense, actually the 'purest' future form of English in (b).

The analysis of Manipuri verb **təu-** 'do' in (63) and **-təu** as a suffix in (64) may be done from the view of English verb *is going to*. Along with the following aspect marker the grammaticalized suffix **-təu** has also developed into an aspect marker as **-təu-ri** and **-təu-re** 'is going to'. The different meanings of the two suffixes are discussed below.

The verb form with the suffix **-təu-ri** in (64) may be examined minutely. Here another suffix **-kə** 'potential' is found to have occurred just after the verbal root. But now-a-days, this construction is rarely found in spoken form and it is retained in written form only. In spoken form, this **-kə** is almost dropped. Still, it is found in the underlying sentence structure. The verb form after the deletion of **-kə** in (64) will be as **-təu-dəu-ri** 'is going to do' (for deletion see **4.3)**

Another point that is worth to be mentioned here in the variations of **-təu** as **-təu ~ dəu** is, as a general rule **-təu** occurs after morphemes that end in unaspirated voiceless stops **/p/, /t/, /k/** and **-dəu** follows morphemes that end in voiced sounds.

Now, coming to the difference in meaning between the two aspect markers **-təu-ri** and **-təu-re**, consider some examples. The sequence **-təu-ri** 'is going to' has different meanings when it occurs with different verb classes. When it is attached to action verbs, it denotes a planning.

64. **thoŋ-** 'cook'
ŋəsi-di tombi-nə cak thoŋ-dəu-ri
today-PART Tombi-NOM rice cook-do-PROG-SAM
'Today Tombi is going to cook'

65. **ləi-** 'buy'
həjeŋ-di əi phurit əmə ləi-dəu-ri
tomorrow-PART I shirt one buy-do-PROG-SAM
'Tomorrow I am going to buy a shirt'

The examples given above have a temporal adverb. Sentence (64) implies that 'Tombi' is going to cook for today only and that she does not cook regularly in the house. In sentence (65), the referent is going to buy a shirt for the day only and it implies that the action is occasional. The adverbs, in one sense, show an implication of the occasional happening or planning.

Another sense implied by the suffixation of **-təu-ri** to action verbs is when the referent responds as a denial to something asked/proposed against his routine-work. As for instance, when cooking is the referent's inevitable routine work in the morning then, as a denial, he may use the following sentence if he is asked/proposed to do some other work.

66. əi əjuk-tə cak thoŋ-dəu-ri
I morning-LOC rice cook-do-PROG-SAM
'I am going to cook in the morning (so I'll be unable to do another work)'

The suffixation of the sequence suffix **-təu-ri** with stative and process verbs gives another reading which is totally different from action verbs. They show a kind of prediction or assumption with the two verb types.

67. **phəɟə-** 'be beautiful'
    əŋaŋ-si məsək phəɟə-dəu-ri
    child-DEM 3PP-face beautiful-do-PROG-SAM
    'The child is going to be beautiful'

68. **isiŋ cau-** 'be flooded'
    kumsi-di isiŋ cau-dəu-ri
    this year-PART flood-do-PROG-SAM
    'There will be flood this year'

In (67), the speaker assumes about the child's beauty in future as he might have noticed some particular feature in the anatomy of the child. Similarly, in (68), the speaker predicts about a flood as there might be heavy rainfall.

The sequence suffix **-təu-re** have the meaning 'is ready to do something or is likely to happen shortly'. Both **-təu-ri** and **-təu-re** denote an action or happening which is going to take place in the future. But the sense of futurity is different in the sense that **-təu-re** is closer to the realization than **-təu-ri**. In other words, it can be said that **-təu-re** has a higher probability of realization than **-təu-ri**.

69. **noŋ-cu** - 'rain'
    noŋ-cu-dəu-re pərəp pərəp cət-həu-rə-si
    rain-do-PERF-SAM quickly go-INCP-PROS-SUG
    'It is about to rain, so let's go quickly.'

70. **tho-rək-** 'come out'
    əi tho-rək-təu-re ŋaihak-təŋ ŋai-rəm-mu
    I come out-DEIC-do-PERF-SAM a while-only wait-COMP-COM
    'I am coming out, wait for a few minutes only.'

71. **cət-** 'go, visit'
    nira taŋ təranithoi-də məhisur cət-təu-ri
    Neera date twelve-LOC Mysore go-do-PERF-SAM
    'Neera is ready to go to Mysore on the 12th of this month.'

The verbs in the above examples show a near future that an action or a happening is about to be realized while sentence (71) is worth to be discussed. The referent is planning to go to Mysore within this month and her plan is about to be realized or it is confirmed on the 12th of that month and another implication is that the speaker is also aware of the plan.

Both suffixes can occur in negative environment also.

72. **jau-** 'join'
    pisək-ti ŋəsi cak ca-nə-bə jau-roi-dəu-ri
    Pishak-PART today rice eat-REC-NMZ join-NPOT-do-PROG-SAM

'Today Pishak is not going to attend the feast.'

73. **skul ka-** 'attend school'
əŋaŋ-si ŋəsi skul ka-roi-dəu-re
child-DEM today school attend-N.POT-do-PERF-SAM
'The child is not going to attend school today.'

Verbal Derivative Suffixes: Non-grammaticalized suffixes may be studied under the following sub-heads:

(1) Deictic suffixes
(2) Multifunctional suffixes
(3) Suffixes **-sin**, **-thok**, **-khət** and **-thə**
(4) Modifiers
(5) Other derivative suffixes.

Deictic Suffixes ***-rə, -ru, -rək, -khi***: The notion of deixis (which is merely the Greek word for 'pointing' or 'indicating' – it has become a technical term of grammatical theory) is introduced to handle the 'orientational' features of language which are relative to the time and place of utterance (Lyons, 1968: 275). In linguistics, a deictic expression is an expression that refers to the personal, temporal, or spatial aspect of an utterance, and whose meaning therefore depends on the context in which it is used (Wikipedia). Bhat and Ningomba (1997: 172) observed three different semantic parameters which help to differentiate between the four suffixes (**-rə**, **-ru**, **-rək**, **-khi**) as (1) motion or orientation of the event ('towards' versus 'away') from the speaker, (2) place of occurrence of the event ('at the place of the speaker' versus 'at a place which is away from him') and (3) relative positions of these two (event 'preceding' versus 'following' the motion of orientation).

Suffixes	Motion of orientation	Place of occurrence	Relative position
-rə	towards the speaker	at the speaker's place	event follows the motion
-ru	away from the speaker	away from the speaker's place	event follows the motion
-rək	towards the speaker	away from the speaker's place	event precedes the motion
-khi	away from the speaker	at the speaker's place	event precedes the motion

It may be noted that **-khi** will come under the sub-section Multi-functional Suffixes next to deictic suffixes. Another point to be noted is that deictic suffixes can be attached to any given verbal base (Bhat & Ningomba, 1997: 172) is not true (see **3.2**)

Suffix ***-lə***: The semantic structure of the suffix **-lə** is to come and perform an action at the speaker's place with the event following the motion. It involves physical displacement of the agent. As the suffix indicates, it generally goes with action verbs only, not with stative and process verbs. The suffix has six allomorphic variations as **-lə ~ rə ~ pə ~mə ~ ŋə ~ə**

(i) -*lə*: it follows morphemes that end in /**n**/ and /**t**/, /**n**/ changes to /**l**/ and the suffix **-lə** follows it.

kət-lə	offer + deictic
phot-lə	mend + deictic
khəl-lə	select + deictic, etc.

(ii) -*rə*: it comes after morphemes that end in voiced sounds.

ta-rə	listen to + deictic
su-rə	work + deictic
phəu-rə	dry in the sun + deictic, etc.

(iii) -*pə*: it occurs after morphemes that end in /**p**/.

nəp-pə	stick + deictic
lep-pə	stand + deictic
hap-pə	put + deictic, etc.

(iv) -*mə*: it follows morphemes that end in /**m**/.

təm-mə	learn + deictic
tum-mə	sleep + deictic
khom-mə	collect + deictic, etc.

(v) -*ŋə*: it follows morphemes that end in /**ŋ**/.

jeŋ-ŋə	watch + deictic
haŋ-ŋə	open + deictic
thoŋ-ŋə	cook + deictic, etc.

(vi) -ə: it occurs after morphemes that end in /**k**/.

nek-ə	hire + deictic
hek-ə	pluck + deictic
khik-ə	sprinkle + deictic, etc.

74. **ca-** 'eat'

bino	horen	nuŋdaŋ	əi-khoi-də	cak	ca-rə-gəni
Bino	after sometime	night	I-PL-LOC	cooked rice	eat-DEIC-NREAL

'Bino will come to my place and have dinner.'

75. **kəu-** 'call'

əi-nə	santi-hoi-də	ləi-riŋəi-də	i-ma-nə	kəu-rə-i
I-NOM	Shanti-PL-LOC	stay-SPFD-LOC	1PP-mother-NOM	call-DEIC-SAM

'Mother came and called me while I was at Shanti's house.'

In the sentences above, there is no word for 'come' in the surface structure. Still, the sentences have the meaning of 'come'. This is because of the deictic suffix **-lə** which implies the motion of the speaker. The suffixation **-lə** to action verbs indicates spatial orientation as well as that the event is performed after the motion.

Suffix *-lu*: The semantic structure of the suffix **-lu** is to go somewhere, perform an action and come back. In this case also, the event follows the motion, that is to say, the action is performed after going somewhere. The motion of orientation is away from the speaker. The suffix has the possibility of occurring with stative and process verbs (for stative verbs see **3.2**). The suffix has also six allomorphic variations: **-lu ~ ru ~ pu ~ mu ~ ŋu ~ u**. The occurrence of the allomorphs are same to **-lə** 'deictic'.

76. **cət-** 'go'
    əi kolej-də cət-lu-re
    I college-LOC go-DEIC-PERF-SAM
    'I have gone to college (and I have returned)'

77. **jeŋ-** 'look, watch'
    əi i-thəntə sinema-du jeŋ-lu-rə-ge
    I 1PP-alone movie-DEM watch-DEIC-PROS-INT
    'I will go alone and watch the movie'

The verb in (77) **je-lu-rə-ge** is not realized. In such constructions, the referent will go, perform the action and come back. The sense of motion of the referent away from the speaker may not be literally seen in the sentence. In such cases the deictic suffix **-lu** is used.

The suffix can also go with process verbs like **tek-** 'break', **tum-** 'sleep', **ken-** 'fall', **na-** 'fall ill', etc. Unlike action verbs, no physical displacement is involved in the case of process verbs as they lack agents.

78. **tek-** 'break'
    cəuki-si məkhoŋ namə tek-u-re
    chair-DEM leg one break-DEIC-PERF-SAM
    'One leg of this chair had been broken (but now it has been repaired)'

The semantic structure of **-lu** with process verbs is different from that of action verbs. It is obvious that no physical displacement is involved in the underlying meaning of the verbs. It can also be studied under three points supposing A, B and C as in the following diagram.

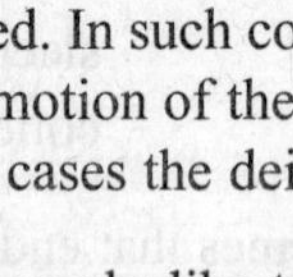

In sentence (78) the verb **tek**- 'break' with -**lu** implies that the leg of the chair was intact before it was broken and this is represented by point A. At point B, the leg of the chair was broken and it has got repaired at point C. Similarly, the leg of this chair was broken and it came to an utilizable position after repair. The same analysis applies to stative verbs also (see also **3.2**).

Suffix -*lək*: The semantic structure of -**lək** may be studied from three different points of view *viz*., (i) purely deictic sense with the dimension of both space and time, (ii) narrating about an event or about somebody or something and (iii) towards a goal (somebody or something). The suffix has five morphological variations as -**lək** ~ **rək** ~ **pək** ~ **mək** ~ **ŋək**.

-**lək**, as a deictic meaning, occurs in both dimensions of space and time. As mentioned above, the suffix originates from the verbal root **lak**- 'come' and thus, the suffixation of -**lək** to a verbal root implies coming back after performing an action. The motion of orientation is towards the speaker and place of occurrence is away from the speaker.

79. **ca**- 'eat'
    əi lәta-hoi-də cak ca-rək-i
    I Lata-PL-LOC meal eat-DEIC-SAM
    'I took meal at Lata's place'

80. **cen**- 'run'
    əŋaŋ-du əwaŋ-lom-dəgi cel-lək-i
    child-DEM north-side-ABL run-DEIC-SAM
    'The child came running from the northern side'

The verb in (79) implies that the referent took meal at somewhere and came back. In (80) the verb **cel-lək**- 'came running' indicates that 'the referent came running towards the speaker'. The verbs involve physical displacement of the referent. There are also some verbs (stative verbs) which do not show physical displacement when combined with the suffix. They occur in the dimension of time and they show continuity of an event.

81. **noi**- 'be fat'
    əŋaŋ-si pik-liŋəi-dəgi noi-rək-i
    child-DEM small-SPFD-since fat-DEIC-SAM
    'The boy has been fat since his childhood'

82. **ŋəu**- 'be fair'
    nupi-məca-si pokpə-dəgi ŋəu-rək-i
    woman-small-DEM birth-since fair-DEIC-SAM
    'This girl has fair complexion since her birth'

The sentences given above have a temporal adverb which indicates a point of time without which the sentences are incomplete. This is because of the semantic component of the meaning carried by the suffix -**lək**. It may be observed that the suffix involves a continuation of an action, process or state from a time in the past. There are also selectional restrictions in the temporal adverbs, for instance, **ŋəsai** 'today's recent past', **ŋəraŋ** 'yesterday', **nəhan** 'day before yesterday' cannot go with stative verbs since they are not semantically matched with the verbs and one cannot acquire the state of being fat, being black or dark complexioned, being fair and so on within such a short time. On the other hand, action and process verbs can take the temporal adverbs **ŋəsai** 'today's recent past' as in the sentences below:

83. **noŋ cu-** 'rain'
noŋ-si ŋəsai əjuk-təgi cu-rək-li
rain-DEM today's recent past morning-since rain-DEIC-PROG-SAM
'It has been raining since today morning'

84. **su-** 'wash'
əi ŋəsai puŋ təra-dəgi phi su-rək-li
I today's recent past hour ten-since cloth wash-DEIC-PROG-SAM
'I have been washing clothes since 10 o'clock today'

The sentences have a temporal adverb **ŋəsai** 'today's recent past' as well as a particular point of time along with it to indicate that the action has been continuing since a recent past (in the day itself) upto the present time of uttering the sentence. The difference between stative and dynamic verbs is only the use of temporal adverbs which show a longer or shorter time period.

Another interesting fact which has been discovered during the analysis is that the suffix **-lək** is vastly used in the language. As a part of survey for the original source, when a book of short stories **'Cherei' /cerəi/** by Manihar Singh (2006) was studied, almost all the verbs in every sentence were found to have the suffix **-lək**. It has been observed from the data available on the book that the suffix indicates a sort of directional meaning 'towards' somebody or something. Secondly, it is found out that the suffix is used in the narrative system. This indirectly implies that all the events or actions are realized. It can also occur in non-realized aspect also. To make it clear consider the following sentences from the book.

85. **hen-** 'be excess'
əjuk-ki puŋ təramathoi khərə hel-lək-pə mətəm-ni
morning-GEN hour eleven some past-DEIC-NMZ time-COP
'The time was around some minutes past eleven in the morning'

(***Cherei***, p.1,)

86. **thəu-** 'drive'
mohendro ma-gi saikəl sumaŋ ta-nə thəu-ɟil-lək-i
Mohendro he-GEN cycle lawn upto-ADV ride-IN-DEIC-SAM
'Mohendro rode his cycle towards/to the lawn'

(p.1)

87. **kəu-** 'call'
səna hai-nə ma-gi nupi nimisəna kəu-rək-i

Sana say-ADV he-GEN wife Nimisana call-DEIC-SAM
'He called his wife Nimisana by the name Sana'

88. **ta-** 'fall'
khədaŋ ta-rək-pə-du jam-nə rasi ləi
chin fall-DEIC-NMZ-DEM much-ADV cute-SAM
'The area around the chin is very cute'

The verbal root **hen-**'be excess' is used in the nominalized form in (85) and it shows some narration. In (86) the verb shows the direction of riding the cycle towards the lawn which is both directional as well as narration. The verb in (87) implies a person to whom the referent is addressing and the direction is towards the wife. The verb **ta-** 'fall' in sentence (88) with **-rək** indicates a direction which is downward from the upper part of the face.

Multifunctional Suffixes ***–khi, -həu, -ləm, -sin, -thok, khət, -thə, -ləgə***. Out of these the first three suffixes function as deictic and somewhere else as non-deictic.

Suffix *-khi*: The suffix has two allomorphs as **-khə** and **-khi**. **-khə** occurs before command marker '**-o**', perfective **-rə** and **–re** whereas **-khi** occurs elsewhere. The suffix has deictic meaning when the action is realized. The motion of orientation is away from the speaker and the action occurs at the speaker's place and the event precedes the motion. In other words it can be said that somebody has done an action at the speaker's place and then went away.

89. **cət-** 'go'
məhak həuɟik-tə əwaŋ-lom-də cət-khi
he now-LOC north-side-LOC go-DEF-SAM
'He went towards the north just now'

90. **pu-** 'carry'
tombə-nə tjusən cət-pə-də lairik-tu pu-khi
Tomba-NOM tuition go-NMZ-LOC book-DEM take-DEF-SAM
'Tomba took away the book when he went for tuition.'

91. **ca-** 'eat'
məni-du ŋəraŋ əi-khoi-də cak ca-khi
Mani-DEM yesterday I-PL-LOC meal eat-DEF-SAM
'Mani took meal at my house yesterday'

The verbs in the above examples imply physical displacement of the referent. The verb **cət-khi-**'went' in (89) indicates that the referent was at the speaker's place a while ago before the utterance of the sentence. All the sentences imply two implications: (i) definiteness- the actions were definitely performed and evidentiality- the speaker eyewitnessed the actions (here, definiteness entails evidentiality and vice-versa) and (ii) the actions are spatial oriented *i.e.* they involve physical displacement.

The suffix gives other implications when it is followed by non-realized suffix **-kəni ~ gəni**.

92. **ca-** 'eat'
əi cak ca-khi-gəni
I rice eat-DEF-NREAL
'I will take meal'

The verb **ca-khi-gəni** 'will take meal' in (92) expresses three different meanings. It may be a situation where the referent is still eating and is asked to do some other work or to stop eating, then the referent might have replied *I will keep on eating* as a denial. The second meaning may be *I will eat here and go away*, and the last meaning may be *I will eat first and then do the work*. The situation is true for other non-realized suffixes like **-si** 'suggestive' and **-sənu** 'let permission' and interrogative environment.

93. **ca-** 'eat'
əi-khoi cak ca-khi-si
I-PL rice eat-DEF-SUG

(i) 'Let us keep eating'
(ii) 'Let us take meal here and go away'
(iii) 'Let us take meal first and then do the work'

94. **pa-** 'read'
əŋaŋ-siŋ-du pa-khi-sənu
child-PL-DEM read-DEF-PERM

(i) 'Let the children keep reading'
(ii) 'Let the children read here and go away'
(iii) 'Let the children read first and then do the work'

95. **ca-** 'eat'
nəŋ cak ca-khi-gə-də-ra
you rice eat-DEF-POT-SPF-INTR

(i) 'Will you certainly take meal (after the feast)?'
(ii) 'Will you keep eating?'
(iii) 'Will you take meal (or may I throw it away)'
(iv) 'Will you take meal here and go away?'
(v) 'Will you take meal first and do the work?'

The suffix can occur in negative environment also as in **tum-khi-roi** 'will not sleep right now'(for more detail see **1.1**).

There is another construction where **-khə** can occur with **-loi ~ roi** which means a serious promise for not doing something again (see **1.1)**

The suffix -**khə** when followed by **-o** 'command' the vowel /ə/ is deleted and it becomes **-kho**.

96. **thək**- 'drink'
ca thək-kho
tea drink-DEF-COM
'Have tea (before you go or before you start the work)'

97. **ŋai**- 'wait'
ŋai-kho! cət-khi-nu
wait-DEIC-COM go-DEF-PROH
'Wait! don't go away'

The verbs in the above sentences do not merely mean a simple command but give the implication of commanding to do something before doing another work or to do something first at the the speaker's place before going away (see **5.2**). Sentence (97) has another negative construction of –**khi** with prohibitive suffix –**nu** which implies not to go at the time of uttering the sentence. Another implication is to perform the action after sometime.

98. **ui**- 'doze off'
para pha-də-riŋəi-də ui-khi-nu
lesson by heart-NEG-SPFD-LOC doze off -PROH
'Do not doze off before getting the lesson by heart'

In (98) the speaker warns somebody not to doze off before getting the lesson by heart.

The suffix also denotes definiteness and evidentiality of an action but without deictic sense.

99. **pathə**- 'overflow/over run'
ca-du məi-thək-tə khərə pathə-khə-re
eat-DEM fire-on-LOC some spill-DEF-PERF-SAM
'The tea spilt over the fire (while it was boiling)'

100. **khənnə**- 'discuss'
mə-ma mə-pa-nə waphəm-du khənnə-khə-re
3PP-mother 3PP-father-NOM matter-DEM discuss-DEF-PERF-SAM
'The parents discussed the matter'

The verbs in the above sentences show definiteness of the actions because of the suffixation of -**khə** but without any displacement of the actors.

Suffix *-həu*: The suffix has three different functions:

(i) the sense of deictic
(ii) opportunity and
(iii) separation.

The sense of deictic is as follows:

(i) The event or action may have happened in the past or around the time of the reporting.
(ii) The event or action is happened somewhere else and not at the place around the speaker.
(iii) The speaker is the eyewitness of the event.
(iv) The speaker is reporting about a third person.
(v) The speaker is reporting something of an action or an event.

101. **isiŋ cau**- 'be flooded'
əi-nə həl-lək-pə-də əsam-di isiŋ cau-həu-ri
I-NOM return-DEIC-NMZ Assam-PART flooded-INCP-PROG-SAM
'Assam was still flooded when I returned'

102. **loi**- 'finish'
memi cak ca-bə loi-həu-re
Memi meal eat-NMZ finish-INCP-PERF-SAM
'Memi has finished taking her meal (when I left the place)'

103. **jeŋ**- 'watch'
əŋaŋ-siŋ imuŋ-də ti-bhi jeŋ-həu-ri
child-PL inside the house-LOC television watch-INCP-PROG-SAM
'Children were still watching TV inside the house (when I came out)'

All the sentences imply that the speaker has eyewitnessed a situation/happening or something being done. Sentence (101) show the implication of the speaker to have eyewitnessed the situation of flood . In (102), the speaker has the evidence that 'Memi's taking meal' has been over and he is reporting this to another person and at the time of reporting he is most probably away from her. In (103) the speaker has eyewitnessed the children still watching TV inside the house and this implies that the speaker is outside the house.

The speaker may report about a second person and in this case, the listener is also the person itself. In other words, the speaker is talking about having eyewitnessed some of the listener's activities.

104. **pa-** 'read'
ŋəraŋ puŋ əhum ədu-wai-də nəŋ laibreri-də lairik pa-həu-i
yesterday hour three that-around-LOC you library-LOC book read-INCP-SAM
'I saw you reading in the library around 3 o'clock yesterday'

105. **cət-** 'go'
nəŋ ŋəsai əjuk kancipur-də cət-həu-i
you a few hours ago morning Canchipur-LOC go-INCP-SAM
'I saw you going somewhere in Canchipur in the morning (I was also going somewhere)'

The speaker is reporting about having eyewitnessed some activity of the listener (the second person) in (104). Sentence (105) implies both speaker and the referent were going on the road. The speaker has the evidence that the referent was also going but the referent might have not seen him. Another case may be that the speaker saw the referent going there without the latter's knowledge and the speaker was not going (as for instance, sitting in a hotel or shop or waiting for a bus). In such a case the following sentence might be used:

106. nəŋ ŋəsai əjuk kancipur-də cət-khi
you a few hours ago morning Canchipur-LOC go-DEF-SAM
'You went somewhere in Canchipur in the morning (I was also at Canchipur)'

The sentences (105) and (106) clearly show the difference in meanings of the suffixes **-həu** and **–khi**

The sense of opportunity: The suffix **-həu** may also give the meaning of 'opportunity' when it goes with **-ke ~ ge**, **-si**, **-ro**, etc. The situations in which it can occur are when:

(i) The speaker may be talking about himself.

(ii) The action may be realized or non-realized.

107. **tum-** 'sleep'
nəŋ ŋaihak tum-həu-ro
you for a while sleep-INCP-COM
'(You) sleep for a while (as you have a lot of works later)'

108. **phəŋ-** 'get'
əi-su phi əmə phəŋ-həu-re
I-also cloth one get-INCP-PERF-SAM
'I have also got a cloth (luckily)'

109. **təu-** 'do'
əi-khoi thəbək khərə təu-həu-si
I-PL work some do-INCP-SUG
'Let us do some work (instead of sitting idly or for the benefit of future generation)'

The sense of separation : The suffix **-həu** may also occur in a situation apart from the above mentioned; it may also denote a sense of separation and do something in the absence of somebody. The situations for this meaning are postulated below:

(i) The verbs may occur either in a non-realized or realized aspect (in certain contexts).

(ii) The verbs may imply someone to stay behind and someone separating from the other.

(iii) The person who stays behind may perform something in the absence of the other.

110. **thoŋ-** 'cook'
əi cak thoŋ-həu-rə-ge
I rice cook-INCP-PROS-INT
'Let me cook (while you are away)'

111. **pa-** 'read'
mala-di lairik pa-ɟə-həu-rə-sənu
Mala-PART book read-REF-INCP-PROS-PERM
'Let Mala stay behind and study'

112. **ləihəu-** 'stay behind'

a. əi ləi-həu-rə-ge nəŋ cət-lo
I stay-INCP-PROS-INT you go-COM
'You go, let me stay behind'

b. memca-di siŋəməi kəithel-də ləi-həu-re
Memcha-PART Singjamei market-LOC stay-INCP-PERF-SAM
'Memcha stayed behind at Singjamei market'

The verbs in the above sentences imply two senses: to stay behind *i.e.* not joining a party or trip and perform an action in somebody's/others' absence. The verbs can be put separately in the root form while the verb in sentence (112) is different. **ləihəu-**'stay behind' can be treated as a single unit (see **2.2**). Similar verb forms are **purək-** 'bring', **puthok-** 'discover', **thorək-** 'come out', etc.

Suffix ***-ləm***: The suffix has six allomorphic variations as **-ləm** ~ **rəm** ~ **pəm** ~ **məm** ~ **ŋəm** ~**əm**. The occurrences of these allomorphs are same to **-lə** 'deictic'. The semantic structure of **-ləm** is to perform something *not here and not now*. All the possible combinations of **-ləm** with other suffixes will come under either one of the semantic scope.

-ləm + **i** may give a different meaning when they are attached to action and stative verbs. With action verbs the combination of the suffixes gives the meaning of an action that is realized or completed and thus, they come under the scope of *not now*.

113. **təm-** 'learn'
əi sər ɟiten-də hindi təm-məm-mi
I Sir Jiten-LOC Hindi learn-COMP-SAM
'I learnt Hindi from Sir Jiten'

The combination of suffixes **-ləm** + **i** may also imply another meaning where it refers to an action which is in progress in the past. The sentence structure may either be a complex one where the verb of the matrix clause takes the suffixes or a simple sentence. Still, it implies another clause in the underlying structure which highlights a sense of evidentiality of the action (see **5.1**). With stative verbs **-ləm** + **i** may give another reading where it implies a change of situation (see **5.1**).

Another context where **-ləm** occurs is with progressive suffix **-li̩**. It can be attached to both action and stative verbs (see **5.1**).

The suffix **-ləm** when followed by **-kəni** ~ **gəni** shows uncertainty of an action which covers the scope *not here*.

114. **cət-** 'go'
əŋaŋ-du həuɟik skul cət-ləm-gəni
child-DEM now school go-COMP-NREAL
'The child might have gone to school'

In the above sentence it may be observed that the 'completive' suffix **-ləm** occurs with a 'non-realized' suffix **-kəni** ~ **gəni** and this feature is not exceptional to Manipuri only. English has also this feature where non-realized action goes with a past form of the auxiliary verb 'may'. The combination of **-ləm** + **kəni** ~ **gəni** gives a sense of uncertainty; yet, the speaker assumes that the referent may be performing something *not here* on the basis of his daily routine or habit. In (114) the speaker assumes that the referent might be in school as usual, yet he is not certain about it. It covers the semantic scope *not here*. **-ləm** + **kəni** ~ **gəni** can also indicate another scope of *not now*.

115. **lak-** 'come'
məhak ŋəraŋ məphəm-si-də lak-ləm-gəni

he yesterday place-this-LOC come- COMP-NREAL
'He might have come here yesterday (in my absence)'

Another occurrence of **-ləm** may be with some suffixes which are not yet realized: **-u/-o** 'command', **-ke~ge** 'intentive' and **-si** 'proposal', etc. which refer to perform something in somebody's absence and perform something first before doing another action.

116. **in**- 'feed'
əŋaŋ. cak il-ləm-mu
child rice feed-COMP-COM
'Feed the child (before you do something or while I am away)'

117. **pi**- 'give'
lairik-tu əmuk-tə pi-rəm-mu
book-DEM once-only give-COMP-COM
'Give me the book (before you leave)'

118. **cət**- 'go'
əi kəithen cət-ləm-mə-ge (-lə-ge)
I market go-COMP-PROS-INT
'Let me go to the market (without you)'

119. **ca lon**- 'make tea'
ca glas əmə lol-ləm-ge
tea glass one make-COMP-INT
'Let me make a cup of tea for you (before I leave)'

120. **ŋai**- 'wait'
nə-khoi əi-bu ca thək-pə-də ŋai-rəm-mə-nu
you-PL I-ACC tea drink-NMZ-LOC wait-COMP-PROS-PROH
'(You) don't wait for me for the tea break'

121. **hai**- 'say'
pau-si han-nə hai-rəm-si
message-DEM earlier-ADV say-COMP-SUG
'Let us convey the message first to him (before we leave)'

Suffixes *-sin, -thok, -khət, -thə*: These suffixes may be studied under the following ways accordingly:

(1) directional meaning
(2) class changing derivative
(3) comparative meaning and

(4) other meanings as repetition, completive, start and continuation respectively.

Directional meaning: Most appropriately, the suffixes may be attached to directional verbs to denote the following directions: **-sin** 'inward directional', **-thok** 'outward directional', **-khət** 'upward directional' and **-thə** 'downward directional'. They have the following allomorphic variations as: **-cin ~ ɟin ~ sin**, **-kət ~ gət ~ khət** and **-thə**. **-kət ~ cin ~ ṫok** occur after any morpheme that begins with an aspirated sound and ends in a stop sound.

hut-kət-	bore + upward direction
hut-cin-	bore + inward direction
hut-tok-	bore + outward direction
thek-kət-	bend + upward direction
thek-cin-	bend + inward direction
thek-tok-	bend + outward direction

-gət, **-ɟin** and **-dok** occur after any morpheme that begin with an aspirated stop sound and ends in a vowel or a nasal sound.

hon-gət-	carry + unward direction
hon-ɟin-	carry + inward direction
hon-dok-	carry + outward direction
thaŋ-gət-	carry + upward direction
thaŋ-ɟin-	carry + inward direction
thaŋ-dok-	carry + outward direction

The suffix **-thə** has no allomorphic variation except in one case that is **thadə**- 'drop (down)'. The original form is **tha** + **thə** > **thadə**- 'release + downward direction'. The suffix **-thə** cannot be attached to disyllabic verbs.

Class changing derivative: The suffixes **-sin**, **-thok**, **-khət**, **-thə** have an important role in the shifting of verb's meaning from one category to another. The addition of these suffixes gives a stative verb a process meaning and sometimes, an action meaning thereby introducing an agent (for more detail see **3.5**).

The four suffixes **-sin**, **-thok**, **khət** and **-thə** when attached to stative verbs may also give another meaning that is comparative sense.

pik-	be small	> pik-thə-	be relatively small
cau-	be big	> cau-khət-	be relative big
pa-	be thin	> pa-thə-	be relatively thin
pəu-	be coarse	> pəu-khət-	be relative coarse

kup-	be fine	>	kup-thə-	be relatively fine
wau-	be light- coloured	>	wau-thok-	be relatively light-coloured
jak-	be deep- coloured	>	jak-sin-	be relatively deep-coloured
pan-	be fair-complexioned	>	pan-thok-	be relatively fair complexioned
ləi-	be a little dark complexioned	>	ləi-sin-	be relatively a little dark-complexioned
səŋ	be green	>	səŋ-ɟin-	be relatively green
mu-	be black	>	mu-sin-	be relatively black
pet-	be soft	>	pet-thok-	be relatively soft
kən-	be hard	>	kən-sin	be relatively hard, etc.

122. **pəu-khət-** 'be relatively coarse'
peket-tə jon-bə cini-si-nə khərə pəu-khət-li
packet-LOC sell-NMZ sugar-DEM-CONT some coarse-UP-SAM
'The sugar which is sold in packet is coarser (as compared to others)'

123. **kup-thə-** 'be relatively fine'
thum peket-si-nə khərə kup-thə-i
salt packet-DEM-CONT some fine-DOWN-SAM
'This packet of salt is finer (as compared to others)'

124. **pan-thok**- 'be relatively fair-complexioned'
ma-gi mə-ca-nupi ətombi-si-nə mə-ce-dəgi
she-GEN 3PP-offspring-woman younger-DEM-CONT 3PP-sister-ABL

kucu khərə pan-thok-i
complexion some fair-OUT SAM
'Her younger daughter is fairer than her elder sister'

125. **kən-sin**- 'be relatively hard'
jam ətotpə-si-nə khərə kən-sil-li
dough-DEM-CONT some hard-IN-SAM
'This dough is harder (as compared to others)'

The verbs with the four suffixes **-sin**, **-thok**, **-khət** and **-thə** imply a sense of comparision in the above sentences. Though the compared things may not be present in the sentences, the meaning is conveyed in the sentence structures.
Some extended meanings of the suffix **-sin** are as follows:

(i) *joining somebody in an action,*

(ii) *putting additional things,*

(iii) *doing something at random or which is undesirable,*

(iv) *doing something intentionally and*

(v) *pretending to do something.*

Joining somebody in an action:

cəi-	scold	>	cəi-sin-	joining others in scolding
ŋaŋ-	speak	>	ŋaŋ-sin-	joining when somebody is speaking
kəp-	cry	>	kəp-sin-	joining others in weeping
jau-	join	>	jau-sin-	joining others in doing something
paŋ-	help	>	paŋ-sin-	joining or lending help in something, etc

126. **cəi-sin-** 'joining others in scolding'
mə-jambə-du-nə-su caubə-də cəi-sil-li
3PP-elder brother-DEM-NOM-also Chaoba-LOC scold-IN-SAM
'His elder brother also joined the group in scolding Chaoba'

127. **paŋ-sin-** 'join or help others in doing something'
thəba-su əi-khoi-gi thəbək-tə paŋ-sil-li
Thaba-also I-PL-GEN work-LOC help-IN-SAM
'Thaba helps us in our work (by joining the working team)'

Putting additional things:

soi-	cut	>	soi-ɟin-	put additional things in the cutting
khəŋ-	know	>	khəŋ-ɟin-	know something extra
pha-	learn by heart	>	pha-ɟin-	learn extra lessons by heart
jeŋ-	look	>	jeŋ-sin-	prepare extra lessons
phut-	boil	>	phut-cin-	put additional things in the boiling
təm-	learn	>	təm-sin-	learn something extra
tak-	teach	>	tak-sin-	teach extra lesson, etc.

128. **pha-ɟin-** 'learn extra lessons by heart'
səireŋ əsi-su pha-ɟil-lu
poem this-also learn by heart-IN-COM
'Learn this poem also by heart (in addition to others)'

129. **tm-sin-** 'learn something extra'
ərembə-də mətəm maŋ-hən-gənu sinphəm əmə təm-sil-lu

waste-LOC time waste-CAUS-PROH profession one learn-IN-COM
'Do not waste time. Instead, learn a profession'

Doing something at random or which is undersirable:

thəm-	put	>	thəm-ɟin-	put something out of order
jek-	paint/draw	>	jek-sin-	paint something at random
təi-	apply	>	təi-sin-	apply something at random
lon-	embroider	>	lon-sin-	embroider a pattern or something at random
nəm-	press	>	nəm-sin-	place something out of order
nəi-	torture	>	nəi-sin-	stay at one's place which is not desirable
lep-	stand	>	lep-sin-	stand in front of others and obstruct the view (which is not desirable)
phəm-	sit	>	phəm-ɟin-	sit for a long time (which is not desirable)
lak-	come	>	lak-sin-	visit by somebody (who is not welcome or when the host is busy), etc.

130. **thəm-ɟin-** 'put something without order'
tebəl məthək-tə phi-siŋ-si kəna-nə thəm-ɟil-li
table on-LOC cloth-PL-DEM who-NOM put-IN-SAM
'Who put these clothes on the table?'

131. **jek-sin-** 'draw something at random'
lairik məkhum-də jek-sin-gənu
book cover-LOC draw-IN-PROH
'Don't draw anything on the cover of the book'

Note: The verb **thəm-ɟin-** may also mean 'to put something safely'.

Doing something intentionally:

lau-	shout	>	lau-sin-	shout intentionally
jeŋ-	watch	>	jeŋ-sin-	watch/supervise intentionally
laŋ-	make noise	>	laŋ-sin-	make noise intentionally
təm-	inform	>	təm-sin	inform intentionally
məral si-	blame	>	məral si-ɟin-	blame intentionally
thəŋ-	blame	>	thəŋ-ɟin-	blame intentionally, etc.

132. **təm-sin-** 'inform intentionally'
memi-nə pau-du mə-ma-də təm-sil-li
Memi-NOM news-DEM 1PP-mother-LOC inform-IN-SAM
'Memi informed her mother about the news intentionally'

133. **lau-sin-** 'shout intentionally'

mi-jam-nə	pulis-tə	lau-sil-ləm-mi
people-many-NOM	police-LOC	shout-IN-COMP-SAM

'The people shouted intentionally at police'

Pretending doing something

The suffix **-sin** when followed by **-nə** gives the meaning of 'pretend'.

təu-	do	>	təu-sin-nə-	pretend doing
tum-	sleep	>	tum-sin-nə-	pretend sleeping
jən-	look	>	jeŋ-sin-nə-	pretend looking
sau-	be angry	>	sau-ɟin-nə-	pretend to be angry
kəp-	cry	>	kəp-sin-nə-	pretend to be crying
cəi-	scold	>	cəi-sin-nə-	pretend scolding
phu-	beat	>	phu-ɟin-nə-	pretend beating
kau-	forget	>	kau-sin-nə-	pretend to forget, etc.

134. **tum-sin-nə-** 'pretend sleeping'

əŋaŋ-du	lairik	təu-niŋ-də-dunə	tum-sin-nə-i
child-DEM	book	read-wish-NEG-due to	sleep-IN-REC-SAM

'The child pretends to sleep as to avoid reading'

135. **khəŋ-ɟin-nə-də-** 'pretend not to recognize'

nupi-du-nə	əi-bu	u-bə-də	khəŋ-jin-nə-de
woman-DEM-NOM	I-ACC	see-NMZ-LOC	recognize-IN-REC- NEG-SAM

'The woman pretends not to recognize me when she saw me'

The suffix **-thok** when added to non-directional action verbs gives the meaning of completeness.

ca-	eat	>	ca-thok-	eat + completeness
təu-	do	>	təu-thok-	do + completeness
i-	write	>	i-thok-	write + completeness
pa-	read	>	pa-thok-	read + completeness
jeŋ-	look	>	jeŋ-thok-	look + completeness
kəp-	cry	>	kəp-thok-	cry + completeness
təm-	learn	>	təm-thok-	learn + completeness
phut-	boil	>	phut-tok-	boil + completeness
tum-	sleep	>	tum-thok-	sleep + completeness, etc.

136. **ca**- 'eat'
cak-si han-nə ca-thok-ə-ro (-lə-ro)
rice-DEM advance-ADV eat-OUT-PROS-COM
'Come and take your meal first (before doing something)'

137. **phut**- 'boil'
əlu-si phut-tok-ə-si (-lə-si)
potato-DEM boil-OUT-PROS-SUG
'Let us boil the potato'

The verbs in the above sentences give a sense of 'completeness' when they go with -**thok** 'out'.

The suffix -**khət** when attached to durative action verbs gives the meaning of 'starting of an action' (see also **3.2**).

su-	wash	>	su-gət-	wash + start
ca-	eat	>	ca-khət-	eat + start
thoŋ-	cook	>	thoŋ-gət-	cook + start
i-	write	>	i-khət-	write + start
hap-	load	>	hap-kət	load + start
sa-	build'	>	sa-gət-	build + start
lon-	pile	>	lon-khət-	pile + start
seŋ-	clean	>	seŋ-gət-	clean + start
cam-	wash	>	cam-khət-	wash + start

138. **su**- 'wash'
nəŋ phi su-gət-ləm-mo (-o)
you cloth wash-UP-COMP-COM
'(You) start washing clothes (while I am eating or doing something)'

139. **lon**- 'knit'
əi phurit əmə lon-khət-lc
I sweater one knit-UP-PERF-SAM
'I have started knitting a sweater'

The suffix -**thə** gives the meaning of 'continuation' when it is added to some durative verbs.

cət-	go	>	cət-thə-	go + continue
pa-	read	>	pa-thə-	read + continue
i-	write	>	i-thə-	write + continue
sək-	sing	>	sək-thə-	sing + continue
tak-	teach	>	tak-thə-	teach + continue

təm-	learn	>	təm-thə-	learn + continue
pi-	supply	>	pi-thə-	supply + continue
ləu-	take	>	ləu-thə-	take + continue
jen-	distribute	>	jen-thə-	distribute + continue, etc.

140. **cət-** 'go'
əi-khoi-gi thəbək ədu məkha cət-thə-ri
I-PL-GEN work that further go-DOWN-PROG-SAM
'We are continuing our work'

141. **təm-** 'learn'
əi-di lairik məkha təm-thə-khi-gəni
I-PART book further learn-DOWN-DEF-NREAL
'I will continue my study further'

Suffix ***-ləgə***: The suffix has six allomorphic variations as **-lə ~ rə ~ pə ~ mə ~ ŋə ~ ə** and their condition of occurrence is same as **-ləm**. The suffix has three different functions which would mean:

(i) doing something earlier

(ii) manner of doing something

(iii) Conjunction joining two verbs.

Doing something earlier : The suffixation of **-ləgə** to action or stative verbs (which refer to the result of an action – see **3.3**) in a subordinate clause imply that the action has been/ will be performed first than another action.

142. **ca-** 'eat'
əi cak ca-rəgə skul cət-li
I rice eat-CPART school go-SAM
'I go to school after taking meal'

143. **iruɟə-** 'take bath'
nə-khoi nuŋti-gi iru-jə-rəgə skul cət-kədəbə-ni
2PP-PL everyday-GEN take bath-CPART school go-must-COP
'You must go to school after taking bath everyday'

The verb form **ca-rə-gə** 'after eating' in (142) indicates that the action of 'eating' has been performed earlier before going to school. The verb **iruɟə- rəgə** in (143) implies an action 'to bath' which is commanded or advised to be done before performing some other action *i.e.* 'to go to school'. In the sentences given above, the verbs show that two actions occur next to each other. There are also sentences when two action verbs occur simultaneously.

Manner of doing something : When two action verbs occur simultaneously in a sentence the verb which takes the suffix **-ləgə** imply a sort of manner *i.e.* how does he come, how does he speak, how does he read, how does he watch and so on.

144. **sai-** 'chew'

pot	sai-rəgə	wa	ŋaŋ-gənu
thing	chew- CPART	speech	speak-PROH

'Don't speak while chewing something'

145. **phəm-** 'sit'

ma-di	mə-sa	cəp tiŋ-nə	phəm-məgə	lairik	pa-i
he-PART	3PP-body	MOD-straight-ADV	sit-CPART	book	read-SAM

'He reads by sitting straight'

In (145) the referent's 'sitting straight' denotes the manner or the way how he sits while reading. Both the actions of sitting and reading occur at the same time. In the above sentences the answer to the question as to how an action is performed by the referent is given by another action. In other words, the referent is performing two actions at the same time.

Conjunction joining two verbs: The suffix **-ləgə** also functions as a conjunction while expressing a quality or state of somebody or something.

146. **mu-** 'be black'

nupa	əsi	mu-rəgə	waŋ-ŋi
man	this	black-CPART	tall-SAM

'This man is black and tall'

147. **pik-** 'be small'

lairik	əsi	pik-əgə (-ləgə)	məgun	ləi
book	this	small-CPART	quality	have-SAM

'This book is small but useful'

Sentence (146) expresses the appearance of a person as black and tall while in (147) the suffix **-ləgə** functions as a conjunction 'but' expressing the size and quality of the book.

Modifiers: There are suffixes denoting modifier meaning which may be divided into two groups: (i) modifiers expressing 'slightly' and (ii) modifiers expressing 'superlative degree'.

Modifiers expressing 'slightly': This modifier may further be sub-divided into three divisions as: (i) modifiers occurring in reduplicative form only, (ii) modifiers occurring in non reduplicative form only and (iii) modifiers occurring in both environments. It may or may not cause disturbance in the semantic structure of the sentence. They are attached to stative verbs only.

Modifiers occurring in the reduplicative form only: The suffix **-li** which functions as a modifier in a sentence cannot occur in a non-reduplicative environment and it has two variations as **-li** ~ **ri**. **-li** occurs after **/m/**, **/n/**, **/ŋ/**, **/p/**, **/t/** and **/k/** while **-ri** occurs after vowel sounds.

thum-	be sweet	>	thum-li thum-li	slightly sweet
pet-	be soft	>	pet-li pet-li	slightly soft
ŋu-	be white	>	ŋəu-ri ŋəu-ri	slightly white
pa-	be thin	>	pa-ri pa-ri	slightly thin
tek-	be broken	>	tek-li tek-li	slightly broken
nop-	be weak	>	nop-li nop-li	slightly weak
mon-	be soft	>	mol-li mol-li	slightly soft
kut-	be low	>	kut-li kut-li	slightly low
nəŋ-	be thick	>	nəŋ-li nəŋ-li	slightly thick
ŋaŋ-	be red	>	ŋaŋ-li ŋaŋ-li	slightly red
mu-	be black	>	mu-ri mu-ri	slightly black, etc.

148. **thum**- 'be sweet'
ca əsi thum-li thum-li təu-i
tea this sweet-MOD sweet-MOD do-SAM
'This tea tastes slightly sweet'

149. **mon**- 'be soft'
sopha əsi mol-li mol-li (mon-li mon-li) təu-i
sofa this soft-MOD soft-MOD do-SAM
'This sofa is slightly soft'

Another suffix which can occur in reduplicative environment is **-pet**. It has two variations as **-pet** ~ **phet**.

thum-	be sweet	>	thum-pet thum-pet	slightly sweet
lup-	sink	>	lup-phet lup-phet	ready to sink
nok-	smile	>	nok-phet nok-phet	smilingly
			ci-phet ci-phet	frequently
			ku-phet ku-phet	twinkling

The first three forms have bases from which they are derived whereas the last two modifiers have no bases and they are always collocated with certain verbs *e.g.* **ci-phet ci-phet na**- 'be sick frequently' and **ku-phet kaphet ŋanb**ə 'twinkling (of stars)'. Another form of reduplication is also possible where the verb is not reduplicated. Instead, the suffix only gets reduplicated.

thum-pet lak-pet	slightly sweet
lup-phet lak-phet	ready to sink

Modifier occurring in non-reduplicative form only: The suffix **-phat** is the only modifier occurred in non-reduplicative form which gives the meaning 'slightly'. It always occurs in a negative environment.

seŋ-	be clear	>	seŋ-phat-tə-	not clear enough
mun-	be properly cooked	>	mun-phat-tə-	not yet properly cooked
ca-	be fit	>	ca-phat-tə-	not properly fitting
lum-	be warm	>	lum-phat-tə-	not warm enough
kən-	be hard	>	kən-phat-tə-	not hard enough
nəŋ-	be thick	>	nəŋ-phat-tə-	not thick enough
saŋ-	be long	>	saŋ-phat-tə-	not long enough
jəu-	arrive	>	jəu-phat-tə-	not yet reached
noŋ ta-	rain	>	noŋ ta-phat-tə-	not yet rained
loi-	finish	>	loi-phat-tə-	not yet finished, etc.

150. **ca**- 'be fitting'
khoŋup-si əi-ŋon-də ca-phat-te
shoe-DEM I-DIR-DAT fit-MOD-NEG-SAM
'This shoe is slightly unfit for me'

151. **seŋ**- 'be clear'
nəŋ-nə pi-rək-pə photo-si seŋ-phat-te
you-NOM give-DEIC-NMZ photograph-DEM clear-MOD-NEG-SAM
'The photograph that you have given me is slightly unclear'

The verbs in the above given examples imply that the degree/quality of something expected is not yet satifactory enough or something which is bound to happen for sure has not yet happened. The verb **ca**- 'be fitting' in (150) gives a negative meaning when it goes with the negative modifier -**phat**. Similarly, the expected degree of clearness or quality of the photograph is not yet achieved in (151). The semantic structure of **-phat** restricts it from occuring with dynamic verb (as action and process verbs do not indicate quality).

Modifiers which can occur in both environments: The suffixes which can occur in both environments *i.e.* in reduplicative as well as non-reduplicative environments are **-ləp**, **-tək** and **-kum ~ gum**.

The suffix **-ləp** has two allomorphs as **-ləp ~ rəp**. Vowel ending morphemes take **-rəp** while **-ləp** occurs elsewhere.

ŋaŋ-	be red	>	ŋaŋ-ləp/ŋaŋ-ləp ŋaŋ-ləp	slightly red
mu-	be black	>	mu-rəp/mu-rəp mu-rəp	slightly black
saŋ-	be long	>	saŋ-ləp/saŋ-ləp saŋ-ləp	slightly long

kon-	bend	>	kol-ləp/kol-ləp kol-ləp	slightly bend
kop-	be dent	>	kop-ləp/kop-ləp kop-ləp	slightly dent
məm-	be dark	>	məm-ləp/məm-ləp məm-ləp	slightly dark
pet-	be soft	>	pet-ləp/pet-ləp pet-ləp	slightly soft
pa-	be thin	>	pa-rəp/pa-rəp pa-rəp	slightly thin
noi-	be fat	>	noi-rəp/noi-rəp noi-rəp	slightly fat
cau-	be big	>	cau-rəp/cau-rəp cau-rəp	slightly big, etc.

152. **saŋ-** 'be long'
əŋaŋ-du-gi pa-du saŋ-ləp saŋ-ləp təu-i
child-DEM-GEN eyelash-DEM long-MOD long-MOD do-SAM
'The child's eyelash is slightly long'

153. **pa-** 'be thin'
nupi-du mə-sa pa-rəp təu-i
woman-DEM 3PP-body thin-MOD do-SAM
'The woman is slightly thin'

The reduplicative form denotes plural meaning.

154. **pa-** 'be thin'
nupi-siŋ-du mə-sa pa-rəp pa-rəp təu-i
woman-PL-DEM 3PP-body thin-MOD thin-MOD do-SAM
'The women are slightly thin'

Another suffix which denotes 'slightly' is **-tək.**

sin-	be sour	>	sin-tək/sin-tək sin-tək	slightly sour
kha-	be bitter	>	kha-tək/kha-tək kha-tək	slightly bitter
kən-	be hard	>	kən-tək/kən-tək kən-tək	slightly hard
pet-	be soft	>	pet-tək/pet-tək pet-tək	slightly soft
mot-	be dirty	>	mot-tək/mot-tək mot-tək	slightly dirty
nəŋ-	be thick	>	nəŋ-tək/nəŋ-tək nəŋ-tək	slightly thick
ten-	be short	>	ten-tək/ ten-tək ten-tək	slightly short
pik-	be small	>	pik-tək/ pik-tək pik-tək	slightly small, etc.

155. **sin-** 'be sour'
sem-si sin-tək təu-i
apple-DEM sour-MOD do-SAM
'This apple is slightly sour'

156. **laŋ**- 'be thin'
ca-si laŋ-tək təu-i
tea-DEM thin-MOD do-SAM
'The tea is slightly thin (it is of less milk)'

It may be noted that the reduplication of -**ləp** and -**tək** gives plural meaning when they modify animates.

Another suffix denoting 'slightly' is -**kum** ~ **gum**. In this construction, only the first word takes the verb and it is not reduplicated unlike the other constructions so far studied. The second word takes **lak**- which is added throughout the construction with any kind of verb.

thot-	be soft	>	thot-kum/thot-kum lak-kum	slightly soft
jak-	be salty	>	jak-kum/jak-kum lak-kum	slightly salty
man-	be similar	>	man-gum/man-gum lak-kum	slightly resemble
tha-	be thick	>	tha-gum/ tha-gum lak-kum	slightly thick
tiŋ-	be straight	>	tiŋ-gum/tiŋ-gum lak-kum	slightly straight
jaŋ-	be light	>	jaŋ-gum/jaŋ-gum lak-kum	slightly light
kem-	be crispy	>	kem-gum/kem-gum lak-kum	slightly crispy
lu-	be clean	>	lu-gum/lu-gum lak-kum	slightly clear, etc.

157. **lu**- 'be clear'
ŋəsi-di toti isiŋ-si lu-gum təu-i
today-PART tap water-DEM clear-MOD do-SAM
'Today the tap water is slightly clear (than before)'

158. **tha**- 'be thick'
təl-si tha-gum lak-kum təu-i
roti-DEM thick-MOD do-SAM
'This roti is slightly thick (than others)'

Modifiers expressing intensity: There are some modifiers which are attached to stative verbs only. They are very specific and not productive (Yashawanta, 2000: 39). They occur only in reduplicative environment as listed below:

cum-	be straight	>	cum-driŋ cum-	be very straight
waŋ-	be tall	>	waŋ-droŋ waŋ-	be very tall
saŋ-	be long	>	saŋ-droŋ saŋ-	be very long
pak-	broad	>	pak-throk pak-	be very broad
cau-	be big	>	cau-throk cau-	be very big
ŋu-	be white/fair	>	ŋəu-rok ŋəu-	be very white/fair

ŋu-	be white/fair	>	ŋəu-srok ŋəu-	be very white/fair
ŋaŋ-	be red	>	ŋaŋ-səŋ ŋaŋ-	be very red
mu-	be black	>	mu-sin-mu-	be very black
pik-	be small	>	pik-tru pik-	be very small
səŋ-	be green	>	səŋ-trik səŋ-	be very green
khu-	be narrow	>	khu-drik khu-	be very narrow
kut	be low	>	kut-sit kut-	be very low
hən-	be new	>	hən-trik hən-	be very new
ten-	be short	>	ten-trik ṭen-	be very short
pa-	be thin	>	pa-drit pa-	be very thin
tai-	be pale	>	tai-phet tai-	be very pale, etc.

159. **pik**- 'be small'
nəŋ-gi khoŋ-di pik-tru pik-i
you-GEN feet-PART small-MOD small-SAM
'Your feet is very small'

160. **cum**- 'be straight'
ucan pambi-si cum-driŋ cum-mi
pine tree-DEM straight-MOD straight-SAM
'This pine tree is very straight'

Other derivative suffixes *-nə, -minnə, -hən, -lə, -tə, -ləbədi, -nə, -liŋəi, -kə, -loi, -cə, -ləmdai, -pi, -pə, -nə*: The derivative suffixes which are not multifunctional are: -**nə** 'reciprocal'. **minnə** 'associative', -**hən** 'causative', -**lə** 'prospective, -**tə** 'negative', -**ləbədi** 'if', -**nə** 'adverbial', -**liŋəi** ~ **riŋəi** 'specific duration', -**kə** 'potential', -**loi** 'non-potential', -**cə** 'reflexive', -**ləmdai** 'about to do something', -**pi** 'honorific', -**pə** 'nominalizer', -**nə** 'purposive'.

***-nə* 'reciprocal'**: The suffix is homophonous with -**nə** 'purposive' and adverbial -**nə**. The reciprocal suffix -**nə** is attached to dynamic verbs and it implies two or more than two persons or things.

phu-	beat	>	phu-n	beat each other or one another.
khən-	think	>	khən-nə	discuss
ja-	agree	>	ja-nə	agree with each other or one another
on-	change	>	on-nə	exchange with each other or one another
lau-	shout	>	lau-nə	shout at each other or one another
jeŋ-	look	>	jeŋ-nə	look at each other or one another
lə-	throw	>	ləŋ-nə	throw at each other or one another, etc.

161. **wari sa-** 'talk'
oɟa-siŋ wari sa-nə-ri
teacher-PL talk-REC-PROG-SAM
'The teachers are talking'

162. **ca-** 'eat'
ŋəraŋ əi-khoi cak ca-nə-i
yesterday I-PL rice eat-REC-SAM
'We had a feast yesterday'

163. **pau phau-** 'keep in touch'
əi-khoi əni-di pau phau-nə-i
I-PL two-PART keep in touch -REC-SAM
'We (two) keep ourselves in touch'

In the examples given above, the suffix **-nə** is attached to the verbs to convey the meaning of 'each other or one another'.

***-minnə* 'together'**: The addition of this suffix to an action verb gives the 'associative' meaning *i.e.* to perform an action together. It is the combination of two suffixes **-min-nə** which is taken as a sequence of suffixes as **-min** cannot stand alone without the reciprocal suffix **-nə**.

cət-	go	>	cət-minnə	go together
thək-	drink	>	thək-minnə	drink together
phəm-	sit	>	phəm-minnə	drink together
jeŋ-	look	>	jeŋ-minnə	look together
sannə-	play	>	sannə-minnə	play together
cen-	run	>	cen-minnə	run together
ləi-	buy	>	ləi-minnə	buy together
təm-	learn	>	təm-minnə	learn together
thaŋ-	carry	>	thaŋ-minnə	carry together
pa-	read	>	pa-minnə	read together, etc.

164. **thək-** 'drink'
əi-khoi əni ca thək-minnə-ru-i
I-PL two tea drink-together-DEIC-SAM
'We (two) went to a hotel and had tea'

165. **təm-** 'learn'
i-bani hindi təm-minnə-i
1PP-two Hindi learn-together-SAM
"We (two) learn Hindi together'

166. **ləi-** 'buy'
i-bani kəithen-dəgi khoŋup əmə ləi-minnə-ru-i
1PP-two market-ABL shoe one buy-together-DEIC-SAM
'We went to the market together and bought a shoe'

***-hən* 'causative'**: The suffixation of the causative suffix **-hən** implies to make somebody to do or cause to happen something. The resulting verb of the suffixation of **-hən** may be either class-changing or class-maintaining. In class-changing category, it brings a change in the verb class from stative or process meaning to action meaning by enforcing an agent to perform something to get some result. For instance, the stative verb **cot-** 'be wet' may be changed to an action verb by adding the suffix **-hən** as **cot-hən** 'make somebody or something wet' which demands an agent (for more detail see **3.5**).

The suffix may also be attached to action verbs and it does not bring any change in the verb class, *i.e.*, the resulting verb is class-maintaining derived verb.

kəp-	cry	>	kəp-hən-	make somebody cry
nok-	laugh	>	nok-hən-	make somebody laugh
sau-	get angry	>	sau-hən-	make somebody angry
thək-	drink	>	thək-hən-	make somebody drink
təu-	do	>	təu-hən-	make somebody do
phəm-	sit	>	phəm-hən-	make somebody sit
pha-	catch	>	pha-hən-	make somebody catch something
tannə-	chase	>	tannə-hən-	make somebody chase, etc.

167. **tannə-** 'chase'
əi-nə tombə-də sən-du tannə-həl-li (-hən-li)
I-NOM Tomba-LOC COW-DEM chase-CAUS-SAM
'I made Tomba chase the cow'

168. **phot-** 'stitch/mend'
əi-nə muci-də khoŋup phot-həl-li (-hən-li)
I-NOM cobbler-DAT shoe stitch-CAUS-SAM
'I made the cobbler mend my shoe'

169. **ŋai-** 'wait'
əi-nə hema-bu puŋ-khai əmə ŋai-həl-li (-hən-li)
I-NOM Hema-ACC hour-half one wait-CAUS-SAM
'I made Hema wait for me for half an hour'

***-lə* 'prospective'**: The suffix is homophonous with perfective **-lə**. Both the suffixes have six allomorphic variations as **-lə ~ rə ~ pə ~ mə ~ ŋə ~** ə. The distribution of the allomorphs is same to **-lə** 'deictic'. The suffixation of **-lə** to a verb form indicates that the action will be done shortly or an event will take place shortly.

170. **həu-** 'start'
nuŋthil-gi puŋ əmə-də pərikhja həu-rə-ni (-lə-gəni)
afternoon-GEN hour one-LOC examination start-PROS-NREAL
'Examination will start at 1 o'clock (shortly)'

171. **həŋ-** 'ask'
əi waphəm-si-gi mətaŋ-də mə-ŋon-də həŋ-ŋu-rə-ge
I matter-DEM-GEN about-LOC 3PP-DIR-LOC ask-DEIC-PROS-INT
'I will enquire about the matter to him'

The prospective suffix of the above sentences shows that the action will be performed shortly. In (170) the examination is going to be started shortly.

In a negative construction with **-loi**, the suffixation of -lə implies a sense of promise or certainty of something (see **1.1**). But in case of stative verbs, there is no meaning of promise since there is no agent to make a promise.

172. **cau-** 'be big'
a. u əsi cau-rə-roi
tree this big-PROS-NPOT-SAM
'This tree will grow no more (It has stopped its growth)'

b. u əsi cau-rə-roi
tree this big-PROS-NPOT-SAM
'This tree is not a big tree (according to its species)'

173. **ŋəu-** 'be white'
a. phi əsi ŋəu-rə-roi
cloth this white-PROS-NPOT-SAM
'This cloth will be no more white as expected'

b. phi əsi ŋəu-rə-roi
cloth this white-PROS-NPOT-SAM
'This is not a white cloth (according to the materials)'

***-tə* 'negative'**: The suffix has two allomorphs as **-tə ~ də**. A verbal root can be derived to negative by the suffixation of **-tə~də** (for detail see **1.1**).

-liŋəi: It is the combination of two morphemes -**li** and -**ŋəi**. -**li** is the progressive suffix while -**ŋəi** alone indicates duration or time. The combination or sequence of morphemes -**liəi** denotes a specific duration and in such cases -**li** cannot stand alone while -**ŋəi** alone indicates duration or time.

kəidəuŋəi	which day
əduŋəi	that time (referring to the past time)
məmaŋŋəi	once upon a time
ləisemŋəi	the time of creation
jelhəuŋəi	time immemorial

It can be observed that in the above given examples the words have the status of a free form as they are not attached to verbal roots. Another point to be noted here is that **-ŋəi** alone cannot be attached to verbal roots.

ca-	eat	>	ca-riŋəi-	while eating
thək-	drink	>	thək-iŋəi-	while drinking
kəp-	cry	>	kəp-piŋəi-	while crying
tum-	sleep	>	tum-miŋəi-	while sleeping
hiŋ-	be alive	>	hiŋ-ŋiŋəi-	while alive
cət-	go	>	cət-liŋəi-	while going
khən-	think	>	khəl-liŋəi-	while thinking
nəu-	be new	>	nəu-riŋəi-	while something is new
noi-	be fat	>	noi-riŋəi-	while somebody is fat
kəŋ-	be thin/ slim	>	kəŋ-ŋiŋəi-	while somebody is thin/slim, etc.

The allomorphic variations can be seen from the above examples as **-li ~ ri ~ pi ~ mi ~ ŋi ~ i** and their occurrence is conditioned in the same way as **-lə** 'deictic'.

It is true that the addition of the sequence of suffixes denotes a specific duration but the degree of specification varies according to the meaning of the verbs to which the suffix is added. The most specific duration is indicated when the suffix is attached to action verbs.

174. **ca**- 'eat'

əi-nə cak ca-riŋəi-də memə lak-i
I-NOM rice eat-SPFD-LOC Mema come-SAM
'Mema came to my house while I was taking meal'

175. **su**- 'wash'

əi-nə phi su-riŋəi-də əŋaŋ-du kəp-pək-i (-lək-i)
I-NOM cloth wash-SPFD-LOC child-DEM cry-DEIC-SAM
'The child cried while I was washing clothes'

Now consider some examples of stative verbs which have temporal meanings:

176. **noi**- 'be fat'

əi-nə noi-riŋəi-də phurit-si ca-rəm-mi
I-NOM fat-SPFD-LOC blouse-DEM fit-COMP-SAM
'This blouse fitted me while I was fat'

177. **kəŋ-** 'be thin/slim'
phurit-si mala-nə jaŋ kəŋ-ŋiŋəi-də lit-ləm-bə-ni
shirt-DEM Mala-NOM back thin-SPFD-LOC wear-COMP-NMZ-COP
'Mala used to wear this shirt while she was thin'

178. **na-**'be ill/sick'
ləta na-riŋəi-də ei-khoi məjam həŋ-bə cət-lu-i
Lata ill-SPFD-LOC I-PL many ask-NMZ go-DEIC-SAM
'We all went to see/visited Mala during her illness'

Consider the following sentences which have stative verbs with no temporal meaning.

179. **nəha oi-** 'be in one's youth'
a. nəha oi-riŋəi punsi-du nuŋŋai-bə-ni-də
youth be-SPFD life-DEM happy-NMZ-COP-EMP
'The days of youth were very enjoyable'

b. nəha oi-riŋəi-də məhak əphəbə səisəkpə əmə oi-rəm-mi
youth be-SPFD-LOC he talented singer one be-COMP-SAM
'He was a talented singer in his days of youth'

180. **əŋaŋ oi-** 'be in one's childhood'
a. əŋaŋ oi-riŋəi mətəm haibə-si mi khudiŋ-nə kəllək-nə-i
child be-SPFD time say-DEM man every-NOM envy-REC-SAM
'Everybody envies childhood time'

b. əi-khoi-nə əŋaŋ oi-riŋəi-də pukhri əmədi turel-də jam-nə
I-PL-NOM child be-SPFD-LOC pond and river-LOC much-ADV

iroi-rək-i
swim-DEIC-SAM
'We used to swim a lot in the ponds and river in our childhood'

The duration implied by the action verbs as **ca**- and **su**- in (174 and 175) is more specific in the sense that the duration occurred in doing the actions are rather short compared to that of the stative verbs as **noi-**, **kəŋ-**, **na-** in (176-178). They are stative verbs with temporal meanings in the sense that a person does not remain fat throughout his lifetime; he may become slim due to some reasons. Similarly, a thin or a slim person may also become fat within a short time (see **3.2** for more detail). The duration implied by these temporal stative verbs is rather short *i.e.* they are more specific than the verbs **nəha oi-** 'be in one's youth', **əŋaŋ oi-** 'be in childhood' in (179) and (180). The duration implied by the two verbs is longer than others shown above. The derived words in sentence (179a) and (180a) *i.e.* **nəha oi-riŋəi punsi** 'life of youths' and **əŋaŋ oi-riŋəi mətəm** 'in one's childhood' occur in a noun phrase in the sentences. From the above analysis, it can be concluded that the degree of specification is different according to the semantic structure of the verbs. With action verbs, the duration is most specific, stative verbs with temporal meaning are less specific and then, the stative denoting a time span of one's childhood or youth have lesser degree of specification while words with **-ŋəi** only (as shown above) have the least degree of specification. In other words, it can be said that it shows duration only (without any specific period).

-ləbədi: The suffix **-ləbədi** 'if' occurs in a subordinate clause of a complex sentence. The suffix is the combination of three suffixes as **-lə**, **-bə** and **-di**. In the present context it has been treated as a sequence of suffixes as the desired meaning cannot be provided when they are separated. When they are treated as separate morphemes, the meaning is completely different from **-bədi** 'if'. Consider some examples of **-ləbədi** which has also six allomorphic variations as **-lə.**

tak-	teach	>	tak-əbədi	teach + if
təm-	learn	>	təm-məbədi	learn + if
jon-	sell	>	jol-ləbədi	sell + if
təu-	do	>	təu-rəbədi	do + if
ki-	fear	>	ki-rəbədi	fear + if
cəŋ-	enter	>	cəŋ-ŋəbədi	enter + if
təp-	be slow	>	təp-pəbədi	be slow + if
nən-	press	>	nəl-ləbədi	press + if
lot-	hide	>	lot-ləbədi	hide + if
phəm-	sit	>	phəm-məbədi	sit + if
pha-	catch	>	pha-rəbədi	catch + if
kai-	break	>	kai-rəbədi	break + if

181. **u**- 'see'
nəŋ u-rbədi məhak cen-sil-lək-kəni (-sin-lək-kəni)
you see-if he run-IN-DEIC-NREAL
'He will run to you if he sees you'

182. **ta**- 'hear'
pau-du ta-rəbədi məhak əi-ŋon-də phon təu-rək-kəni
news-DEM hear-if he I-DIR-LOC phone do-DEIC-NREAL
'He will ring me if he hears the news'

183. **ŋəm**- 'can do'
pərikhja əsi-də nəŋ-nə məkok thoŋ-bə ŋəm-ləbədi
examination this-LOC you-NOM top get-NMZ can do-if

saikəl əmə ləi-bi-gəni
cycle one buy-BEN-NREAL
'I will buy a bicycle for you if you can top the examination'

***-nə* 'adverbial'**: The suffixation of **-nə** to stative verbs denotes manner of adverb which can occur in both reduplicative and non-reduplicative while with action verbs it is reduplicated.

kən-	be hard	>	kən-nə/kən-nə kən-nə	fast, quickly
təp-	be slow	>	təp-nə/təp-nə təp-nə	slowly
ŋən-	be early	>	ŋən-nə/ŋən-nə ŋən-nə	early
thu-	be quick	>	thu-nə/thu-nə thu-nə	quickly
theŋ-	be late	>	theŋ-nə/theŋ-nə theŋ-nə	late
nəu-	be new	>	nəu-nə/nəu-nə nəu-nə	newly
cet-	be tight	>	cet-nə/cet-nə cet-nə	tightly
həu-	be loud	>	həu-nə/həu-nə həu-nə	loudly
sau-	be angry	>	sau-nə/sau-nə sau-nə	angrily
cen-	run	>	cen-nə cen-nə	by running
kəp-	cry	>	kəp-nə kəp-nə	by crying
sai-	chew	>	sai-nə sai-nə	by chewing
ui-	take a nap	>	ui-nə ui-nə	by taking a nap, etc.

184. **təp**- 'be slow'
əhən-du təp-nə lak-i
old man-DEM slow-ADV come-SAM
'The old man comes slowly'

185. **həu**- 'be loud'
əŋaŋ-du həu-nə kəp-pi
child-DEM loud-ADV cry-SAM
'The child cries loudly'

186. **kui**- '(of time) be long'
ma-nə nəŋ-bu kui-nə ŋai-rəm-mi
he-NOM you-ACC long-ADV wait-COMP-SAM
'He waited for you for a long time'

The adverbs when reduplicated gives a sense of habituality or an event occurring frequently while non-reduplicative adverbials imply that the events occur only once. Consider the following sentences to observe the semantic differences between reduplicative and non-reduplicative forms of adverbs.

187. **təp**- 'be slow'
əhən-du təp-nə təp-nə ŋaŋ-ŋi
old man-DEM slow-ADV slow-ADV speak-SAM
'The old man usually speaks slowly'

188. **theŋ**- 'be late'
suni-di theŋ-nə theŋ-nə lak-i

Suni-PART late-ADV late-ADV come-SAM
'Suni comes late (as usual)'

The adverbials in the above sentences give a sense of repetition, habitual when they occur in reduplicative form. For examples, the adverb **təp-nə təp-nə** in (187) implies that the event occurs repeatedly.

Adverbs derived from action verbs always occur in reduplicated forms. They cannot occur in a non-reduplicative environment.

189. **cət-** 'go'
əi-nə ləmbi-də cət-nə cət-nə wakhən khəl-li (khən-li)
I-NOM road-LOC go-ADV go-ADV thought think-SAM
'I thought of something while I was going'

190. **thoŋ-** 'cook'
memə-nə cak thoŋ-nə thoŋ-nə kon pheŋ-ŋi
Mema-NOM rice cook-ADV cook-ADV utensil scour-SAM
'Mema scours utensil while cooking'

***-kə* 'potential/non-realization'**: The suffix has two variations as **-kə ~ gə**. **-kə** comes after any morpheme that ends in unaspirated stop sounds /**p**/, /**t**/, /**k**/ while **-gə** follows any morpheme that ends in vowels and nasal sounds. The suffix can occur in three combinations which form a sequence of suffixes as **-kəni ~ gəni** which denotes non-realization, **-kənu ~ gənu** which gives the meaning of prohibitive and **-kədəbə ~ gədəbə** which means 'is to do/has to do/ have to do'. In the first two contexts **-kə ~ gə** can be dropped while in the last context it is present obligatorily.

ca-	eat	ca-gni	>	ca-ni	will eat
thom-	hit	thom-gəni	>	thom-ni	will hit
tu-	fall	tu-gəni	>	tu-ni	will fall
cak-	burn	cak-kəni	>	cak-ni	will burn
tət-	break	tət-kəni	>	tət-ni	will break
təp-	be slow	təp-kəni	>	təp-ni	will be slow
ten-	be short	ten-gəni	>	ten-ni	will be short
saŋ-	be long	saŋ-gəni	>	saŋ-ni	will be long, etc.

191. **thək-** 'drink'
əi səŋgom thək-kəni
I milk drink-NREAL
'I will drink milk'

192. **tət-** 'break'
ləŋ əsi thu-nə tət-kəni
thread this quick-ADV break-NREAL
'This thread will break easily'

Some examples of **-kənu** are given below:

cət-	go	cət-kənu	>	cət-nu	don't do
kəp-	cry	kəp-kənu	>	kəp-nu	don't cry
nok-	laugh	nok-kənu	>	nok-nu	don't laugh
pa-	read	pa-gənu	>	pa-nu	don't read
hai-	swing	hai-gənu	>	hai-nu	don't swing, etc.

192. **kau-** 'kick'
kəuta-du kau-gənu
can-DEM kick-PROH
'Don't kick the can'

193. **ca-** 'eat'
həkcaŋ sok-kədəbə pot ca-gənu
health harm-have to thing eat-PROH
'Don't consume anything that is harmful to health'

Some examples of **-kədəbə** with some verbal roots are given below:

ta-	listen	>	ta-gədəbə	to be listened
i-	write	>	i-gədəbə	to be written
lon-	knit	>	lon-gədəbə	to be knitted
hap-	put	>	hap-kədəbə	to be put
khənnə-	discuss	>	khənnə-gədəbə	to be discussed, etc.

194. **in-** 'follow'
əi-khoi-nə əphaubə mi-siŋ-gi khuduŋ in-gədəbə-ni
I-PL-NOM famous man-PL-GEN way follow-have to-COP
'We must follow the way of famous personalities'

195. **niŋ-siŋ-** 'remember'
nə-khoi nə-sa-gi nə-thəu niŋsiŋ gədəbə-ni
you-PL 2PP-body-GEN 2PP-duty remember-have to-COP
'You should remember your duties'

-loi **'non-potential'**: The suffixation of **-loi** to verbal roots denotes negative sense. It has six allomorphic variations as **-loi ~ roi ~ poi ~ moi ~ ŋoi ~ oi** and their occurrence is same with the conditioning factor of **-lə** 'deictic'. The suffix is often contrasted with **-kə** 'non-realization'. The contrastive meaning may be observed from the following sentences:

196. **lon-** 'prepare tea'
a. əi ca lon-gəni
I tea prepare-NREAL
'I will make tea'

b. əi ca lol-loi (-lon-loi)
I tea prepare-NPOT-SAM
'I will not make tea'

The contrast can also be seen in the question answer forms.

197.a. nəŋ ca lon-gədəbə-ra (lon-gədəbə-ra > lon-gədra)
you tea prepare-have to-INTR
'Will you make/prepare tea?'

It is to be noted that -**bə** from -**gədəbə** is deleted by applying -**bə**/ə deletion rule as (-**gə-dəbra**/ **gədəbə-ra** > **gədəra**). The same -ə deletion rule deletes -ə from -**də** and whereby resulting **lon-gədə-bə-ra** > **lon-gədəbra/lon-gədəra** > **lon-gədra**.

b. əi ca lol-loi (lon-loi)
I tea prepare-NREAL-SAM
'I will not make tea'

Another possible construction where the contrast may be seen is given below.

ca- 'eat' ca-gədəbə-ni 'have to/ ought to/ supposed to/ must eat'
ca-roi-dəbə-ni 'have not to/ ought not to/ not supposed to/ must not eat'
It may be used in sentences as:

198. **ca-** 'eat'
a. noŋmə-də həi khərə khərə ca-gədəbə-ni
daily-LOC fruit some some eat-have to-COP
'We ought to eat a small amount of fruit everyday'

b. na-riŋəi-də-di həi khək ca-roi-dəbə-ni
sick-SPFD-LOC-PART fruit never eat-NPOT-have to-COP
'You ought not to eat fruit when you are sick'

The suffix -**loi** gives different meanings which are conditioned by its neighbouring suffixes *i.e.* the suffixes which precede it. When -**khi** precedes -**loi**, the combination of the suffixes imply a temporal negative (see **1.1**).

Another construction is with -**lə** 'prospective' where the speaker's intension is not to do something. It may be a simple negative statement or stoppage of a habit and sometimes, a sense of promise (see **1.1**).

The addition of -**khə** 'definitive' to -**rə-roi** intensifies the statement by giving a sense of promise (see **1.1**).

***-pə ~ bə* 'nominalizer'**: It is a nominalizer suffix which changes the word class of the verb to a nominal form. The word resulting from the suffixation of **-pə ~ bə** is also known as verbal noun. **-pə** comes after unaspirated voiceless stops /**p**/, /**t**/, /**k**/ while **-bə** follows morphemes that end in voiced sounds *i.e.* vowels and nasal sounds.

cət-	go	>	cət-pə	going/to go
kət-	offer	>	kət-pə	offering/to offer
kək-	cut	>	kək-pə	cutting/to cut
nəp-	stick	>	nəp-pə	sticking/to stick
hop-	be loose	>	hop-pə	loose
nok-	laugh	>	nok-pə	laughing/to laugh
pi-	give	>	pi-bə	giving/to give
pu-	carry	>	pu-bə	carrying/to carry
təm-	learn	>	təm-bə	learning/to learn
ken-	fall	>	ken-bə	falling/to fall, etc.

199. **cət-** 'go'
əŋaŋ-sa! nə-khoi cət-pə ja-re
child-PL you-PL go-NMZ agree-PERF-SAM
'Children! you may go'

200. **su-** 'wash'
əi phi su-bə həu-də-ri
I cloth wash-NMZ start-NEG-PROG-SAM
'I have not yet started washing clothes'

The verbal noun or derived noun can be followed by copula **-ni** as seen in the following sentences.

201. **ca**-'eat'
ma-di sa ca-bə-ni
he-PART meat eat-NMZ-COP
'He is a non-vegetarian'

202. **sək-** 'sing'
isəi-du ma-nə sək-pə-ni
song-DEM he-NOM sing-NMZ-COP
'The song is sung by him'

Adjectives are formed by adding attributing ə- to the derived noun, *e.g.* **cət-** 'go' > **əcət-pə** 'one who goes'. Verbal nouns which are derived from disyllabic verbal roots like **hərau-** 'be happy', **ciŋ-nə-** 'hesitate, suspect, doubt', **pakhət-** 'become nervous', etc. do not take the prefix ə-. The derived nouns as **hərau-bə**, **ciŋnə-bə**, **pakhət-pə** can also become adjectives (see **1.3**). Derived forms like **ca-ri-bə** 'one who is eating', **ca-rəm-bə** 'one who was eating', **ca-rə-bə** 'one who has eaten', **ca-ru-bə** 'one who went somewhere to eat', **ca-rə-bə** 'one who came here to eat', etc. are adjectives which are normally found in a relative clause construction. They can also occur with copula **-ni**.

The derived word which have **-pə ~ bə** are generally followed by interrogative marker **-la ~ ra** and **-ke ~ ge**, **-no**.

203. **həi-** 'know, experienced, skilled'
nəŋ cak thoŋ-bə həi-bə-ra
you rice cook-NMZ know-NMZ-INTR
'Do you know how to cook?'

204. **phəŋ-** 'find'
səŋai hai-bə sa əsi məphəm kədai-də phəŋ-bə-ge
bow-antlered deer connector animal this place where-LOC find NMZ-INTR
'Where is the bow-antlered deer (***Cervus eldi eldi***) found ?'

205. **sat-** 'bloom'
siroi lili kəri tha-də sat-pə-ge
Siroy Lili which month-LOC bloom-NMZ-INTR
'In which month does Siroy Lily bloom?'

206. **sai-** 'chew'
nəŋ kəri sai-ri-bə-no
you what chew-PROG-NMZ-Q
'What are you chewing?'

Sentences (203-206) in the above examples show that they are interrogative sentences which are formed by adding interrogative markers (**-la**, **-ke**, and **-no**) to a nominal form. It may be observed that the nominalizer **-pə ~ bə** takes an important role in the formation of interrogative sentences.

***-cə* 'reflexive/ request'**: It is the reflexive suffix which has a variant form **-ɟə**. **-cə** occurs before unaspirated voiceless stops /**p**/, /**t**/, /**k**/ while **-ɟə** occurs after voiced sounds. It can go with all the verb types, where it implies to perform or experience something by the self.

207. **sək tak-** 'introduce'
məhak mə-sa-nə mə-sa-bu sək tak-cə-i
he 3PP-body-NOM 3PP-body-ACC introduce-REF-SAM
'He introduced himself'

208. **pen-** 'satisfy'
satrə-siŋ-nə pukniŋ cəŋ-nə ta-bə-du-də oɟa-du
student-PL-NOM attentive-ADV listen-NMZ-DEM-LOC teacher-DEM

pen-ɟə-rm-mi
satisfy-REF-COMP-SAM
'The teacher was satisfied when the students listened to his lecture attentively'

The verb **sək-tak**- 'introduce' in (207) is an action verb and the suffixation of **-cə** to it gives the meaning of performing an action by the self while the verb **pen**- 'satisfy' in (208) is a stative verb and the addition of **-ɟə** to it implies that the referent experiences the effect.

It may be noted that the suffix **-cə ~ ɟə** is also used as a request marker. The following sentences will show the difference in meaning between reflexive and request form.

209. **jeŋ**- 'look'
lairik əsi əi əmuk-tə jeŋ-ɟə-ge
book this I once-only look-REF-INT
'Please allow me to have a look at the book'

210. **lak**- 'come'
əi həjeŋ əjuk lak-cə-rə-ge
I tomorrow morning come-REF-PROS-INT
'Let me visit you tomorrow morning'

Sentences (209) and (210) have verbs indicating request to an elder person in the form of seeking permission to do something. The suffixation of **-cə** also gives a sense of warning to someone for doing something bad or unfavourable as found in the following sentences:

211. **curuŋ**- 'happen to oneself what he dislikes in others'
mi noknə-gənu curuŋ-ɟə-ni
man laugh at-PROH happen to oneself -REF-COP
'Don't laugh at others; you will get what you dislike in them'

212. ləm hel-ləbədi pulis-ki cəi ça-ɟə-ni
arrogant if police-GEN stick eat-REF-COP
'If you are arrogant, you will get a beating from the police'

The use of this suffix can be found in a different syntactic construction also.

213. lairik kən-nə pau-o nət-tə-rəbədi phel oi-ɟə-ni
book hard-ADV read-COM not-NEG-if fail be-REF-COP
'Study hard or you will fail (in the examination)'

***-pi* 'honorific'**: It is an honorific marker which is homophonous with benefactive **-pi** (see grammaticalized suffixes). The suffix has another variant form **-bi** and the conditioning factor of occurrence is same with benefactive **-pi**. The suffix is commonly associated with honorific verb forms given below.

Honorific	**Common**	
leŋ-	cət-	go
lan-	pi-	give

ha-	ca-	eat
phan-	thək-	drink
caithə-	iruɟ-	take bath
cep-	hip-	lie down
mitjeŋ ta-	jeŋ-	look
leŋkhət-	həugət-	wake up, etc.

214. **leŋ-sin**- 'take a seat'
phida som-də leŋ-sin-bi-ju
seat direction-LOC take seat-POL-COM
'Please take the seat'

215. **phan**- 'drink'
ca-si phan-bi-ju
tea-DEM drink-POL-COM
'Please have the tea'

The polite form with honorific lexical items is not a common practice in day-to-day use. They are replaced by common lexical items while the polite marker **-pi** is still retained.

216. **phəm**- 'sit'
phida-sidə phəm-bi-ju
seat-DEM-LOC sit-POL-COM
'Please take the seat'

217. **cəŋ**- 'enter'
imuŋ-lom-də cəŋ-bi-ju
inside the house-direction-LOC enter-POL-COM
'Please enter inside the house'

***-lə* 'perfective'**: It is the perfective suffix which is homophonous with **-lə** 'prospective'. It has the same variations with the same conditionaing factors. The suffix **-l** when followed by **-gə** becomes a sequence of suffixes and it has multiple functions. With the perfective meaning it implies that the action is finished or completed as **ca-rəgə** 'after finished eating', **thək-ləgə** 'after finished drinking', etc.

The participal form of -lə is **ca-rə-bə** 'one who has eaten', **jeŋ-lə-bə** 'something that has been seen', **ləi-rə-bə** 'something that has been bought', etc. These forms may be followed by a copula **-ni**.

218. **ca**- 'eat'
əŋaŋ-du cak ca-rə-bə-ni
child-DET rice eat-PERF-NMZ-COP
'The child has taken meal'

219. **tət**- 'be torn'
phi-du tət-lə-bə-ni
cloth-DEM torn-PERF-NMZ-COP
'The cloth is torn'

220. **iŋ**- 'be cold'
isiŋ-du iŋ-ŋə-bə-ni (-ləbə-ni)
water-DEM cold-PERF-NMZ-COP
'The water has become cold'

The verb **ca**- 'eat' in (218) is an action verb and the suffixation of **-lə** indicates that the action of eating has been finished while **tət**- 'be torn' in (219) is a process verb. The sentence implies that the process of 'being torn' is completed and it simply shows a state or condition of the cloth. Thus, in the present context, the sentence is a stative sentence. The verb **iŋ**- in (220) implies that a change has taken place in the sense that the water was hot earlier but it has become cold. It shows process of some change. Hence, it is to be treated as process verb.

***-nə* 'purposive'**: This suffix indicates purpose or intention of doing or achieving something. It may be attached to both monosyllabic and disyllabic or polysyllabic verbal roots.The suffixation of **-nə** to monosyllabic verbal roots may be followed by nominalizer **-pə** ~ **bə** and verbal inflectional markers. When **-nə** is attached to a monosyllabic verbal root, there is a difference in the pronunciation of the verbal root, *i.e*, the vowel of the verbal root is lengthened (which occurs in this case only). This does not happen when the verbal root or the preceding morpheme is disyllabic or polysyllabic and when the suffix is followed by derivative markers or inflectional suffixes except by nominalizer **-pə** ~ **bə**, *e.g*. in **thoŋ-nə-re** '(of a pot) used as a cooking pot'. When **-nə** is repeated (which will come just after nonosyllabic verbal root followed by single **-nə**) the vowel lengthening does not occur as well. Examples of verbs that have nominalizer and again followed by nominal free forms are given below:

thək-nə-bə isiŋ	water (meant) for drinking
i-nə-bə ce	paper (meant) for writing
pa-nə-bə lairik	book (meant) for reading
phot-nə-bə ləŋ	thread (meant) for stitching
pun-nə-bə thəuri	rope (meant) for binding
jom-nə-bə phi	cloth (meant) for wrapping, etc.

221. **thək**- 'drink'
thək-nə-bə isiŋ khərə pu-rək-u
drink-PUR-NMZ water some bring-DEIC-COM
'Bring some water for drinking'

222. **phot**- 'stitch'
phi-si phot-nə-bə ləŋ khərə pi-rək-u
cloth-DEM stitch-PUR-NMZ thread some give-DEIC-COM
'Give me a piece of thread to stitch this cloth'

The copula **-ni** can also follow the sequence of suffixes **-nə-bə** as given in the following sentence.

223. **təi**- 'apply'
thau-si kok-tə təi-nə-bə-ni
oil-DEM head-LOC apply-PUR-NMZ-COP
'This oil is meant for applying on hair *i.e.* this is hair oil'

Another possible occurrence of **-nə** is with verbal inflectional suffixes, *i.e.* with aspect marker **-i**.

224. **su**- 'wash'
khudeŋ-də phi su-nə-i
tub-LOC cloth wash-PUR-SAM
'Clothes are washed in washing tubs'

225. **tau**- 'fry'
khaŋ-də ŋa tau-nə-i
frying pan-LOC fish fry-PUR-SAM
'Fish are fried in frying pans'

The suffix **-nə** may be used in repeated forms with nominalized constructions only. The derived form may be followed by either a nominal or a verb. With nominals, it gives a sense of emphasis or the meaning is enhanced while with verbs, it implies that an extra effort is given in order to meet the purpose or intention of doing or achieving something.

təm-nə-nə-bə lairik	books meant for learning only (textbook)
thoŋ-nə-nə-bə ceŋ	rice meant for cooking meal only
i-nə-nə-bə ce	paper meant for writing only
hon-nə-nə-bə gari	vehicles meant for carrying load only
soi-nə-nə-bə thaŋ	knife meant for cutting vegetables only
toŋ-nə-nə-bə khoŋ-up	shoe meant for wearing only
sup-nə-nə-bə phəiɟ up	blanket meant for covering only
hap-nə-nə-bə khau	bag meant for putting things only, etc.

226. **təm**- 'learn'
klas siks-tə təm-nə-nə-bə lairik phoŋ-le
class six-LOC learn-PUR-PUR-NMZ book publish-PERF-SAM
'Text books for class-VI have been published/ released'

227. **hap**- 'put'
lairik-siŋ-si hap-nə-nə-bə khau əmə ləi-rək-u
book-PL-DEM put-PUR-PUR-NMZ bag one buy-DEIC-COM
'Buy a bag to put these books'

The repetition of **-nə** in the above sentences gives a sense of emphasis on the verb to which they are added. The phrase **təm-nə-nə-bə lairik** means 'books for learning in schools, *i.e.* textbooks' only. Similarly, the phrase **hap-nə-nə-bə khau** also means 'a bag for putting the books' only and not for other purposes. Some examples of the derived forms followed by a verb are given below:

nəŋ-nə-nə-bə cət-li	goes quickly in order to reach in time
phəŋ-nə-nə-bə tan-nəi	chase hard in order to catch
khəŋ-nə-nə-bə jeŋ-ŋi	look carefully in order to know
pha-nə-nə-bə pa-i	read hard in order to learn by heart
cət-nə-nə-bə təu-ri	tries to get ready to go/set off
ja-nə-nə-bə ŋaŋ-nə-ri	persuing hard in order to agree/get permission, etc.

228. **phəŋ-** 'catch'
pulis-nə huranbə-du phəŋ-nə-nə-bə tan-nə-i
police-NOM thief-DEM catch-PUR-PUR-NMZ chase-REC-SAM
'Police chased the thief in order to arrest him'

229. **nəŋ-** 'be in time'
məhak klas nəŋ-nə-nə-bə cel-li
he class in time-PUR-PUR-NMZ run-SAM
'He runs in order to reach school in time'

The repetition of **-nə** in (228 and 229) gives the implication that an extra effort has been used in order to achieve something. In (228), the policemen give an extra effort while chasing the thief. In (229), the referent gives an extra effort while running all the way to school.

The suffix -**nə** can also be attached to disyllabic or polysyllabic roots. It can also follow a derived verbal root which contains a monosyllabic verbal root and one or two verbal derivative suffix and so on.

Disyllabic or polysyllabic verbal roots with ***-nə***.

sannə-nə-bə bol	ball (meant) for playing
khətnə-nə-bə mərəm	cause for quarrelling
khənnə-nə-bə waphəm	topic (meant) for discussion
niŋsiŋ-nə-bə photo	photograph for memory
tuŋsin-nə-bə sel/pəisa	money for saving
pottha-nə-bə məphəm	place for taking rest
siŋtha-nə-bə thəbək	work worth to be appreciated
irulə-nə-bə isiŋ	water for bathing, etc.

230. **sannə-** 'play'
əŋaŋ-də sannə-nə-bə bol-du pi-ju
child-DAT play-PUR-NMZ ball-DEM give-COM
'Give the ball to the child for playing'

231. **tuŋsin-** 'save'
əi-gi tuŋsin-nə-bə sel ləi-te
I-GEN save-PUR-NMZ money have-NEG-SAM
'I have no money for saving'

-nə can be preceded by other derivatives also which is again followed by a verb as given below:

232. **həi-** 'be experienced, skilled'
əŋaŋ-du lairik həi-niŋ-nə-bə tak-u
child-DEM book experience-wish-PUR-NMZ teach-COM
'Motivate the child to learn more'

233. **hai-** 'say'
məhak-nə əi-ŋon-də wa-du hai-dok-nə-bə tək-i
he-NOM I-DIR-LOC matter-DEM say-OUT-PUR-NMZ insist -SAM
'He insisted me to disclose the matter to him'

-ləmdai: The addition of this suffix to a verbal root gives the meaning of 'about to start' doing or becoming something. As the meaning indicates it can go with dynamic verbs only, *i.e.* with action verbs and process verbs. The suffix has six allomorphic variations as **ləmdai** ~ **rəmdai** ~ **pəmdai** ~ **məmdai** ~ **ŋəmdai** ~ **əmdai** and the conditioning factor of these variations is same to **-ləm**.

234. **cət-** 'go'
əŋaŋ skul cət-ləmdai-də əi phi su-ri
child school go-about to-LOC I cloth wash-PROG-SAM
'I was washing clothes while my child was ready to go to school'

235. **mun-** 'be ripe'
kəphoi-du mul-ləmdai-də hek-tət-kənu
pomegranate-DEM ripe-about to-LOC pluck-DEST-PROH
'Do not pluck the pomegranate when it is about to ripe'

236. **səu-** 'boil'
isiŋ səu-rəmdai-də əi kəu-rək-u
water boil-about to-LOC I call-DEIC-COM
'Call me when the water is about to boil'

The verb **cət-** 'go' to which the suffix is added in (234) is an action verb while the verb **mun-** in (235) is a stative verb by virtue of its semantic structure. The reason why it can go with this suffix is that it implies a natural process of becoming ripe from unripe which is already present in our conscience.

-kum: The suffix can occur with two different grammatical forms, *viz* (i) with verbal nouns (nominalized verbs formed by adding **-pə ~ bə** to verbal roots) (ii) with a verb where it is always followed by **-si** 'suggestive'.

***-kum* with nominalized verbs**: It can occur with all verb types *i.e.* stative, process and action. When the suffix is attached to a verb it gives the meaning of uncertainty of an action. In normal speech this **-pə ~ bə** is often deleted and it seems to be attached to a verbal root directly. The suffix is always associated with a verb **təu-**. The suffix has two variations as **-kum ~ gum**. **-kum** comes after voiceless sounds while **-gum** follows any voiced sounds.

237. **man-** 'look like or resemble'

nupi-məca-si	mə-ma	man-bə-gum	təu-i
woman-small-DEM	3PP-mother	resemble-NMZ-uncertain	do-SAM

'The girl seems to resemble her mother'

238. **səm-** 'be short'

ləmbi	əsi-nə	səm-bə-gum	təu-i
street	this-CMP	short-NMZ-uncertain	do-sam

'This street seems to be a short cut'

239. **cət-** 'go'

məhak	ŋəraŋ	dili	cət-khi-bə-gum	təu-i
he	yesterday	Delhi	go-DEF-NMZ-uncertain	do-SAM

'It seems to me that he left for Delhi yesterday'

The verb forms **man-bə-gum** 'seems to resemble', **səm-bə-gum** 'seems to be short' in (237 and 238) are stative verbs. They express uncertainty of a state or condition. **cət-khi-bə-gum** 'seems to have left' in (239) denotes uncertainty of the action. It may also mean that it is not certain when and where he went.

When the nominalizer **-pə ~ bə** is deleted or dropped the suffix **-kum ~ gum** is repeated where a dummy verb **lak-** takes the place of the second element of the repeated form to which **-kum** is attached. Some examples of the reduplicated form of **-kum ~ gum** are shown below:

thək-	drink	>	thək-kum lak-kum	seems to drink
cen-	run	>	cen-gum lak-kum	seems to run
nok-	laugh	>	nok-kum lak-kum	seems to laugh
sau-	be angry	>	sau-gum lak-kum	seems to be angry
ui-	be drowsy	>	ui-gum lak-kum	seems to be drowsy, etc.

The dummy verb **lak-** in the above construction may be replaced by another dummy word **kəri**.

hərau-	be happy	>	hərau-gum kəri-gum	seems to be happy
tum-niŋ-	feel sleepy	>	tum-niŋ-gum kəri-gum	seems to be sleepy
purək-	bring	>	purək-kum kəri-gum	seems to bring
hai-	swing	>	hai-gum kəri-gum	seems to swing
sit-	sweep	>	sit-kum kəri-gum	seems to sweep
pu-khi-	taken away	>	pukhi-gum kəri-gum	seems to have taken away
hap-pəm-	put inside	>	hap-pəm-gum kəri-gum	seems to have put inside, etc.

All the reduplicated verb forms are also followed by **təu-** as found in non-reduplicated form and they convey the same meaning.

***-kum* with a verb where it is always followed by -si 'suggestive'** : **-kum** with verbal roots has a restriction in the selection of suffixes with which it can occur. It is always followed by the suggestive suffix **-si** and the combination of the suffixes denote negative proposal of a verb. Since proposal to do or not to do something is always associated with action oriented verbs (*i.e.* with controllable verbs), it cannot occur with uncontrollable verbs (see **1.1**).

4.3 Deletion or Contraction

David (2003: 106) defined contraction as a term used in linguistics to refer to the process or result of phonologically reducing a linguistic form so that it comes to be attached to an adjacent linguistic form or fusing a sequence of forms so that they appear as a single form. It is a phonological process whereby a syllable or part of a syllable is dropped or deleted. The deletion of the latter type (dropping of a part of a syllable) may result in the contraction of the adjacent consonants (when followed by **/r/** sound). It may also bring about a sound change *e.g.* voicing of unaspirated stops.

Deletion or Dropping of a Syllable: Manipuri, being an agglutinating type of language, a verbal root may take a string of suffixes and for the language, it is quite normal to drop some of the suffixes from the string without disturbing the semantic structure of the derivational process. Nominalizer suffix **-pə ~ bə** and **-kə** of non-realizational marker **-kəni** can be dropped.

Deletion of *-pə ~ bə*: The nominalizer **-pə ~ -bə** may be dropped in certain environments. It may be dropped in the following circumstances where it occurs between **-də** and **-ra**.

cət-kə-də-bə-ra	>	cət-kə-də-ra	Will you go?
jau-gə-də-bə-ra	>	jau-gə-də-ra	Will you join?
pa-gə-də-bə-ra	>	pa-dgə-də-ra	Will you read?
nəp-kə-də-bə-ra	>	nəp-kə-də-ra	Will you stick?
sem-gə-də-bə-ra	>	sem-gə-də-ra	Will you repair?
khok-kə-də-bə-ra	>	khok-kə-də-ra	Will you peel out?

ca-roi-də-bə-ra	>	ca-roi-də-ra	Will you not eat?
tum-moi-də-bə-ra	>	tum-moi-də-ra	Will you not sleep?
phot-loi-də-bə-ra	>	phot-loi-də-ra	Will you not stitch?
tak-loi-də-bə-ra	>	tak-loi-də-ra	Will you not teach?
ka-roi-də-bə-ra	>	ka-roi-də-ra	Will you not climb?, etc.

-pə ~ **bə** may also be deleted when it is followed by **-kum** ~ **gum** which gives the meaning of uncertainty.

cət-pə-gum təu-i	>	cət-kum təu-i	seems to go
hən-bə-gum təu-i	>	hən-gum təu-i	seems to be older
ta-khi-bə-gum təu-i	>	ta-khi-gum təu-i	seems to have heard
khəŋ-bə-gum təu-i	>	khəŋ-gum təu-i	seems to know
cau-bə-gum təu-i	>	cau-gum təu-i	seems to be big
mən-bə-gum təu-i	>	mən-gum təu-i	seems to be old
kəp-pə-gum təu-i	>	kəp-kum təu-i	seems to cry, etc.

The suffix **-pə** ~ **b** may also be deleted when the word **man-li** > **mal-le** 'uncertaintity' follows it.

ca-rə-bə mal-le	>	carə mal-le	seems to have eaten
i-rə-bə mal-le	>	i-rə mal-le	seems to have written
thək-pə mal-le	>	thək mal-le	seems to drink (liquor)
təu-bə mal-le	>	təu mal-le	seems to do
loi-khə-rə-bə mal-le	>	loi-khə-rə mal-le	seems to have finished
ca-niŋ-bə mal-le	>	ca-niŋ mal-le	seems that he wishes to eat
ŋaŋ-gən-bə mal-le	>	ŋaŋ-gən mal-le	seems to be talkative, etc.

There are also two other environments where **-pə** ~ **bə** is deleted. This is interpreted in a wrong way by Shobhana (1997, see p. 156). They are **-ɟat** and **-pot** which she considered to be nominalizers. But the fact is that both the words are preceded by nominalizer **-pə** ~ **bə** but deleted in the surface structure.

ca-bə ɟat-ni	>	ca-ɟat-ni
jeŋ-bə ɟat-ni	>	jeŋ-ɟat-ni
lak-pə ɟat-ni	>	lak-cat-ni
həu-bə ɟat-ni	>	həu-ɟat-ni
lon-bə ɟat-ni	>	lon-ɟat-ni

Examples with the word **-pot** are also given below:

ŋəm-bə pot nətte	>	ŋəm pot nətte
ja-bə pot-ni	>	ja-pot-ni
həu-bə pot-ni	>	həu-pot-ni
pa-niŋ-bə pot-ni	>	pa-niŋ-pot-ni

Deletion of *-kə ~ gə*: The suffix **-kə** of non-realization marker **-kəni ~ gəni** and prohibitive marker **-kənu ~ gənu** may be dropped without any disturbance in the meaning.

lak-kəni	>	lak-ni	will come
ləi-gəni	>	ləi-ni	will buy
təu-gəni	>	təu-ni	will do
sannə-gəni	>	sannə-ni	will play
iroi-gəni	>	iroi-ni	will swim
phut-kəni	>	phut-ni	will boil, etc.

Shobhana (1997: 232) did not mention about the deletion rule and she considered **-ni** (when **-kə ~ gə** is dropped from **-kəni ~ gəni)** as copula and explained that the copula **-ni** alone indicates that the action will certainly take place.

The suffix **-kə ~ gə** may also be dropped from the prohibitive marker **-kənu ~ gənu**.

cət-lə-gənu	>	cət-lə-nu	don't go (as the plan is dropped)
ca-gənu	>	ca-nu	don't eat
ca-ru-gənu	>	ca-ru-nu	don't go and eat there
kəu-gənu	>	kəu-nu	don't call
ŋaŋ-gənu	>	ŋaŋ-nu	don't speak
phu-gənu	>	phu-nu	don't beat
phu-bi-gənu	>	phu-bi-nu	don't beat (unnecessarily)
cət-minnə-gənu	>	cət-minnə-nu	don't go together
pən-ɟə-gənu	>	pən-ɟənu	don't mention
phu-nə-gənu	>	phu-nə-nu	don't beat each other
təu-khi-gənu	>	təu-khi-nu	don't do it now, etc.

The suffix **-kənu ~ gənu** is obligatory when certain suffixes precede it. Some of them are **-sin** 'inward directional', **-thok** 'outward directional', **-khət** 'upward directional', **-hən** 'causative', **-niŋ** 'wish' etc. A hypothesis can be formulated from the above examples that **-kə ~ gə** can be dropped when it is preceded by verbal suffixes which end in vowels (as seen in the examples above) while **-nu** can be attached directly after any verbal root. **-kə ~ gə** cannot be dropped in **-kədəbə ~ gədbə** 'ought to'.

There is also another instance where **-kə ~ gə** can be dropped. The grammaticalized suffix **-təu-ri** or **-təu-re** 'is going to do something' is always preceded by **-kə ~ gə** which may, sometimes be deleted. Still the meaning is not disturbed (see **4.2**).

cət-kə-dəu-ri	>	cət-təu-ri	is going to visit
paŋthok-kə-dəu-ri	>	paŋthok-təu-ri	is going to perform
khənnə-gə-dəu-ri	>	khənnə-dəu-ri	is going to discuss
phəŋ-gə-dəu-ri	>	phəŋ-dəu-ri	is going to receive
siɟinnə-gə-dəu-ri	>	siɟinnə-dəu-ri	is going to use
həu-gə-dəu-ri	>	həu-dəu-re	is going to start shortly
loi-gə-dəu-re	>	loi-dəu-re	is going to finish shortly
mun-gə-dəu-re	>	mun-dəu-re	is going to be ripe
i-gə-dəu-re	>	i-dəu-re	is going to write shortly
thom-gə-dəu-re	>	thom-dəu-re	is going to hit, etc.

Deletion of a part of a syllable: A peak (usually vowels) of a syllable having no coda or a coda (usually consonants) of a syllable may be dropped. The first type of deletion is the deletion of /ə/ which generally occurs with verbal suffixes like **-pə ~ bə**, **-də**, **-khə** and **-tə ~ də** while the latter type occurs in verbal root itself.

Deletion of /ə/: The deletion may occur in suffixes as **-pə ~ bə**, **-də**, **-khə**, **-tə ~ də** when they are followed by **-ra** 'interrogative suffix'.

Deletion of /ə/ **in –pə ~ bə**

ca-bə-ra	>	ca-bra	do you eat?
cət-pə-ra	>	cət-pra	do you go?
tok-niŋ-bə-ra	>	tok-niŋ-bra	do you want to quit?
jau-hən-bə-ra	>	jau-hən-bra	do you let him join?
loi-khə-rə-bə-ra	>	loi-khərə-bra	has it been finished?
ca-ri-bə-ra	>	ca-ri-bra	are you eating?
ca-rə-bə-ra	>	ca-rə-bra	have you eaten?
ləŋ-thok-pə-ra	>	ləŋ-thok-pra	do you throw it out?
su-minnə-bə-ra	>	su-minnə-bra	do you work together?
khətnə-bə-ra	>	khətnə-bra	do you quarrel?
sannə-ru-bə-ra	>	sannə-ru-bra	did you go and play there?
pu-rək-pə-ra	>	pu-rək-pra	did you bring it?, etc.

Deletion of /ə/ **in** *–də*: When the sequence of suffixes **-kədəbə ~ gədəbə** 'ought to do something' undergoes a deletion and **-kədə ~ gədə** is remained. When the interrogative marker **-ra** follows this sequence of suffixes **-kədə ~ gədə**, the /ə/ of **-də** is generally omitted and /**d**/ and /**ra**/ is contracted in the following way.

cət-kədə-ra	>	cət-kədra	will you go?
ca-gədə-ra	>	ca-gədra	will you eat?

lak-kədə-ra	>	lak-kədra	will you come?
hai-gədə-ra	>	hai-gədra	will you say?
pu-gə-də-ra	>	pu-gədra	will you carry?
tət-kədə-ra	>	tət-kədra	will it break?
ləu-gədə-ra	>	ləu-gədra	will you take?, etc.

/ə/ of -**də** in -**loidə-bə** 'not ought to' which is a counterpart of -**kədəbə** ~ **gədəbə** may also be deleted where -**ra** follows and have the same form as above.

tət-loidəbə-ra	>	tət-loidra	will it not break?
kut-loidə-ra	>	kut-loidra	(surface) will it not be low?
thət-loidə-ra	>	thət-loidra	(of flower) will you not pluck it?
phəm-moidə-ra	>	phəm-moidra	will you not sit?
təŋ-ŋoidə-ra	>	təŋ-ŋoidra	will you not have a taste (a curry)
thap-poidə-ra	>	thap-poidra	will it not be far (from here), etc.

Deletion of /ə/ **in** ***-khə***: The suffix -**khə** 'definitive' may be followed by -**rə** 'perfective', -**re** (-**rə-i**) 'perfective' and -**ri** 'progressive' and in such situation, the /ə/ of -**khə** is generally deleted and the combination of **kh**- and -**rə**/-**ri**/-**re** forms a fusion like -**khrə**, -**khri**, -**khre**.

pai-khə-rə-bə	>	pai-khrə-bə	(a bird) that has flawn away
jot-khə-rə-bə	>	jot-khrə-bə	(something) that has been swallowed
kau-khə-rə-bə	>	kau-khrə-bə	(something) that has been forgotten
loi-khə-rə-bə	>	loi-khrə-bə	(something) that has been finished
mut-khə-rə-bə	>	mut-khrə-bə	(something) that has been extinct
pha-khə-rə-bə	>	pha-khrə-bə	(something) that has been got by heart
səŋ-khə-rə-bə	>	səŋ-khrə-bə	(something) that has been dyed
sən-dok-khə-ri	>	sən-dok-khri	(of trees on hills) has spread from here to places where the eyesight cannot reach
cət-khə-ri	>	cət-khri	has gone to somewhere and not yet returned
pai-khə-ri	>	pai-khri	as been flying in one after another and is not yet finished
jon-khə-re	>	jon-khre	(something) that has been sold
thəu-khə-re	>	thəu-khre	(vehicle) that has been driven
ken-khə-re	>	ken-khre	(leaves) that have been fallen
ləŋ-khə-re	>	ləŋ-khre	(ball) that has been thrown
cen-khə-re	>	cen-khre	(someone) who has run away
jəu-khə-re	>	jəu-khre	(someone) who has reached his destination, etc.

Deletion of /ə/ in negative *-tə ~ də*: The negative suffix -tə ~ **d**ə may be followed by **-ra** 'interrogative', **-ri** 'progressive' and **-re** 'perfective' and in such a situation, the vowel /ə/ of -tə ~ **d**ə is optionally dropped and the following contracted forms are produced as: **-dra**, **-dri** and **-dre**.

ca-də (-bə)-ra	>	ca-dra	don't you eat?
hot-tə (-bə)-ra	>	hot-tra	don't you scratch?
kət-tə (-bə)-ra	>	kət-tra	don't you offer (sweets to God)
sok-tə (-bə)-ra	>	sok-tra	don't you touch it?
nop-tə (bə)-ra	>	nop-tra	is it not weak?
phut-tə-ri	>	phut-tri	not yet boil
lak-tə-ri	>	lak-tri	not yet come
ja-də-ri	>	ja-dri	not yet agreed
pa-də-ri	>	pa-dri	not yet read
cət-tə-re	>	cət-tre	have not gone
lap-tə-re	>	lap-tre	is not too far
kau-də-re	>	kau-dre	have not forgotten
pi-də-re	>	pi-dre	have not given, etc.

Deletion of coda in verbal roots: Certain vebal roots may delete coda obligatorily when particular suffixes follow them. Some of them may be devoiced while some retain the previous sounds. Examples are given below.

hot-khai	>	ho-khai	>	hogai	scratch out
set-khai	>	se-khai	>	segai	tear apart
thət-tət	>	thə-tət	>	thədət	pull apart
kot-khət	>	ko-khət	>	kokhət	pull up
khot-khət	>	kho-khət	>	khokət	drag up
thok-lək	>	tho-lək	>	thorək	come out
thəm-ləm	>	thə-ləm	>	thəməm ~ thənəm	put down, etc.

In case of the last verbal root **thəm-** 'place' it may have the three forms as variations: **thmləm ~ thəməm ~ thənəm**.

The semantic components of the verbal derivative affixes with their various forms and functions have been studied in this chapter. The analysis of the inflectional suffixes, as a further study of the suffixes, comes in the next chapter.

CHAPTER 5

VERBAL INFLECTIONAL SUFFIXES

It has been discussed in Chapter-IV that Manipuri language is a tense less language. However, traditional grammarians studied Manipuri language on the grammatical framework of Indo-Aryan languages like Sanskrit, Hindi, Bengali, etc. There is the gross imposition of Sanskrit grammatical rules to the study of Manipuri language (Yashawanta, 2000). They analysed that Manipuri language has three tense forms: present, past and future. This traditional concept has been challenged by modern linguists like Bhat and Ningomba (1997), Madhubala (1979) and they claimed that Manipuri has two tense distinctions namely future and non-future while English has past and non-past. Tense distinction is not uniform in all languages. In some languages, there may be only two distinctions like future and non-future, past and non-past, etc. while some languages display three-fold system like present, past and future. This clearly shows that tense is not a universal phenomenon whereas both the concepts of time and aspect are universal. Some languages may be tenseless and in such languages the time concept is expressed by other time references.

Future tense, according to modern linguists, is indicated by **-kəni** ~ **gəni** while non-future tense (present and past) is expressed by **-i**. In further analysis, it is found that Manipuri verbs are not grammatically marked by tense as found in English (*He goes* and *He went*). The verbal suffixes that are attached to verbal roots indicate aspect only as they indicate the temporal frame of the action or event. Time reference is, of course, expressed by adverbials like **ŋəraŋ** 'yesterday', **nəhan** 'day before yesterday', **ŋəsai** 'today's recent past', etc. The inflectional suffixes that express aspectual meaning may broadly be divided into two: realized and non-realized.

5.1 Realized Suffixes

The suffix **-i** is the realized suffix that indicate various temporal structure of the verbs. It may be studied under two scopes: the individual occurrence of the suffix without any other aspectual suffixes and the combination of other aspectual suffixes with **-i**.

Realized *–i*: The attachment of this suffix to a verbal root indicates that the action is realized. It can be attached to all types of verbs.

1. **pai-** 'fly'
   ucek-nə   ətija-də   pai

bird-NOM sky-LOC fly-SAM
'Birds fly in the sky'

2. **su**- 'work'
ləumi-nə ləbuk-tə thəbək su-i
farmer-NOM field-LOC work work-SAM
'Farmers work in the field'

3. **mənəm nuŋsi**- 'smell good'
ləi əsi mənəm nuŋsi
flower this smell good-SAM
'This flower smells good'

4. **həugət**- 'wake up'
əi nuŋti-gi puŋ məŋa-də həugət-li
I everyday-GEN hour five-LOC wake up-SAM
'I wake up at 5 o'clock everyday'

5. **thok**- 'come out, rise'
numit-nə noŋpok-tə thok-i
sun-NOM east-LOC rise-SAM
'The sun rises in the east'

The verb **mənəm nuŋsi-** in (3) is a stative verb while the verbs in the other sentences are action verbs. Sentence (1) has the verb **pai**- that indicates a universal truth (except for some birds). Sentence (2) illustrates the fact that farmers work in the field. Sentence (4) indicates a habitual fact of the speaker. There are some process verbs which normally take perfective suffix **-le** instead of realized **-i**. Some of them are **pət**- 'be rotten', **pum**- 'be rotten', **sat**- 'bloom', etc. When they take **-i**, they give another implication that the verbs no more give the meaning of process. Instead, they denote a condition or a state of something (for more detail see **3.2**). The suffix has eight allomorphic variations as **-i** ~ vowel deletion~ merged into a diphthong ~ **li** ~ **pi** ~ **mi** ~ **ŋi** ~ **wi**.

-i comes after /**k**/ ending morphemes

lak-	come	>	lak-i	comes
nok-	laugh	>	nok-i	laughs
cik-	bite	>	cik-i	bites
tak-	teach	>	tak-i	teaches
hik-	be loose	>	hik-i	is loose, etc.

-i is deleted by identical vowel deletion rule when it occurs after /**i**/, /**ai**/, /**oi**/, /**ui**/, /**əi**/

pai-	fly	>	pai (i)	flies
pi-	give	>	pi (i)	gives
kai-	breaks	>	kai (i)	is broken
khoi-	be curly	>	khoi (i)	is curly
koi-	go round	>	koi (i)	goes round
thoi-	be proud	>	thoi (i)	is proud
kui-	take long time	>	kui (i)	takes long time
ləi-	buy	>	ləi- (i)	buys
nəi-	be unclean	>	nəi (i)	is unclean, etc.

-i is merged into diphthong when it is preceded by /**a**/, /**u**/, /**o**/

pa-	read	>	pai	reads
na-	be ill	>	nai	is ill
u-	see	>	ui	sees
tu-	fall	>	tui	falls
lu-	be deep	>	lui	is deep
o-	vomit	>	oi	vomits
ho-	be hollow	>	hoi	is hollow, etc.

-li occurs after /**t**/ and /**n**/ ending morphemes

kət-	offer	>	kət-li	offers
sat-	bloom	>	satli	blooms
mot-	be dirty	>	motli	is dirty
mən-	be old	>	məl-li	is old
hən-	be new	>	həl-li	is new
pən-	mention	>	pəl-li	mentions, etc.

-pi follows morphemes that end in /**p**/

kəp-	cry	>	kəp-pi	cries
lap-	be far	>	lap-pi	is far
kop-	be dent	>	kop-pi	is dent
nop-	be inferior	>	nop-pi	is inferior
khop-	hem	>	khop-pi	hems
thup-	fold	>	thup-pi	folds, etc.

-mi comes after /**m**/ ending morphemes

təm-	learn	>	təm-mi	learns

səm-	be brief	>	səm-mi	is brief
nem-	be short	>	nem-mi	is short
kom-	be loose	>	kom-mi	is loose
thom-	hit	>	thom-mi	hits
lum-	be warm	>	lum-mi	is warm, etc.

-ŋi occurs after /ŋ/ ending morphemes

təŋ-	taste	>	təŋ-ŋi	tastes
həŋ-	ask	>	həŋŋi	asks
ləŋ-	throw	>	ləŋ-ŋi	throws
cəŋ-	enter	>	cəŋ-ŋi	enters
məŋ-	dream	>	məŋ-ŋi	dreams
jaŋ-	be fast	>	jaŋ-ŋi	is fast
ləŋ-	be bright	>	ləŋ-ŋi	is bright, etc.

-i~wi follows morphemes that end in /**əu**/ and /**au**/. **-wi** is used only in spoken form while **-i** is retained in texts.

nəu-	be new	>	nəu-wi/i	is new
həu-	grow	>	həŋ-wi/i	grows
pəu-	be coarse	>	pəu-wi/i	is coarse
səu-	boil	>	səu-wi/i	boils
hau-	be tasty	>	hau-wi/i	is tasty
sau-	be angry	>	sau-wi/i	is angry
cau-	be big	>	cau-wi/i	is big, etc.

Realized *-i* attached to other aspectual suffixes: A theoretical framework may be constructed from the suffixes that denote realization of an action, event or state. The realized suffix **-i** is always incorporated with other aspectual suffixes to denote the internal temporal structure of the event (as complete or ongoing, beginning or ending, etc.). The progressive suffix **-li**, perfective suffix **-le** and many other suffixes take the suffix **-i** which is merged into the preceding suffix and it is represented by a zero morpheme in the surface level.

Progressive Suffix *-li*: The progressive suffix **-li** is a medial suffix that denotes progressiveness of an action or event. The progressive aspect is denoted by the suffix **-li** plus realized **-i** and the combination of **-li + i** (which is not preceded by any other aspectual suffixes) denote progressive in the present reading. The suffix is often contrasted with the realized **-i** as both of them have the same variation as **-li ~ pi ~ mi ~ ŋi**. Progressive suffix has level tone which can be distinguished from the realized **-i**. The suffix has six allomorphic variations as **-li ~ ri ~ pi ~ mi ~ ŋi ~ i** while **-li** is rather formal and it almost takes the place of the variations while writing.

Progressive aspect in the present reading may give two implications. It always indicates an activity continuing both before and after the time indicated. For present reading, the activity started before now and continuing till now. It suggests that the activity is unfinished and it gives the *right now* meaning, *i.e.* at the time of speaking the event is in progress. The use of the progressive suffix does not necessarily imply an unbroken activity (Palmer, 1965: 55-58).

6. **i**- 'write'

a. əi cithi əmə i-ri
I letter one write-PROG-SAM
'I am writing a letter'

b. əi lairik əmə i-ri
I book one write-PROG-SAM
'I am writing a book'

Sentence (6a) implies that the activity of writing is going on at the moment of speaking while sentence (6b) gives the meaning that the speaker is not necessarily doing the act of writing the book at the present moment.

It may be noted that stative verbs in English cannot go with progressive aspect (see Lyons, 1968). He also suggests that the majority of English verbs which occur freely in the progressive may be called 'verbs of action'. Thus, progressive aspect has become one of the contrastive features of classifying the verb types in English. Linguists often suggest a two-way classification of English verbs on the basis of progressive aspect as progressive verbs (activity verbs) and non-progressive verbs (stative verbs). Palmer (1965: 56-58) postulated five points of difference in the use of progressive and non-progressive verbs. Lyons (1965: 7.5.7) also suggests that verbs like *think, know, understand, hate, love, see, taste, feel, possess, own, etc.* are non-progressive verbs (for further detail see Chapter-III). Manipuri verbs show a unique feature that allows stative verbs to occur with progressive suffix **-li**. It may be noted here that action verbs can normally take this suffix. Consider the following sentences which illustrate a present reading of the progressive form:

7. **mu**- 'be black'
ma-gi mə-səm-si (həuɟik phau-bə) mu-ri
3PP-GEN 3PP-hair-DEM now upto-NMZ black-PROG-SAM
'Her hair is still black'

8. **kut**- 'be low'
ləmbi-si (həuɟik phau-bə) kut-li
road-DEM now upto-NMZ low-PROG-SAM
'This road is still low'

9. **noi**- 'be fat'
əŋaŋ-si həuɟik phau-bə noi-ri

child-DEM now upto-NMZ fat-PROG-SAM
'The child is still fat'

10. **pai-** 'fly'
ucek əmə ətija-də pai-ri
bird one sky-LOC fly-PROG-SAM
'A bird is flying in the sky'

11. **tum-** 'sleep'
əŋaŋ-du phəmuŋ-də tum-mi
child-DEM bed-LOC sleep-PROG-SAM
'The child is sleeping in the bed'

The verbs **mu-ri** 'is black', **kut-li** 'is low', and **noi-ri** 'is fat' in (7-9) are stative verbs which confer that the blackness of the hair , the condition of the road's being low and the fatness of the child remain the same as time goes on (showing unchanged states). All the verbs in the three sentences indicate that no change has taken place in the state or condition of the referents. Verbs in sentences (10) and (11) are action verbs and they simply mean that the activities of **pai-** and **tum-** are still going on.

Some process verbs that inherently possess duration like **noŋ cu-** 'rain', **nuŋsit sit-** 'blow wind', etc. can take progressive suffix **-li** but process verbs of momentary actions like **tu-** 'fall', **kinthə-** 'crumble', etc. cannot.

12. **noŋ-cu-** 'rain'
həuɟik kəithen-də noŋ kən-nə cu-ri
now market-LOC rain heavy-ADV rain-PROG-SAM
'It is raining heavily in the market now'

13. **(nuŋsit) sit-** 'blow'
həuɟik nuŋsit kən-nə sit-li
now wind hard-ADV blow-PROG-SAM
'The wind is blowing hard now'

Dynamic verbs that denote momentary actions like **(thoŋ) thin-** 'knock', **jəi-** 'hit', **si-** 'die', etc. may take the progressive suffix **-li** when the actions are performed repeatedly.

14. **thin-** 'knock'
əi thoŋ-də thil-li
I door-LOC knock-PROG-SAM
'I am knocking at the door'

15. **si-** 'die'
həuɟik mənipur-də mi jam-nə si-ri

now Manipur-LOC man much-ADV die-PROG-SAM
'In Manipur nowadays many people are dying everyday (unnaturally)'

The verb **thin**- 'knock' is a momentary action but in (14) it gives the sense that the action of knocking is repeated. The verb **si**- 'die' in (15) is also a momentary verb. But in the sentence, the occurrence of the progressive aspect implies that the activity of dying occurs regularly (see **3.2**).

Progressive aspect *–li* occurring in the past: The addition of other aspectual suffixes like -**ləm**, -**lək**, etc. to simple aspect marker -**i** or progressive -**li** may denote progressive action or event or state occurring in the past. They are discussed in detail in the following section.

-ləm+i: The combination of -**ləm** 'completive' and -**i** 'realized/simple aspect marker may mean that an action or event occurred in the past. When the suffixes are attached to action verbs, it may be interpreted in two ways.

16. **thoŋ**- 'cook'
 a. memə-nə cak thoŋ-ŋəm-mi
 Mema-NOM rice cook-COMP-SAM
 'Mema cooked rice'

 b. əi-nə jum jəu-bə-də memə-nə cak thoŋ-ŋəm-mi
 I-NOM house reach-NMZ-LOC Mema-NOM rice cook-COMP-SAM
 'Mema was cooking rice when I reached home'

Sentence (16a) implies that the cooking of rice was performed by Mema and after finishing it she might have left the place or been engaged in doing something else. This may also be an answer to the question like **kəna-nə** 'who cooked rice/who prepared meal?' It simply gives a statement of an action that occurred in the past and bears no sense of progressiveness. On the other hand, the same verb form **thoŋ-ŋəm-mi** in (16b) gives the meaning that the action of cooking was going on at the moment of the speaker's reaching home. It may be observed that the two actions (Mema's cooking and the speaker's reaching home) occur simultaneously and in such cases, the combination of **-ləm+i** denote progressiveness of an action that occurred in the past.

17. **su**- 'wash'
 əi-nə sila-hoi-də cət-lu-bə-də məhak phi su-rəm-mi
 I-NOM Sheela-place-LOC go-DEIC-NMZ she cloth wash COMP-SAM
 'When I went to Sheela's house she was found washing clothes'

18. **pa**- 'read'
 əi isəi ta-nə ta-nə lairik pa-rəm-mi
 I song listen-ADV listen-ADV book read-COMP-SAM
 'I was reading while listening to songs'

19. **jeŋ-** 'watch'

kəməla-du	ŋəraŋ	hol-də	sinema	jeŋ-ŋəm-mi
Kamala-DEM	yesterday	hall-LOC	cinema	watch-COMP-SAM

'Kamala was watching a movie in the hall yesterday'

The above sentences refer to two actions occurring simultaneously. In (17), the activities were performed by two persons while in (18, the two activities were performed by a single person simultaneously. Sentence (19) is a simple sentence having one verb only. But, the underlying structure of the sentence implies that the speaker had some evidence of the action which was in progress in the past. The speaker found the referent watching a movie in a hall which indicates that the speaker was also present in the hall. Even though the presence of the speaker at the place where the action was in progress is not mentioned in the sentence, the meaning is conveyed in the underlying structure of the sentence. The analysis done so far shows that the suffix **-ləm** has some aspectual as well as evidential meanings. The combination of the suffixes may also mean a non-progressive action occurred in the past and it will be studied under a different head in this section

-ləm+li: It is the combination of two suffixes: **-ləm** 'completive' and **-li** 'progressive' and it may be attached to both action and stative verbs. Consider the following sentences:

20. **su-** 'wash'

əi-nə	kəithen-dəgi	həl-lək-pə	phau-bə	tombi-du	phi
I-NOM	market-ABL	return-NMZ	upto-NMZ	Tombi-DEM	cloth

su-rəm-li
wash-COMP-PROG-SAM

'Surprisingly I found that Tombi was still washing clothes even when I returned from the market (It was not yet finished)'

21. **pa-** 'read'

rani-si	həujik	phau-bə	lairik	pa-rəm-li
Rani-DEM	now	upto-NMZ	book	read-COMP-PROG-SAM

'I found it surprising that Rani was still reading'

The different implications given by **su-ri** 'is washing', **su-rəm-mi** 'was washing' and **su-rəm-li** 'was still washing' may be analysed by asking questions like the following. For a question like *What is he doing?*, the answer may be **məhak phi su-ri** 'She is washing clothes'. It gives the present reading that while uttering the sentence, the action of washing is going on. For another question like- *'What was she doing when you reached there?* The answer to this question may be *She was washing clothes (when I reached there)*. It indicates that the speaker reached there when the action of washing was going on. Thus, it gives a past reading. Consider that the speaker was questioned like- *What has she been doing from the time you left her to the instant you came back?* The answer may be *She was still washing*. The question demands to show different time references: the instant when the speaker left the actor and the time of uttering the sentence and amidst the time references, the action was still going on. It gives another strong indication that the action occurred beyond the speaker's expectation. In other words, the action was not yet finished contradictory to the speaker's expectation that it might have been finished long time back.

The combination of the suffixes **-ləm** 'completive' and **-li** 'progressive' may also be attached to stative verbs.

22. **ŋəu-** 'be white'
    phi-du həuɟik phau-bə ŋəu-rəm-li
    cloth-DEM now upto-NMZ white-COMP-PROG-SAM
    '(It is surprising that) the cloth is still white'

23. **phəɟə-** 'be beautiful'
    nupi-du həuɟik phau-bə phəɟə-rəm-li
    woman-DEM now upto-NMZ beautiful-COMP-PROG-SAM
    '(It is surprising that) the woman is still beautiful'

Sentence (22) implies that the colour of the cloth remained as white as before while the speaker expected that it might have become dull. In sentence (23), the speaker is surprised to see the referent still beautiful as before. It is quite natural that everything (living and non-living) are subject to change with the factor of time. This made the speaker think that some changes might have taken place to the referents but the unchanged states surprised him. Here, the inference is that the speaker has past relevance (evidence) of the event. He had already seen the whiteness of the cloth which is still reflected in his mind and when he sees the cloth for a second time (*i.e.* now) he is surprised to see the whiteness still there in the cloth. The utterance was made by the speaker to recall a past event that he had encountered. In other words, the explanation may be that the speaker has the knowledge of the past condition of the whiteness of the cloth or the woman's beauty.

The adverbial **həuɟik phaubə** 'till now' identifies an interval spanning of a past time and till the present time containing the event. The reported event sets up a result state which still holds at the present time (Kate, 2000:160).

-lək+i: It is the combination of a deictic suffix and realized **-i**. The addition of the suffix to an action verb denotes that an action is realized and it gives a past reading (which will be studied just after this paragraph). It gives another interpretation when it goes with stative verb as the suffix **-lək** is studied under the scope of time. When it goes with action verbs, it gives the meaning of physical displacement while it shows a sense of continuation of a state, condition or quality of something when it occurs with stative verb.

24. **mu-** 'be dark-skinned'
    nupi əsi ləisa-riŋəi-dəgi mu-rək-i
    woman DEM before marriage-SPFD-ABL dark-skinned-DEIC-SAM
    'This woman has been dark-skinned since she was a bachelorette/damsel'

25. **khoi**- 'be curly'
nupi-məca-si pik-liŋəi-dəgi mə-səm khoi-rək-i
woman-small-DEM small-SPFD-ABL 3PP-hair curly-DEIC-SAM
'This girl has curly hair since she was very small'

26. **lairik phə**- 'be good at studies'
məhak əŋaŋ oi-riŋəi-dəgi lairik phə-rək-i
he child be-SPFD-ABL good at studies-DEIC-SAM
'He has been good at studies since his childhood'

Predicates for state verbs have a quite different reading which describes a state of affair beginning in the past and continuing up to the present. The verb forms **mu-rək-i** 'has been dark-skinned', **khoi-rək-i** 'has curly hair' and **lairik phə-rək-i** 'has been good at studies' in (24-26) refer to the continuation of a condition or state or quality. Sentence (24) implies that the speaker has the knowledge of the woman's dark skin in the past. In sentence (25) and (26), the speaker has the familiarities of the girl's curly hair and the boy's brilliance in his studies in sentence (26). To make such a comment like the above sentences, the speaker definitely requires a previous knowledge of the referents.

-lək+li: It is the combination of two suffixes: **-lək** 'deictic' and **-li** 'progressive'. It gives the meaning that an action or event started in the past and continuing up to the present time. It normally occurs with dynamic verbs.

27. **noŋ cu**- 'rain'
ŋəraŋ-dəgi noŋ cu-rək-li
yesterday-ABL rain-DEIC-PROG-SAM
'It has been raining since yesterday'

28. **thi**- 'search'
polis-nə huranbə-du ŋəraŋ-dəgi thi-rək-li
police-NOM thief-DEM yesterday-ABL search-DEIC-PROG-SAM
'Police has been searching for the thief since yesterday'

The verbs in the given examples are dynamic verbs. The verb **noŋ cu-** 'rain' is a process verb while **thi**- 'search' is an action verb. Sentence (27) indicates that the act of raining started since a time period **ŋəraŋ** 'yesterday' and continues up to the present time of uttering the sentence. The verb **thi**- 'search' implies two references of time: the past time and the present time. Kate (2000: 160) observed that if there is a temporal adverbial such as since a time period, today or this week, the adverbial must identify an interval spanning a past time and the present, containing the reported event.

Aspectual suffixes that indicate actions or events occurring in the past: There are seven aspectual suffixes that occur before realized **-i** and the combination of the suffixes indicates that an action or event takes place in the present but not at the place of the speaker and a past reading as well.

-ləm+i: The combination of the suffixes to an action verb may give two interpretations as seen above (sentence 16a and b). When these suffixes are attached to stative verbs they give a different meaning.

29. **mu-** 'be black'
    məhak han-nə-di mu-rəm-mi
    he early-ADV-PART black-COMP-SAM
    'He was dark earlier'

30. **phəɟə-** 'be beautiful'
    tutu-du han-nə-di phəɟə-rəm-mi
    Tutu-DEM early-ADV-PART beautiful-COMP-SAM
    'Tutu was beautiful earlier'

The verb form **mu-rəm-mi** 'was dark' in (29) implies that the referent was dark-complexioned earlier. But now he is no longer dark and he has become fair-complexioned. The verb form **phəɟə-rəm-mi** 'was beautiful' in (30) gives the meaning that the referent was beautiful earlier. But now she is no longer beautiful. It may be observed that the two sentences imply a change of state, condition or quality of something.

-lək+i: It has already been studied in this section where the combination of the suffixes is attached to stative verbs. It gives another implication when it goes with action verbs. The suffix **-lək** gives the deictic meaning which involves physical displacement when it goes with action verbs like **ca-** 'eat', **pu-** 'carry', **in-** 'push', **kau-** 'kick', **ləŋ-** 'throw' (for detail see **4.2**).

31. **ca-** 'eat'
    əi-khoi hotel-də cak ca-rək-i
    I-PL hotel-LOC rice eat-DEIC-SAM
    'We took meal from a hotel'

32. **wai-** 'borrow'
    əi-nə libreri-dəgi lairik əmə wai-rək-i
    I-NOM library-ABL book one borrow-DEIC-SAM
    'I borrowed a book from the library'

Sentence (31) implies that the referents did the action of eating somewhere (not at the speaker's place) and came back. At the time of uttering the sentence, the action of eating is already finished and thus, it gives a past reading. Similarly, **wai-rək-i** 'borrowed' in (32) indicates that at the time of uttering, the action is already performed and it normally gives a past reading.

-lu + i: It is the combination of deictic suffix **-lu** and realized **-i**. As the semantic structure of the suffix **-lu** indicates, the action verb to which the suffix is attached, gives the meaning that at the time of uttering the sentence the action is already performed. The speaker makes the utterance after he has already carried out the action somewhere else. To indicate the exact time reference, the speaker may either take an adverbial like **ŋəraŋ** 'yesterday', **ŋəsai** 'today's recent past', etc.

33. **cət**- 'go'
    əi memə-hoi-də cət-lu-i
    I Mema-PL-LOC got-DEIC-SAM
    'I have been to Mema's house/I have visited Mema'

34. **jeŋ**- 'watch'
    əi hol-də sinema jeŋ-ŋu-i
    I hall-LOC cinema watch-DEIC-SAM
    'I went to the cinema hall and watched a movie'

The sentences imply that the speaker went somewhere and performed the action there as the deictic suffix indicates physical displacement of an action. The same interpretation may be given to stative and process verbs also.

35. **na**- 'become ill'
    əŋaŋ-si mətəm khərə na-ru-i
    child-DEM time some become ill-DEIC-SAM
    'The child has been ill for some time'

36. **ləi**- 'stay'
    əi tha əni məhisur-də ləi-ru-i
    I month two Mysore-LOC stay-DEIC-SAM
    'I have been to Mysore for two months'

The verb **na**- 'become ill' in (35) is a process verb and it gives the implication that the child is no more ill. When the verb is examined carefully, it may be analysed at three different time references: the stage before illness, the stage of illness and the stage after recovery from illness and the utterance is made at the last stage, *i.e*. the recovery stage (for more detail see **4.2**).

-lə+i: It is also the combination of deictic suffix **-lə** and realized **-i**. As mentioned above (see **4.2**), it cannot go with stative verbs. When it is attached to action verbs, it gives a past reading.

37. **thoŋ**- 'cook'
    imo-nə əi-khoi-də cak thoŋ-ŋə-i
    Imo-NOM I-PL-LOC rice cook-DEIC-SAM
    'Imo came and prepared meal for us'

38. **pi**- 'give'

thembi-nə əi-ŋon-də lairik əmə pi-rə-i
Thembi-NOM I-DIR-LOC book one give-DEIC-SAM
'Thembi came and gave me a book'

As the meaning of the suffix **-lə** indicates, the verb **thoŋ-** 'cook' (37) conveys that the referent came at some other place (the place where the utterance is made) and performed the act of cooking and went back. Similarly, Thembi in (38) went back after giving the book to the speaker. Both sentences imply that at the time of utterance, the action has already been performed, thus giving a past reading.

-khi+i: It is the combination of **-khi** 'definitive marker' and realized **-i**. The combination of the two suffixes serves as an aspect marker to denote a completed action. As mentioned above -**khi** ~ **khə** (see **4.2**) is a multifunctional suffix and it serves various purposes. Besides being definitive, it also gives deictic as well aspectual meaning when it goes with certain action verbs.

39. **cət-** 'go'
oȷa ŋəraŋ dili cət-khi
teacher yesterday Delhi go-DEF-SAM
'Teacher went to Delhi yesterday'

40. **pu-** 'carry'
əŋaŋ-du tombi-nə pu-khi
child-DEM Tombi-NOM carry-DEF-SAM
'Tombi carried/took along the child with him'

The above sentences give the following implications. The definitive marker **-khi** serves as a deictic as well as aspectual suffix in sentences (39 and 40). The verb **cət-khi** 'went' in (39) implies a physical displacement and a confirmation that the referent has gone to Delhi and at the time of uttering the sentence the action of going has already been performed. Similarly in (40), the listener instantly presupposes that the actions had occurred in the past.

-həu+i: It is the combination of a multifunctional suffix **-həu** and realized **-i** and it refers to aspectual meaning as in the following sentences (for detail see **4.2**).

41. **lak-** 'come'
səna-du əi-khoi-də lak-həu-i
Sana-DEM I-PL-LOC come-INCP-SAM
'Sana came to my house (when I left)'

42. **pun-** 'gather'
ləmbi-də mi jam-nə pul-həu-i
road-LOC man many -ADV gather-INCP-SAM
'Many people gathered on the road'

The two sentences give the meaning that the speaker personally encountered the event. In (41) the speaker saw that Sana visited his house before he left home and in (42) the gathering of people on the road is encountered by the speaker.

Perfective Aspect: Palmer, F.R. (1974: 50) observed that the perfective is used to indicate a period of time that began before and the action is relevant to something observable at the present. The past perfect may be treated in a similar way activity occurring before, but relevant to a point of time in the past. Kate Kearns (2000: 158) also suggested two points to define perfective aspect as the combination of past and present *i.e.* to describe a past event from a present point of view as being currently relevant and it describes a past event as occurring at an indefinite or unidentified time. In Manipuri perfective aspect marker is **-le** and **-ləm+le**.

The suffix *-le*: The perfective suffix **-le** may be analysed as the combination of **-lə** 'perfective' and realized **-i**. This realized marker is merged into **-lə** and becomes **-le** and **-i** is represented by a zero morpheme in the sentence level. As mentioned above, the perfective aspect shows the present relevance of a past event.

43. thoibi ɟəgoi sa-bə ŋəm-lə-roi, ma-gi
Thoibi dance-NMZ able-PROS-NPOT-SAM she-GEN

mə-khoŋ ləithek-e
3PP-leg twisted -PERF-SAM
'Thoibi would not be able to dance, her leg got twisted'

The meaning that is implied by the speaker is that Thoibi is now injured. This is the chief instance of 'present relevance' conveyed by the present perfective: a past event is currently relevant because its consequences are still in force. In such examples the state of affairs resulting from the reported event is more pertinent than the event itself (Kate 2000: 158).

Similar explanations are also suggested by Quirk *et al* (1985: 193) where they postulate three implications associated with present perfect and each of which may or may not be applicable in a given instance. They are (1) that the relevant time zone leads up to the present; (2) that the event is recent; and (3) that the result of the action still obtains at the present time. To make the points comprehensible, syntactic illustrations are given below:

44. **ca-** 'eat'
tombə-nə sem-siŋ-du loi-nə ca-thok-khə-re
Tomba-NOM apple-PL-DEM all-ADV eat-OUT-DEF-PERF-SAM
'Tomba has eaten all the apples'

45. **nabə phə-** 'recover from illness'
i-ma-du na-bə phə-re
1PP-mother-DEM ill-NMZ good-PERF-SAM
'My mother has recovered from her illness'

The above sentences clearly express the third connotation that result of the action still obtains and they may be explained in such a way: the verb **ca-thok-khə-re** 'has eaten' in (44) implies that there are no apples left and the verb **nabə phə-re** 'recover from illness' in (45) implies that my mother is no longer ill. There are also other verb types which can take the perfective aspect as given below.

46. **tek-** 'break'
    cəuki-si məkhoŋ namə tek-e
    chair-DEM leg one break-PERF-SAM
    'One of the legs of the chair has been broken'

47. **eksiden thok-** 'have an accident'
    a. nəŋ eksiden əmə thok-lu-re
    you accident one happen-DEIC-PERF-SAM
    'You have had an accident'

Sentence (46) implies that the broken leg of the chair has not been repaired at the time of uttering the sentence. But compare the verb in (47a) which has the deictic suffix **-lu** (for detail see **4.2**) may give the following implication that the speaker can see the bruises and after seeing the bruises the speaker utters the sentence. If the referent *i.e.* the person who meets the accident says the following sentence, it may have two implications:

b. əi eksiden əmə thok-lu-re
   I accident one have-DEIC-PERF-SAM
   'I've had an accident

Extended use of Perfective *-le*: The perfective suffix **-le** may be used to indicate different aspects which are conditioned by the internal structure of the verbs. They are: (1) a realized action when it goes with a process verb, (2) an activity that is going on and (3) an activity that is not yet performed but ready, etc. They are discussed one by one in the following way.

***-le* with Process verb**: It is quite normal for process verbs to take the perfective suffix **-le** instead of realized **-i.** In the syntactic constructions given below, the perfective suffix **-le** does not give any perfective meaning to the verbs to which it is attached. It simply means realization of an event.

48. **pət-** 'get rotten'
    uhəi-siŋ-si loi-nə pət-le
    fruit-PL-DEM all-ADV rotten-PERF-SAM
    'These fruit are all rotten'

49. **pum-** 'get rotten'
    ŋa-du pum-me
    fish-DEM rotten-PERF-SAM
    'The fish is rotten'

50. **lo-** 'be ripe'
thaŋɟiŋ-si lo-re
water chestnut-DEM ripe-PERF-SAM
'This water chestnut is ripe'

Activity that is going on: The addition of perfective suffix **-le** to action and process verbs give the progressive meaning. The sentences, in such situations, express suddenness or to some extent, they may be termed as exclamatory sentences.

51. **cət-** 'go'
məni-du adə cət-le
Mani-DEM over there go-PERF-SAM
'Mani is going over there'

52. **səu-** 'boil'
isiŋ-si səu-re
water-DEM boil-PERF-SAM
'The water is boiling'

53. **pathə-** 'spill down'
ca-du pathə-re
tea-DEM spill down-PERF-SAM
'The tea (that is on the stove) is spilling down'

Sentence (51) implies that Mani, the person whom the speaker and his/her party have been looking for quite some time happened to be going on the way. The same situation may also be applied to the verb **lak-e** when the speaker with his party saw the man they had been eagerly waiting for, came towards them. Sentence (52) may give two implications: the speaker is waiting for the water to be boiled or he happened to see the water boiling. In both contexts, the boiling of the water is still going on. Sentence (53) may be analysed as a situation where the speaker happens to see the boiling and spilling down and he suddenly exclaims the sentence.

The perfective suffix **-le** is also used in teaching also while teaching a baby how to write the letters they are taught to draw lines, round shapes, etc. The teachers may say the following sentence.

54. **in-** 'push'
jet-lom-də il-le ədugə məkha-rom-də
right-direction-LOC push-PERF-SAM after this down-direction-LOC

ciŋ-thə-rək-e
draw-DOWN-DEIC-PERF-SAM
'First, your hand is moved towards the right direction and then it is pulled downward'

Activity not yet performed but ready to be performed: Perfective suffix **-le** is also used in a context where the action is not yet performed but ready to be performed. When somebody sets out for something or when somebody is about to go back after a visit to a friend's house, the verb with perfective suffix **-le** serves as giving information to the second person.

55. **cət-** 'go'
    əi koleɟ cət-le
    I college go-PERF-SAM
    'I am going to college'

56. **pheŋ-** 'scour'
    kon-siŋ-du phen-ŋe
    utensil-PL-DEM scour-PERF-SAM
    'I am scouring the utensils'

Sentence (55) simply conveys information that the speaker is going out for something while (56) may be an answer to an inquiry that *Have you scoured the utensils?* and keeping the fact that someone is in urgent need of the utensils, the speaker suddenly utters the sentence. The fact is that he/she hardly starts scouring it.

The perfective suffix **-le** can take a past time adverbial like **ŋəraŋ** 'yesterday'. Such type of occurrence is incompatible in English since the present perfect indicates a period of time that includes the present that it is not possible to further specify by an adverbial past time at which the activity took place (Palmer, 1974:52). Thus *They have come back last Monday* is incorrect while *They came back last Monday* is a correct form. Consider the sentence in Manipuri:

57. **lak-** 'come'
    mə-khoi ŋəraŋ lak-e
    he-PL yesterday come-PERF-SAM
    'They came yesterday'

The addition of perfective suffix **-le** to stative verbs causes a change in the meaning as well as in the verb classes (see **3.5)**.

-ləm + le: The addition of completive suffix **-ləm** to perfective **-le** implies that an action or event occurred behind the speaker, that is to say, the speaker finds something happened in his/her absence or without his knowledge. With dynamic verbs the suffixation gives a past reading while it gives a present perfective reading with stative verbs.

58. **jon-** 'sell'
    tombəgi-gi phi-siŋ-du loi-nə jol-ləm-le
    Tombi-GEN cloth-PL-DEM all-ADV sell-COMP-PERF-SAM
    'Tombi had already sold all the clothes'

59. **phəɟə-** 'be beautiful'
rita-du mə-sək jam-nə phəɟə-rəm-me
Rita-DEM 3PP-face much-ADV beautiful-COMP-PERF-SAM
'Rita has become very beautiful (after an interval of not seeing her)'

60. **cu-** 'get stain'
phi-si cu-rəm-me
cloth-DEM stain-COMP-PERF-SAM
'I found that this cloth has got stain'

The verb **jon-** 'sell' in (58) is an action verb and it gives the implication that the action took place in the absence of the speaker. The referent had sold all the clothes when the speaker came to buy one. The verb **phəɟə-** 'be beautiful' in (59) is a stative verb and the suffixation of -**ləm+me** implies that the speaker finds Rita become very beautiful after an interval. The speaker has the knowledge of Rita's beauty before the interval (maybe days, months or years). Similarly, the verb **cu-** 'get stain' in (60) also implies that the speaker sees the stain at the time of uttering the sentence only. It can be interpreted as follows: the speaker had not noticed the stain and he finds it only when he is ready to use it.

Copula *-ni*: The term copula is generally used to refer to the English verb 'to be' and its corresponding versions in world languages. Copula is a Latin word meaning a link, tie, connection or union (Tomiko Narahara, 2002:16). The most appropriate and exemplified definition of copula as given by Radford (1997) is as follows: 'Copula is a verb used to link a subject with a non-verbal predicate'. Thus, it supplies tense and other verbal inflectional features to non-verbal predicate categories. Webster's Dictionary (1984) provides both syntactic and logico-semantic definitions of copula as a verb. as a form of 'be' or seem, that identifies the predicate of a sentence with the subject. Yashawanta (2000: 166) classified 'be verb' of Manipuri into three forms as given below:

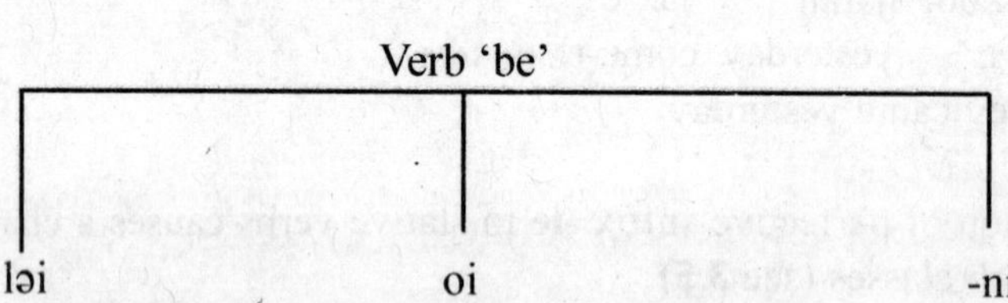

The copula **-ni** has three functions as 'identification, class inclusion and class membership. The existential function of copula is performed by the verb **ləi-** in Manipuri. Syntactic illustrations showing the various functions of copula are given below.

61. məhak caubə-ni (identification)
he Chaoba-COP
'He is Chaoba'

62. həudoŋ jum-də jok-pə sa-ni (class inclusion)
cat house-LOC rear-NMZ animal-COP
'The cat is a domestic animal'

63. tomi həudoŋ-ni (class membership)
Tomy cat-COP
'Tomy is a cat'

64. toni imuŋ-də ləi (location in space)
Tony inside the house-LOC be
'Tony is inside the house'

65. mitiŋ-du puŋ əni-də-ni (location in time)
meeting-DEM hour two-LOC-COP
'The meeting is at two'

It has been reported in the literature (*e.g.* Payne 1997; Schachter, 1985) that in many languages, the copula does not occur in the present sense interpretation, allowing the existence of the sentences with two juxtaposed nominals (Tomiko Narahara, 2002: 36).

66. SWAHILI (Schachter 1985)
a. Hamisi mpishi
Hamisi cook
'Hamisi is a cook.'
b. Hamisi alikuwa/atakuwa mpishi
'Hamisi was/will be cook'

67. RUSSIAN (Payne 1997)
a. Ivan uchit^{j}l^j
John teacher
'John is a teacher'

b. Ivan bil uchit^{j}l^j
John was-MASC teacher
'John was a teacher'

68. YAGUA (Payne 1997)
a. máchituru ráy
teacher ISG
'I am a teacher'

b. ra-vyicha-núú-yanu máchituru
ISG-be-CONT-PST3 teacher
'I used to be a teacher'

69. HUNGARIAN (Kiefer 1968)

a. péter katona
Peter soldier
'Peter is a soldier'

b. péter kotona volt
Peter soldier was
'Peter was a soldier'

In the above examples, sentences (a) have nominals only without any copula to link them in the present tense while sentences (b) have the copula in the past form.

Copula in Manipuri has different functions and forms which may be discussed in the following way.

1. Affirmative -**ni** (**oi**)
2. Interrogative -**ra** ~ **la**
3. Negative **nətte**

Copula *-ni* in affirmative use: Sentences (66-69) given above express affirmative meaning in the present relevance. To indicate progressive and perfective meaning of a copula verb, **oi-** takes place of -**ni** as the latter cannot carry the verbal inflectional features like progressive -**li** and perfective -**le**. The following sentences will indicate the aspectual variations of copula -**ni**.

70. məhak oɟa oi-ri
he teacher be-PROG-SAM
'He is still a teacher/He is still in the teaching profession'

71. ləta-du oɟa oi-re
Lata-DEM teacher be-PERF-SAM
'Lata has become a teacher (Lata has chosen teaching as her profession)'

72. təmpha-du oɟa oi-rəm-mi
Tampha-DEM teacher be-COMP-SAM
'Tampha was a teacher (but now she has quit the job)'

It is to be noted that -**ni** and -**oi** are grammatically different. **oi-** is a verbal root while -**ni** is a suffix.

Interrogative *-la* ~ *ra* as a copula: The suffix -**la** ~ **ra** serves as an interrogative marker and it is always attached to nominals only. Verbal roots are first nominalized by suffixing -**pə** ~ **bə** and then follows interrogative suffix -**la** ~ **ra**.

73. nəŋ bembem-gi mə-buŋ-la
you Bembem-GEN 3PP-elder brother-INTR
'Are you Bembem's elder brother?'

74. nəŋ-nə pa-ri-bə-du ŋəsi-gi pau-ce-ra
you-NOM read-PROG-NMZ-DEM today-GEN newspaper-INTR
'Is it today's newspaper that you are reading?'

75. nəŋ-n pai-ri-bə-du əi-gi kolom-la
you-NOM hold-PROG-NMZ-DEM I-GEN pen-INTR
'Is it my pen that you are holding?'

The sentences in the given examples have strings of nominals and the interrogative marker **-la ~ ra** links the subject with the non-verbal predicates. Sentences (74 and 75) have phrases *e.g.* **nəŋ-nə pa-ri-bə** '(something) that you are reading' in (74) and **nəŋ-nə pai-ribə-du** '(something) that you are holding' in (75) have nominalized verbs in the noun phrases which serve as a noun and the predicative noun as linked by the interrogative marker **-la ~ ra**.

The other form of interrogative is the suffix **-no** which may be attached either to the question words like **kəna** 'who', **kəri** 'what', or other nouns. The condition that restricts the suffixation of **-no** to a noun in a sentence is that the question word should be present in the sentence.

76.a. lairik əsi kəna-gi-no
book this who-GEN-Q
'Whose book is this?'

b. məsi kəna-gi lairik-no
this who-GEN book-Q
'Whose book is this?'

77.a. lairik əsi kərəmbə-no
book this which-Q
'Which type of book is this?'

b. məsi kərəmbə lairik-no
this which book-Q
'Which type of book is this?'

Copula *nətte*: The other form of copula in Manipuri is the lexical negator **nətte** which transforms an affirmative sentence to negative. It may be noted that the definition of copula that is given above does not fit in the negative construction. It links or connects the subject with the non-verbal predicates in other instances except in negative construction. Instead, it separates the subject from the non-verbal predicates. However, it does the same function as the copula does, *i.e.* it takes the role of a verb in the following sentences.

78. məhak tombə nətte
he Tomba NEG-SAM
'He is not Tomba'

79. əi hindi-gi oɟa nətte
I Hindi-GEN teacher NEG-SAM
'I am not a Hindi teacher'

80. məhak mitəi nətte
he Meetei NEG-SAM
'He is not a Meetei'

It may be observed that **nətte** is a negative word. The other forms of copula like **-ni** and **-la ~ ra** are suffixes which are directly attached to the non-verbal predicates while **nətte** occurs as an independent item.

-te: It is the negative suffix which is the combination of a negative suffix **-tə** and an aspect marker **-i**. the addition of this suffix to a verbal root expresses the negative situation of an action or event. The negative suffix **-tə** is a verbal derivative suffix (see **4.2**) and the aspect marker **-i** is merged into **-tə** and becomes **-te**. The use of **-te** has already been discussed in Chapter-I (**1.1**).

5.2 Non-Realized Suffixes

Suffixes that denote non-realization of an action or event come under this section, e.g. suffixes like command marker, suggestive marker, intentive marker, etc. indicate non-realization.

Non-realized *–kəni ~ gəni*: When the suffix **-kəni ~ gəni** is attached to a verbal root, it denotes non-realized aspect. **-kəni** follows morphemes that end in voiceless sounds while **-gəni** occurs after voiced sounds.

81. **pa-** 'read'
əi lairik-tu pa-gəni
I book-DEM read-NREAL
'I shall read the book'

82. **hiŋ-** 'live'
pambi əsi niŋthi-nə sennə-bi-rəbədi soi-də-nə hiŋ-gəni
plant this well-ADV look after-BEN-if mistake-NEG-ADV live-NREAL
'This plant will be certainly be alive if proper care is taken'

83. **theŋ-** 'be late'
khoŋ-nə cət-ləbədi məphəm-du jəu-bə-də theŋ-gəni
foot-INST go-if place-DEM reach-NMZ-LOC late-NREAL
'If you go on foot it will late when you reach there'

The verb **pa-** 'read' in (81)is an action verb while those in (82 and 83) are stative. It may be observed that the first verb in (81) is a controllable verb and it has an agent to perform the action and here the suffix **-kə** alone serves as potential marker as suggested by Shobhana (1997: 232). From this analysis it is evident that the suffix **-kə** may be analysed alone in other instances.

84. nəŋ kəithel cət-kə-də-(bə)-ra (-dra)
you market go-POT-SPF-NMZ-INTR
'Will you go to the market?'

The answer to this question may be as given below:

85. hoi, əi cət-kəni
yes, I go-NREAL
'Yes, I'll go'

86. əi kəithel cət-kə-dəu-ri
I market go-POT-do-PROG-SAM
'I am planning to go to the market'

87. əi kəithel cət-kə-dəu-re
I market go-POT-do-PERF-SAM
'I am ready to go to the market'

In all the above given sentences, the function of **-kə** is evident that it denotes potentiality as well as non-realization and that it can be analysed alone. But in case of sentences like (81-83) **-kəni** ~ **gəni** cannot be analysed separately. The concept of **-kə** still remains intact in **-kəni** ~ **gəni**.

The deletion or contraction of certain morphemes or a sound from a morpheme has been studied earlier in Chapter-IV (see **4.3**).

88. əi lairik-tu pa-ni (-gəni)
I book-DEM read-NREAL
'I shall read book'

The deletion of **-kə** from **-kni** in the above sentence does not have any effect on the semantic structure of the sentence. One of the most common evidence of deletion of **-kə** is found when the suffix **-lə** is also there. It is made clear in the following way:

89. **cət-** 'go'

a. əi ophis cət-lə-gəni
I office go-PROS-NREAL
'I will be going to office (within a few moments)'

b. əi ophis cət-lə-ni (-gəni)
I office go-PROS-NREAL
'I will be going to office (within a few moments)'

The meaning of non-realization which is denoted by the suffixation of **-kəni** ~ **gəni** may be changed when certain suffixes are inserted between the verbal root and **-kəni** ~ **gəni**. For instance, the definitive suffix **-khi** and completive **-ləm (4.2)** may intervene the verb form and give a different reading. The addition of completive suffix **-ləm** before **-kəni** ~ **gəni** gives the meaning of unreal past.

Command marker *-u/-o*: The general concept of command is to ask somebody to execute something and it naturally comes under non-realized group as the action is not yet carried out. In Manipuri, a command is always signified by the suffixation of **-u** and **-o**. The suffixation of -**u** to an action verb (which cannot go with stative and process verbs, see Chapter-III) gives a command in general while the addition of **-o** implies to perform the action right away in the presence of the speaker. The suffix -**u** has eight variations as **-u~lu ~ pu ~ mu ~ ŋu ~ ju ~ u ~** merged as diphthong. **-o** has six variations as **–o ~ lo ~ po ~ mo ~ ŋo ~ ro.**

-u/o occurs after /**k**/ ending morphemes:

lak	come	>	lak-u/lak-o	come
hək-	carve	>	hək-u/hək-o	carve
nik-	shake		nik-u/nik-o	shake
cik	bite	>	cik-u/ck-o	bite, etc.

-lu/lo comes after /**t**/ and /**n**/ ending morphemes:

cət-	go	>	cət-lu/cət-lo	go
pun-	bind	>	pul-lu/pul-lo	bind
hon-	carry	>	hol-lu/hol-lo	carry
thət-	pluck	>	thət-lu/thət-lo	pluck, etc.

-pu/po follows morpheme that end in /**p**/:

kup-	cover	>	kup-pu/kup-po	cover
nəp-	stick	>	nəp-pu/nəp-po	stick
lep-	stand	>	lep-pu/lep-po	stand
khəp-	winnow	>	khəp-pu/khəp-po	winnow, etc.

-mu/mo occurs after /**m**/ ending morphemes:

təm-	learn	>	təm-mu/təm-mo	learn
cam-	wash	>	cam-mu/cam-mo	wash
khum-	cover	>	khum-mu/khum-mo	cover
phəm-	sit	>	phəm-mu/phəm-mo	sit, etc.

-ŋu/ŋo comes after /ŋ/ ending morphemes:

seŋ-	clean	>	seŋ-ŋu/seŋ-ŋo	clean
haŋ-	open	>	haŋ-ŋu/haŋ-ŋo	open
jeŋ-	look	>	jeŋ-ŋu/jeŋ-ŋo	look
cɔ-	enter	>	cəŋ-ŋu/cəŋ-ŋo	enter, etc.

-ju/ro follows morphemes that end in /**i**/, /**ai**/, /**oi**/, /**ui**/, /**əi**/

təi-	apply/ mop	>	təi-ju/təi-ro	apply/ mop
pi	give	>	pi-ju/pi-ro	give
koi	go round	>	koi-ju/koi-ro	go round
ui	doze	>	ui-ju-ui-ro	doze
pai	hold	>	pai-ju/pai-ro	hold, etc.

-u is merged into diphthong when it is preceded by /**a**/ while –**ro** comes after /**a**/

pa-	read	>	pa-u/pa-ro	read
ca-	eat	>	ca-u/caro	eat
ta	listen	>	ta-u/ta-ro	listen
ka	climb	>	ka-u/kau-ro	climb, etc.

-u is deleted when it follows morphemes that end in /**o**/, /**u**/, /**əu**/ and /**au**/ while –**ro** can follow the sounds

po-	carry child on the back	>	po-/po-ro	carry a child on the back
ləu	take	>	ləu/ləu-ro	take
lau	shout	>	lau/lau-ro	shout
pu-	carry	>	pu-/pu-ro	carry, etc.

In the above examples, verbs ending in /**a**/ like **ca-** , **pa-** , **ta-**, etc. have a diphthong when the command marker **-u** is added. In another context, verbs like **po-** , **pu-**, etc. have a zero morpheme when **-u** is attached to them. This is because of the application of identical vowel deletion rule where the rounded back vowels /**u**/ and /**o**/ are of the same origin with the command marker /**u**/. Sometimes, this deletion rule often causes confusion to some linguists like

Yashawanta (2000: 37, 159) and Aruna (2006: 145) where they explain that the suffix **-lu ~ ru** (which is originally a deictic suffix) is a command marker. Of course, it seems to be a command marker when somebody says **ca-ru** 'go and eat', **ləu-ru** 'go and take'. But in the deep structure analysis, the suffix **-lu** is found to be a deictic suffix denoting physical displacement and the addition of the command marker **-u** which cannot be seen in the surface level because of the identical vowel deletion rule.

90. **haibə in-** 'be obedient'
nə-ma nə-pa-nə hai-bə il-lu
2PP-mother 2PP-father-NOM say-NMZ follow-COM
'Be obedient to your parents'

91. **ta-** 'listen'
oʝa-nə tak-pə para pukniŋ cəŋ-nə ta-u
teacher-NOM teach-NMZ lesson attentive-ADV listen-COM
'Listen attentively to what the teacher teaches'

92. **jek-** 'draw'
ucek əmə jek-u
bird one draw-COM
'Draw a bird'

Sentences ending in command marker **–o** are given below:

93. **li-** 'tell'
wari-du məjam-də li-ro
story-DEM people-LOC tell-COM
'Tell the story to the people (maybe to a specified group of people)'

94. **cəŋ-** 'enter'
nəŋ han-nə cəŋ-ŋo
you ahead-ADV enter-COM
'You go/ enter first'

95. **hek-** 'pluck'
puŋton-si nəŋ hek-o
guava-DEM you pluck-COM
'(You) pluck this guava'

Sentences (93-95) imply that the speaker asks the referent to perform the action at the time of speaking and in his presence as well. The verb **hek-** in sentence (95) gives the meaning that the speaker should pluck the guava in front of the speaker right away. In the same way the sentences denote a command to be performed instantly and in the presence of the speaker.

Another form of command is the combination of **-khə** (a variant form of **-khi** 'definitive') and the command marker **-o** > **-kho** which some linguists have mistaken to be a command marker. The meaning implied by **-kho** is given by **-khə** which gives a deictic sense that involves physical displacement; the sense of continuation of an action that has already been started. It may also mean to do something before doing other actions.

96. **pu-** 'carry'
lairik-si pu-kho
book-DEM carry-DEF-COM
'Take this book along with you'

97. **thək-** 'drink'
ca thək-kho
tea drink-DEF-COM
'Have tea before you leave/ do something'

98. **phəm-** 'sit'
ŋaihak-təŋ phəm-kho
a while-only sit-DEF-COM
'Sit for a while' or 'Keep sitting for a while'

Sentence (96) gives a deictic sense while (97) insists someone to take tea before leaving or doing something. Sentence (98) gives two implications: (i) asking the referent to sit for a while or (ii) asking him to continue sitting for some more time in the sense of asking for some more spare time in the company.

It may be observed that in the examples given above, the person to whom the speaker asks to carry out an action is the second person. A command is usually carried out by an agent and this agent is always a second person. In most cases of command sentences, the addressee *i.e.* the second person is understood. Another feature of command is that the verb form is not reflected for tense, number, person and gender in English, *e.g.* the verb *go*, *eat*, is the shortest command form, while in Manipuri, the verbal root takes the command marker **-o**. In both languages and other languages as well, the addressee may, sometimes, be overtly seen in the sentence as seen in (94).

Prohibitive *-kənu ~ gənu*: The suffixation of **-kənu** ~ **gənu** to an action verb gives the meaning of negative command. It prohibits someone from doing something and it implies futurity. **-kənu** follows morphemes that end in voiceless sounds while **-gənu** comes after voiced sounds (see **1.1**).

99. **phu-** 'beat'
əŋaŋ phu-gənu
child beat-PROH
'Don't beat the child'

100. **sannə**- 'play'
nə-khoi ləmbi-də sannə-nu
you-PL road-LOC play-PROH
'Don't play on the road/ path'

Sentence (100) is also prohibitive sentence where the suffix **-kə ~ gə** has been dropped from the sentence. Still, the meaning of prohibition is conveyed by the sentences since the deletion of -**kə** ~ **gə** from -**kənu ~ gənu** does not disturb the semantic structure of the suffix.

Intentive suffix *ke ~ ge*: The intentive suffix **-ke ~ ge** may be translated in English by '*let*' restricting the referent to first person only. When the referent becomes second person or third person, the speaker is talking about them while in case of first person, the speaker talks about himself.

101. **tum**- 'sleep'
əi tum-mu-rə-ge
I sleep-DEIC-PERF-INT
'Let me go to bed and sleep'

102. **pottha**- 'take rest'
ŋaihak-tə pottha-khi-ge
a while-only take rest-DEF-INT
'Let me take rest for a while'

103. **pa**- 'read'
əi pauce ŋaihak-təŋ pa-ge
I newspaper a while-only read-INT
'Let me read newspaper for a while only'

Note: ŋaihak-tə 'a while-only' in (102) and **ŋaihak-təŋ** in (103) is the same word. **-tə** is the shortened form of **-təŋ** 'only'.

In the above examples, the speaker is talking about himself. Consider some constructions which give a different picture:

104. **cət**- 'go'
nəŋ ct-lə-ge hai-bə-ra
you go-PROS-INT say-NMZ-INTR
'Do you want to go (now)?'

105. **lak**- 'come'
ma-su lak-ke hai-ri
he-also come-INT say-PROG-SAM
'He also wants to come'

It is evident that **-ke** ~ **ge** which seems to associate only with first person, can also go with second person and third person on certain conditions. The sentence structures are complex type and the suffix **-ke** ~ **ge** occurs in subordinate clause. Sentence (104) may be analysed in the underlying forms as: (1) **nəŋ cət-lə-ge(-ra)** 'Do you want to go?' and (2) **mədu hai-bə-ra** 'Do you say that?'.

The suffix **-ke** ~ **ge** when attached to an action verb (as it cannot occur with process and stative verbs) it gives three implications: (i) it implies intention in the sense that the speaker as well as the referent intends to carry out an action; (ii) it shows a sense seeking of permission, *i.e.*, the speaker seeks permission from the addressee (*i.e.* the hearer); (iii) the sense of permission is always associated with request and this has been clearly shown in **4.2** where the suffix **-cə** ~ **-ɟə** which indicates a request form, is always followed by **-ke** ~ **ge**.

Suggestive *-si*: The suffixation of **-si** to an action verb indicates suggestion. The semantic structure of the suffix does not allow it to occur with process and stative verbs as they are not action-oriented (for detail see Chapter-III).

106. **ka-** 'climb'
 əi-khoi ciŋ ka-ru-si
 I-PL hill climb-DEIC-SUG
 'Let's go and climb a hill'

107. **tanə-** 'discuss'
 i-bani wa khərə tanə-si
 I-two speech some discuss-SUG
 'Let two of us discuss some matters'

The examples given above are sentences indicating suggestion where the speaker insists others to perform an action along with the speaker himself. The negative version of the sentences is **-kum-si** where the speaker asks others along with himself not to perform the action (see **1.1** and **4.2**).

108. **ja-** 'agree'
 i-bani ma-nə hai-bə ja-gum-si
 I-two he-NOM say-NMZ agree-NEG-SUG
 'Let two of us not agree with what he suggests'
 '(Let two of us object his suggestions)'

In (106) the speaker makes a proposal to his friends to climb a hill, an action which he himself is going to take part. The subject of the sentence **i-bani** 'we two'/ 'two of us' and **əi-khoi** 'we' indicate this inclusion of the speaker in the action. But there is another situation where the speaker may not take part in the action, and the subject of the sentence does not refer to the first person.

109. **pai-** 'take hold'
   məjam ca pai-bi-si/pai-si
   all tea hold-HON-SUG/ hold-SUG
   'Please have tea'

110. **leŋsin-** 'take seat'
   oɟa-siŋ som-də leŋsin-bi-si/leŋ-sin-si
   teacher-PL this way-LOC take seat-HON-SUG/ take seat-SUG
   'Respected teachers! Please come this way and have seat'

The verbs **pai-** and **leŋsin-** in (109 and 110) are honorific verbs of **thək-** 'have/drink' and **phəm-** 'sit'. The suffix **-bi** in the sentences is honorific marker which is a homophonous form of benefactive **-pi ~ bi**. The difference between the two forms may be elucidated as follows: in benefactive form, the subject of the sentence is doing a favour to someone (who takes the suffix **-ki ~ gi/-kidəmək ~ gidəmək** or dative **-tə ~ də**) or someone is benefited by the action performed by the subject of the sentence. But in case of honorific form, the speaker requests an older person to perform an action by using honorific verbs. **–si** in this context, it refers to a request form where the subject is not going to be included in the action. For example, in (109) the speaker requests his/her guests to take tea while he himself is not going to take it. Similarly, in (110), the speaker requests the honourable guests (teachers) to take seat while he is not going to take one.

Permissive *-sənu*: The semantic structure of **-sənu** is to give permission to somebody to perform an action. In this case, the permission is not granted directly to the persons *i.e.*, it is granted through a second person. The listener, *i.e.* the second person is not going to perform the action. It is another person, *i.e.* a third person who gets the relayed permission and he is going to perform the action. Thus, the semantic structure of the suffix does not permit it to occur with first person and second person. The use of this suffix is restricted to third person only.

111. **ca-** 'eat'
   əŋaŋ-du həi ca-sənu
   child-DEM fruit eat-PERM
   'Let the child eat fruit'

112. **ləi-** 'buy'
   ləta-nə phi-du ləi-ru-sənu
   Lata-NOM cloth- DEM buy-DEIC-PERM
   'Let Lata go and buy the cloth'

In (111), the speaker talks to a second person and allows the third person 'child' to eat fruit. In (112), the speaker gives permission to the listener for Lata (not the listener) to go and buy the cloth. The implication given by these examples may be as follows: the speaker takes the role of authority and shows that he is superior to the persons to whom permission is granted. Another suffix may be inserted Manipuri uses a suffix **-cə ~ ɟə** which is a reflexive suffix (see **4.2**) to emphasize the sense of permission. The suffixation shows a sense of caring or love towards the person who gets the permission.

113. **sannə**- 'play'
əŋaŋ-du ŋaihak sannə-ɟə-sənu
child-DEM a while play-REF-PERM
'Let the child play for a while (because he has studied since morning)'

114. **pottha**- 'take rest'
caubə-su ŋaihak pottha-ɟə-sənu
Chaoba-also a while take rest-REF-PERM
'Let Chaoba also take rest for a while (as he deserves it)'

115. **ca**-'eat'
əŋaŋ-du mə-buk thən-nə-bə ca-ɟə-rə-sənu
child-DEM 3PP-stomach fill-PUR-NMZ eat-REF-PROS-PERM
'Let the child eat to its heart's content (because he has not eaten its heart's content for a long time)'

Another construction is also found in Manipuri when the speaker grants permission to the third person after permission is sought. The insertion of the clause makes the sentence a complex type.

116. **tum**- 'sleep'
əŋaŋ-du tum-ge hai-rgə tum-ɟə-sənu
child-DEM sleep-INT connector sleep-REF-PERM
'If the child wants to sleep, let him sleep'

117. **ləu**- 'take'
lairik-tu hema-nə ləu-ge hai-rə-bə-su ləu-ɟə-sənu
book-DEM Hema-NOM take-INT connector take-REF-PERM
'If Hema wants the book let her take it'

118. **ləi**- 'buy'
i-ma-nə ləi-niŋ-bə-məkhəi ləi-ɟə-sənu
1PP-mother-NOM buy-wish-NMZ-all buy-REF-PERM
'Let my mother buy whatever she likes'

Sentences (113-115) are simple sentences while (116 and 118) are complex sentences. In (116) the subordinate clause is **əŋaŋ-du tum-ge hai** 'the child wants to sleep' while **əŋaŋ-du tum-ɟə-sənu** 'let the child sleep' functions as a main clause. It may be noted that the subject of the main clause **ŋaŋ-du** 'the child' is deleted. Sentence (145) may also be analyzed in the same way by applying the deletion rule, the subject is deleted in the main clause **ləu-ɟə-sənu** 'let (her) take it' while **lairik-tu hema-nə ləu-ge hai** 'Hema wants to take the book' is the subordinate clause.

This meaning is extended to process and stative verbs also. There is no intention on the referent's part. In such type of construction the meaning does not refer to permission. Instead, it gives a sense of carelessness or negligence on the speaker's part.

119. **tu**- 'fall'
satin-du tu-ge hai-rəgə tu-ɟə-sənu
umbrella-DEM fall-INT connector fall-REF-PERM
'I don't care whether the umbrella falls or not'

120. **na**- 'become sick'
əŋaŋ-du na-ge hai-rəgə na-ɟə-sənu
child-DEM sick-INT connector sick-REF-PERM
'I don't care whether the child gets sick or not'

121. **noi**- 'be fat'
nupidu noi-ge hairəgə noi-ɟə-sənu
woman-DEM fat-INT connector fat-REF-PERM
'I don't care whether the woman is fat or not' or 'Let the woman be fat'

The verbs in the subordinate clauses above are process and stative. They are **tu**- , **na**- and **noi**-. They fail to indicate desire or intention of falling, becoming sick or fat. Yet, they occur with intentive suffix **-ke** ~ **-ge** in the sentences which may be explained only as an extended use of the suffix. The intention on the speaker's part may also be examined in these constructions. The sentences express the speaker's carelessness/ negligence or helplessness on the events.

Suffixes *-təu-ri* and *-təu-re*: Both the suffixes have been discussed in Chapter-IV (see **4.2**) in detail. The reason why the suffixes come under inflectional suffixes is that both **-ri** 'progressive' and **-re** 'perfective' have the realized **-i**. Yet, they imply futurity, *i.e.* the actions (the verbs to which the suffixes are attached) are not yet realized.

Non-potential suffix *-loi*: The derivative suffix **-loi** with the combination of aspect marker **-i** form this inflectional suffix **-loi** where **-i** is deleted by identical vowel deletion rule and it is represented by a zero morpheme in the surface structure. It can occur with all the three semantic classes of verbs: action, stative and process. With action verbs, it denotes non-potentiality of an action while with stative and process verbs, it simply indicates futurity of an event that an event like this and this will not happen or take place. The variants of this suffix with their occurrences and its various uses are discussed in Chapter-I (see **1.1**).

BIBLIOGRAPHY

Abbi, Anvita. 1992. ***Reduplication in South Asian Languages. An Areal, Typological and Historical Study.*** New Delhi: Allied Publishers Ltd.

___________. 1994. ***Semantic Universals in Indian Languages***. Shimla: Indian Institute of Advanced Study.

Anderson, Stephen R. 1992. ***A Morphous Morphology.*** Cambridge: Cambridge University Press

Arokianathan, S. 1981. ***Tamil Clitics.*** Thiruvenantapuram: Dravidian Linguistics Association.

Bauer, Laurie. ***Word Formation in English***.

Beard, Robert. 2001. Derivation. Andrew Spencer and Arnold Zwicky (Eds.) ***The Handbook of Morphology.*** Oxford: Blackwell Publishers Ltd.

Bhat, D.N.S. and M.S. Ningomba. 1986. ***Chapters from a Manual of Manipuri Grammar (Morphology).*** Imphal: Department of Manipuri Language and Literature, Manipuri University.

Bhat D.N.S. and M.S. Ningomba. 1997. ***Manipuri Grammar.*** München, Newcastle: Lincom Europa.

Bhat, D.N.S. 2007. Typological Study of Language. ***Indian Linguistics***, Vol. 68 No. 3-4.

__________. ***Introduction to Linguistics***. Canchipur: Teachers' Forum, Manipur.

__________. 1991. 'Adjectives in Tibeto-Burman Languages' ***An Introduction to Indian Grammars.*** New Delhi: University Grants Commission.

__________. ***The Prominence of Tense, Aspect and Mood***. Amsterdam: John Benjamins.

__________. 2000. Functional Constraints on Word Formation Rules. Rajendra Singh (Ed.) ***The Yearbook of South Asian Languages and Linguistics.*** Delhi: Sage Publication Private Ltd.

Bhat, Raj Nath. 2002. Compound Verbs in Hindi. ***Indian Linguistics.*** Vol. 63, No. 1 to 4.

Bidyarani, M. 2002. ***Manipuri Verbs.*** Unpublished Ph. D. Thesis. Imphal: Manipur University.

Bloch and Tragor. ***Outlines of Linguistic Analysis.*** New Delhi: Oriental Books Reprint Corporation.

Chellia, Shobhana Lakshmi. 1997. ***A Meithei Grammar***. New York: Mouton De Gruyter.

Comrie, Bernard. 1985. ***Tense***. Cambridge: Cambridge University Press.

_____________. 1985. ***Aspect***. Cambridge: Cambridge University Press.

Crystal, David. 1985. ***A Dictionary of Linguistics and Phonology.*** Oxford: Basil Blackwell.

_____________. 1995. ***The Cambridge Encyclopedia of English Language.*** Cambridge: Cambridge University Press.

_____________. 1997. ***The Cambridge Encyclopedia of Language.*** 2nd Edition, Cambridge : Cambridge University Press.

Dasgupta, P. 1989. ***Projective Syntax: Theory and Application.*** Pune: Deccan College of Post Graduate and Research Institute.

Dolen, H. 2002. ***The Semantic Structure of Manipuri Verbs.*** Unpublished Ph.D. Thesis. Imphal: Manipuri University.

Fabb, Nigel. 2001. Compounding. Andrew Spencer and Arnold M. Zwicky (Eds) ***The Handbook of Morphology.*** Oxford: Blackwell Publishers Ltd.

Fillmore, Charles J. 1971. ***Verbs of Judging: An Exercise in Semantic Description.***

Fillmore Charles, J. and Terrace Langendeon (Eds). ***Studies in Linguistic Semantics.*** Chicago: Holt Rinehart and Winston Inc.

Gerdts, B. Donna. 2001. Incorporation. Andrew Spencer and Arnold Zwicky (Ed.) ***The Handbook of Morphology.*** Oxford: Blackwell Publishers Ltd.

Giridhar, P.P. 1994. ***Mao Naga Grammar.*** Mysore: Central Institute of Indian Languages.

Givon, T. 1979b. ***Discourse in Syntax: Syntax and Semantics***. New York: Academic Press.

Greenbaum, Sydney. 1996. ***Oxford English Grammar.*** Oxford: Oxford University Press.

Grierson, G.A. 1927. ***Linguistic Survey of India***, Vol. III, Part III, Delhi: Motilal Banarasidas (Reprinted 1967).

Halpern, Aaron L. 2001. Clitics. Andrew Spencer and Arnold Zwicky (Eds.) ***The Handbook of Morphology.*** Oxford: Blackwell Publishers Ltd.

Heine, Bernd; Ulrike Claudi and Friederike Hiinnemeyer. 1991. ***Grammaticalization: A Conceptual Framework.*** Chicago: Chicago University Press.

Hook, Peter Edwin. 2001. Where do Compound Verbs Come From? (And Where Are They Going). Peri Bhaskarano and K.V. Subbarao (Eds.) ***The Yearbook of South Asian Languages and Linguistics. Contact, Convergence and Typology.*** Tokyo Symposium on South Asian Languages, National Museum Ethnology, Osaka, Japan.

Horn, Laurence R. 1978. Some Aspects of Negation. Joseph H. Greenberg (Ed.) ***Universals of Human Language***, Vol. 4. **Syntax**. Stanford: Stanford University Press.

Imoba, S. 2004. ***Manipuri to English Dictionary***. Imphal: S. Ibetombi Devi.

James, J. Bauman. 1975. ***Pronouns and Pronominal Morphology in T.B***. Berkeley: University of California.

Kansakar, Tej R. 2001. Typology of Verbal Categories of the Languages of Nepal. Peri Bhaskarano and K.V. Subbarao (Eds.) ***The Yearbook of South Asian Languages and Linguistics. Contact, Convergence and Typology.*** Tokyo Symposium on South Asian Languages, National Museum Ethnology, Osaka, Japan.

Kapoor, Kapil. ***Semantic Structure and the Verb: A Proportional Analysis.*** New Delhi: Intellectual Book Corner.

Katamba,Fransis.1993. ***Morphology.*** Modern Linguistics Series. New York: Palgrave.

Katy, Terrold T. 1977. ***Proportional Structure and Illocutionary Force - A Study of the Contribution of Sentence Meaning to Speech Acts.*** New York: Thomas Y. Crowell Company Inc.

Katz, Jerrold. 1972. ***Semantic Theory***. New York: Harper and Row.

Kavitskaya. 1997. Tense and Aspect in Lai Chin. ***Linguistics of Tibeto-Burman Area.*** Vol. 20.2.

Kearns, Kate. 2000. ***Semantics.*** Modern Linguistics Series. New York: Palgrave.

Loken, Kh. 1997. ***Word Formation in Kuki-Chin Groups***. Unpublished Ph.D. Thesis, Manipur University.

Lyons, John. 1968. ***Theoretical Linguistics.*** Cambridge: Cambridge University Press.

Madhubala, P. 1979. ***Manipuri Grammar.*** Unpublished Ph.D. Thesis. Pune: Deccan College of Post Graduate Studies and Research Institute.

Mathews, P.H. 1991. ***Morphology.*** Cambridge: Cambridge University Press.

Matisoff, A. James. 1973. ***The Grammar of Lahu.*** London: California University Press.

Mc Arthur. 1996. ***The Oxford Companion to the English Language.*** Oxford: Oxford University Press.

McCarthy, Kevin M. 1980. ***Grammar and Usage: A Rapid Review.*** Harcourt Brace Jovanovich, Inc.

Narahara, Tomiko. 2002. ***The Japanese Copula, Forms and Functions.*** New York: Palgrave, Macmillan.

Ningomba, M.S. 1992. ***Meitei Lonmit.*** Imphal: Saraswati Book House.

Nonigopal, N. 1987. ***A Meitei Grammar of Roots and Affixes.*** Unpublished Ph.D. Thesis. Imphal: Manipur University.

Palmer, F.R. 1974. ***The English Verbs.*** London: Longman.

Pardeshi, Prashant. 2003. The Compound Verb in Marathi: Definitional Issues and Criteria for Identification. ***Indian Linguistics.*** Vol. 64 No. 1-4.

Pettigrew, William. 1912. ***Manipuri Grammar.*** Allahabad: The Pioneer Press.

Premabati, B. 1998. Affixation. ***Working Paper Series***. Imphal: Language Cell, Directorate of Education(S), Government of Manipur.

Primrose, A.J. 1987. ***A Manipuri Grammar, Vocabulary and Phrase Book***. Shillong.

Quirk, Randolph; Sydney Greenbaum, Geoffrey Leech and Jan Svartvik. 1985. ***A Comprehensive Grammar of the English Language.*** New York: Longman Group Ltd.

Robins, R.H. 1970. ***General Linguistics: An Introductory Survey.*** New York: Longman Group Ltd.

Sharma, Dwijamani Dev. 1969. ***Manipuri Byakaran***. Imphal: Shekhar Brothers.

Sharma, H. Surmangol. 1998. Classification of Roots. ***Working Paper Series***. Imphal: Language Cell, Directorate of Education(S), Government of Manipur.

__________________. 2006. Negation in Manipuri. ***IJDL*** vol xxxv No. 2.

Sharma, H. Surmangol. 2006. ***Learner's Manipuri-English Dictionary***. Imphal: Sangam Book House.

Sharma, L. Narayan. 1984. ***Meiteilon Byakaran***. Imphal.

Sharma, Nandalal. 1976. ***Meiteilon***. Imphal: Orient Book Depot.

Shastri, Kalachand. 1964. ***Manipuri Byakaran Kaumudi***. Imphal: T. Abir Singh for O.K. Store.

Shyamlakumari, B. 2003. Rigorous Definitions of Verb: An Elusive Effort. ***Languages in India.*** Vol. 3.

Singh, A. Minaketan. 1975. ***Meitei Lonjan.*** Imphal.

Singh, Chungkham Yashawanta. 1996. Tag questions in Meiteilon (Manipuri). ***Mon-Khmer Studies, A Journal of South East Asian Languages***, Vol. XXV.

________________________. 1988. Reduplication in Meiteilon. ***Quarterly Journal of African, Asian and Latin American Studies.*** 56.

________________________. 1992. Causativization in Meiteilon. ***Linguistics of Tibeto- Burman Area*** (LTBA).

________________________. 1992. Negation in Meiteilon. ***Journal of Asian and African Studies.*** No. 44.

________________________. 1994. 'Be' Verb in Manipuri. ***26th International of Sino-Tibetan Languages and Linguistics***.

________________________. 1995. Tense or Aspect in Manipuri. Nishi Yoshio, James A. Matisoff and Yasuhiko Nagano (Eds.) ***New Horizons in Tibeto-Burman MorphoSyntax.*** Osaka, Japan: Senri Ethnological Studies 41, National Museum of Ethnology.

________________________. 2000. ***Manipuri Grammar.*** New Delhi: Rajesh Publications.

Singh, N. Khelchandra. 2004. ***Manipuri to Manipuri and English Dictionary***. Imphal.

Singh, Ningombam Tomba. 1969. ***Meitei Lonmit***. Imphal.

Singh, W. Tomchou. 1976. ***A Study of Meitei Phonology***. Imphal.

Sonamani, L. 1980. ***Meeteilon Phonology with a Supplement of Morphology***. Imphal.

Stump, T. Gregory. 2001. Inflection. Andrew Spencer and Arnold Zwicky (Eds.) ***The Handbook of Morphology.*** Oxford: Blackwell Publishers Ltd.

Thakur, D. 1998. ***Linguistics Simplified Syntax.*** Patna: Bharati Bhawan.

Thoudam, P.C. 1991. ***T.D.C. Remedial Manipuri***. Imphal: S.I. and Co.

Tomba, Sapam. 2000. ***Meetei Lonmit***. Imphal: Writers Form Manipur.

Trask, R.L. 1993. ***A Dictionary of Grammatical Terms in Linguistics.*** London: Routledge.

Underhill, Robert. 1976. ***Turkish Grammar.*** London: The MIT Press.

Van Valin, Robert D. 2006. Some Universals of Verb Semantics. Ricardo Mairal and Juana Gil (Eds) ***Linguistics Universals.*** Cambridge: Cambridge University Press.

Zograph, G.A. 1980. ***Languages of South East Asia: A Guide***. London: Longman Group Ltd.